My Dear Mr. Stalin

To the 405,000 Americans and the
27,000,000 Russians who died in World War II

My Dear Mr. Stalin

The Complete Correspondence Between
Franklin D. Roosevelt and Joseph V. Stalin

Edited, with Commentary, by Susan Butler

Foreword by Arthur M. Schlesinger, Jr.

Yale University Press
New Haven and London

Published with assistance from the foundation established in memory of Philip Hamilton McMillan of the Class of 1894, Yale College.

Set in Sabon Roman type by The Composing Room of Michigan, Inc.
Printed in the United States of America.

Library of Congress Cataloging-in-Publication Data
Roosevelt, Franklin D. (Franklin Delano), 1882–1945.
  My dear Mr. Stalin : the complete correspondence between Franklin D. Roosevelt and Joseph V. Stalin / edited, with commentary, by Susan Butler.
     p.   cm.
  Includes bibliographical references and index.
  ISBN-13: 978-0-300-10854-5 (cloth : alk. paper)
  ISBN-10: 0-300-10854-0 (10-digit)
  1. Roosevelt, Franklin D. (Franklin Delano), 1882–1945—Correspondence.   2. Stalin, Joseph, 1879–1953—Correspondence.   3. Presidents—United States—Correspondence. 4. Heads of state—Soviet Union—Correspondence.   5. World War, 1939–1945— Sources.   I. Stalin, Joseph, 1879–1953.   II. Butler, Susan, 1932– .   III. Title.
  E807.A4 2005
  973.917'092—dc22

                                                                2005012583

A catalogue record for this book is available from the British Library.

The paper in this book meets the guidelines for permanence and durability of the Committee on Production Guidelines for Book Longevity of the Council on Library Resources.

10 9 8 7 6 5 4 3 2 1

Contents

Foreword

It is a curiosity of scholarship that the full correspondence between Franklin D. Roosevelt and Joseph V. Stalin was never published during the Cold War. That correspondence consisted of more than three hundred hot-war letters, beginning with Hitler's surprise attack on the Soviet Union in 1941 and ending with FDR's surprise death in 1945. History owes a debt to Susan Butler for the collection and annotation of these exchanges.

Roosevelt and Stalin met only twice—in Tehran in November 1943 and in Yalta in February 1945. They met each time with the third of the Big Three, British Prime Minister Winston Churchill. By the time they met at Yalta, all three were old and tired. Churchill, who had spent the 1930s in constant frustration, was seventy-one. Stalin at sixty-six had governed his country for seventeen draining years. Roosevelt, who had turned sixty-three the week before the Yalta meeting, had led his country through the worst economic depression and the worst foreign war in its history. Now they were together to lay the foundation for the peace to come.

Was FDR too sick at Yalta to put up a strong U.S. case? His health was poor and his energy level was low; but I do not gather from conversations with persons who were with him at Yalta that his defenses were down. Charles E. Bohlen, a State Department

Soviet expert who served as Roosevelt's interpreter with Stalin, summed up the general testimony: "While his physical state was certainly not up to normal, his mental and psychological state was certainly not affected. He was lethargic but when important moments arose, he was mentally sharp. Our leader was ill at Yalta . . . but he was effective." I interviewed Sir Frank Roberts, later British ambassador to Moscow. "The hand of death was on him," Roberts said, "but it didn't impede his role at Yalta. He was in charge and achieved everything he had come to do. No problem at Yalta derived from Roosevelt's illness." As for the Soviet side, I asked Valentin Berezhkov, Stalin's interpreter, who replied in a letter to me that Roosevelt's health "was certainly worse than in Tehran, but everybody who watched him said that in spite of his frail appearance his mental potential was high. Before he got tired, he was alert, with quick reactions and forceful arguments."

"Stalin treated Roosevelt with great esteem," Berezhkov added, "and as far as I know did not make any comment on FDR's condition. He certainly could have in private with his closest colleagues, but none of them ever mentioned it." Frank Roberts thought that "Roosevelt and Churchill were susceptible to Stalin because he did not fit the dictator stereotype of the time. He was not a demagogue; he did not strut in flamboyant uniforms. He was soft-spoken, well organized, not without humor, knew his brief—an agreeable facade concealing unknown horrors."

Roosevelt had no illusions about Stalin's Russia. "The Soviet Union, as everybody who has the courage to face the fact knows," he told the American Youth Congress in February 1940, "is run by a dictatorship as absolute as any other dictatorship in the world." But FDR, and Churchill too, knew how much the democracies owed the Red Army for the prospective defeat of Adolf Hitler. D-day would never have succeeded if Stalin had not detained most of the Nazy army on Germany's eastern front. By the time the Big Three gathered at Yalta, the Red Army was forty-four miles from Berlin.

Much has been made of Roosevelt's alleged naïveté about the Soviet Union and his alleged conviction that he could charm Stalin into postwar harmony. Certainly FDR had no expert understanding of Leninist ideology or of the terrible internal nature of Stalinist society. He responded to what he saw of Soviet behavior in the world, and he never saw very far into the Soviet Union. Always an optimist, he hoped that the wartime alliance would bridge the ideological chasm and create a new reality for the peace. Even with benefit of hindsight, this still seems a hope worth testing. It had to be tested in any case before the peoples of the democracies could be persuaded that their vital allies were in fact mortal foes.

Did Roosevelt really believe that he could charm Stalin out of the tree? As Walter Lippmann has suggested, he was too cynical for that: "He distrusted everybody. What he thought he could do was outwit Stalin, which is quite a different thing." Perhaps the American president was not so hopelessly naïve after all. For Stalin was not the helpless prisoner of Leninist ideology. The Soviet dictator saw himself less the disciple of Marx and Lenin than their fellow prophet. Roosevelt was surely right in regarding Stalin as the only lever available to the democracies against the rigidities of Leninism. Only Stalin had the power to rewrite Communist doctrine, as he had already rewritten Russian history and Russian science. Roosevelt's determination to court Stalin, to work on and through Stalin, was, I believe, based on the astute reflexes of a master politician. Changing Stalin's mind was the only chance the West had to keep the peace.

Authoritative witnesses—Averell Harriman, U.S. ambassador to the Soviet Union in the last years of the war, and Chip Bohlen and Valentin Berezhkov, the two interpreters—testify that Roosevelt retained to the end a certain capacity to influence Stalin. Harriman contrasted Stalin's evident "deference" to Roosevelt with his constant needling of Churchill and explained it by Stalin's recognition that "Roosevelt represented something entirely new; his New Deal was reforming capitalism to meet the needs and desires of the 'working class.' There was nothing like that in Communist doctrine."

A great foreign policy fear that haunted Roosevelt's generation was the fear of resurgent American isolationism. We sometimes forget how brief an interval separated the two world wars. FDR was thirty-eight years old when the Senate rejected the League of Nations; he was only fifty-seven years old when war broke out again in Europe in 1939—the war predicted by Woodrow Wilson "with absolute certainty" in September 1919 if America did not join the League. During the interwar years the struggle against isolationism consumed much of FDR's time and energy. As foreign policy spokesman for the Democratic Party, he declared in a *Foreign Affairs* article in 1928 that only by actions of international collaboration could the United States "regain the world's trust and friendship."

The experience of an internationalist movement followed by a profound and impassioned isolationist revival had engraved itself indelibly on the consciousness of the old Wilsonians. In the 1942 midterm congressional election, internationalists launched a major campaign for a "win-the-war" Congress, targeting isolationist legislators on a hit list. The leading isolationists in Congress survived the primaries. In FDR's own congressional district, internationalist Republicans like Wendell Willkie and Thomas E. Dewey opposed the renomination of the bitter isolationist Hamilton Fish, but Fish won the primary two to one. In the general election only 5 of 115 congressmen with isolationist records were beaten. The Republicans gained forty-four seats in the House and nine in the Senate—their best performance in years.

After the election, Secretary of State Cordell Hull told Vice President Henry Wallace that "the country was going in exactly the same steps it followed in 1918." Hull, Wallace noted, thought it "utterly important to keep the sequence of events from following the 1918–1921 pattern because he felt if we went into isolationism this time, the world was lost forever."

For Roosevelt the critical task in 1943–45 was to commit the United States to a postwar structure of peace. FDR regarded a permanent international organization, in Chip Bohlen's words, as "the only device that could keep the United States from slipping back to isolationism." The memory, still vivid, of the repudiation of the League two decades before suggested that the task would not be easy. Unilateralism had been the American norm for a century and a half. Internationalism had been a two-year Wilsonian aberration. No one could assume that isolationism would simply wither away. It had to be brought to a definitive end by American commitments to international order, and, as the master politician knew, Congress and the people were more likely to make such commitments while the war was still on. FDR said privately, "Anybody who thinks that isolationism is dead in this country is crazy. As soon as this war is over, it may well be stronger than ever."

He proceeded to lay the groundwork in 1943–45 with the same skill and circumspection with which he had steered the nation away from isolationism in 1937–41. The challenge of contriving a smooth transition from unilateralism to internationalism shaped Roosevelt's diplomatic strategy. He moved quietly to prepare the American people for a larger international role. By the end of 1944 a series of international conferences, held mostly at American initiative and generally with bipartisan American representation, had created a postwar agenda—international organization (Dumbarton Oaks), finance, trade and development (Bretton Woods), food and agriculture (Hot Springs), civil aviation (Chicago), relief and reconstruction (UNRRA). These conferences established a framework for the world after the war—an impressive achievement for a president whom historians used to charge with subordinating political to military goals.

Against this background we can consider Roosevelt's objectives in this last meeting with Stalin. The first priority, I surmise, was to get the United Nations under way before the end of the war on terms that would ensure American and Soviet participation—a result he deemed imperative both to provide the means of correcting any mistake that harassed leaders framing the peace might make and to save his own country from a relapse into isolationism. The second priority was to get the Soviet forces to join the war against Japan by a date certain (the atomic bomb was five months in the future) on terms that would strengthen Chiang Kai-shek's Nationalist regime in China. A third priority was to work out some compromise on Eastern Europe as a test of Soviet intentions; and a fourth, to get a few modest preliminary agreements for the occupation of Germany. "I dislike making detailed plans," Roosevelt explained to Hull in October 1944, "for a country which we do not yet occupy."

Roosevelt achieved his objectives. He established the United Nations organization on terms acceptable both to the American people and to the Soviet Union. Stalin delivered a firm date by which the Red Army would enter the Pacific war, thereby pleasing the American military planners. As for Eastern Europe, Stalin, as Bohlen said, "held all the cards" through the presence of the Red Army, but Roosevelt managed to extract an astonishing document—the Declaration on Liberated Europe, an eloquent affirmation of "the right of all people to choose the form of government under which they will live."

The Soviet commissar for foreign affairs, Vyacheslav Molotov, complained that the declaration "amounted to interference in the affairs of liberated Europe" and warned Stalin against signing it, but Stalin in his provincial way believed, so Harriman always thought, that free elections in Eastern Europe were bound to result in Communist victories. It was a grave diplomatic blunder. The declaration laid down standards for Eastern Europe, and Stalin, in order to consolidate the Soviet position, had to break the Yalta accord. It was indeed a test of Stalin's intentions. The declaration stands too as a refutation of the myth, believed most intensely in France, that Yalta caused or ratified the division of Europe. It was the deployment of armies, not words on paper, that caused the division of Europe.

There are indications that before Yalta, Stalin had decided against postwar collaboration. How else to explain the article by Jacques Duclos, who had been the Comintern official responsible for the Western Communist Parties, in the April 1945 issue of *Cahiers du Communisme*? That article, which was probably written before the Big Three met at Yalta and was certainly planned well before, was an uncompromising attack on the revisionism of the American Communist Party. Duclos specifically rebuked Earl Browder, the CPUSA leader, for favoring class collaboration. He specifically commended Browder's rival William Z. Foster, who later boasted of having said in January 1945, a month before Yalta, "A postwar Roosevelt Administration would continue to be, as it is now, an imperialist government." The Duclos article was Moscow's signal to Communists everywhere that the fun was over and that they should prepare for new confrontations in the postwar world.

For whatever reason, Stalin soon left no doubt that the Soviet Union was striking out on its own unilateral course. Roosevelt's disappointment in the weeks after Yalta has been well documented.

I have come on another document, not, I think, previously noted, that adds to the evidence.

On March 13, 1945, two weeks after his return from Yalta, Roosevelt called Leon Henderson to his office. Henderson was the tough and exceedingly able New Deal economist who had succeeded so brilliantly as director of the Office of Price Administration in keeping wartime inflation under control. Roosevelt had sent Henderson to Europe in December 1944 to check on allied planning for the occupation of Germany, and the president intended to make Henderson the American economic chief for Germany. At their meeting Roosevelt told Henderson that, with reference to Germany,

> We ought not do too much in advance. Didn't I think so? I said, well, no, I thought the Russians were willing to make concessions, that we could get some things settled in advance like coal and transportation and perhaps we ought to move. He said the British, French and ourselves would abide by agreement but the Russians would do to suit themselves! I asked if they were not meticulous on things they agreed to. I remembered the protocols. He said "yes"—on protocols, on anything that would show, but anywhere else, they would go their own way.

So, after Yalta, the Russians indeed went their own way. FDR gained all he had come to Yalta for—Soviet membership in the United Nations, Soviet entry into the Pacific war, a test of Soviet intentions in liberated Eastern Europe. But his vision of the wartime alliance prolonged into peacetime encountered the hard rock of Stalinist ideology. The Second World War left the international order in acute derangement. With the Axis states vanquished, the European allies exhausted, the colonial empires in tumult and dissolution, great gaping holes appeared in the structure of world power. The war left only two states—the United States and the Soviet Union—with the dynamism to flow into these vacuums. The two states were constructed on opposite and antagonistic principles, marvelously incarnated in Franklin D. Roosevelt and Joseph V. Stalin. No one should be surprised by what ensued. The real surprise would have been if there had been no Cold War.

Arthur M. Schlesinger, Jr.

Acknowledgments

This book would not have been possible without the assistance of two people: Robert Clark, supervising archivist at the Franklin D. Roosevelt Library, and Dan Heaton, senior manuscript editor at Yale University Press. Both have given generously of their time and expertise, much beyond the call of duty, and helped me resolve numerous puzzling issues.

Nor would it have been possible without the help of Robert Parks, Mark Renovitch, Alycia Vivona, Karen Anson, and Virginia Lewick at the Library, all of whom were always willing to help me find whatever I needed.

I am indebted to John Lukacs and Arthur Schlesinger, Jr., who both took the time to read the entire manuscript, make valuable suggestions and comments, and rescue me from innumerable errors.

George M. Elsey, Commander, U.S. Naval Reserve, duty officer in the White House Map Room from 1941 to 1946, answered my endless questions about the Map Room.

Jonathan Brent, editorial director of Yale University Press, has given me valuable advice as well as putting the justly famous resources of the Press to work on the manuscript.

I would also like to thank my literary agent, Fredrica Friedman.

David E. Murphy, author of *What Stalin Knew: The Enigma of Barbarossa*, clarified for me the role of Richard Sorge. I want to thank, also, Samuel Clapp and Simon Sebag Montefiore for their invaluable advice.

Last but not least, I would like to thank my husband, Allan C. Butler, another critical reader, who provided the finishing touch: the title.

A Note on the Text

With a few exceptions, all of the messages in *My Dear Mr. Stalin* are from the Franklin D. Roosevelt Library in Hyde Park, N.Y. *My Dear Mr. Stalin* is the first book to contain all of Roosevelt's messages to Stalin, as well as the first book to reproduce these messages in their original wording, properly dated. It is the first book as well to contain all of Stalin's messages to Roosevelt, including the two messages Stalin gave verbally.

The reader will occasionally notice awkward wording in the messages written by Stalin. This is usually due to issues of translation, but since these are Stalin's messages as Roosevelt read them, I have intentionally left them uncorrected.

Unless otherwise noted, italics and line-throughs denote longhand additions and deletions by Roosevelt.

Spellings of place names have changed since the 1940s; indeed, there was no uniformity in spelling in the messages. For the sake of clarity, then, place-name spellings have been regularized.

Introduction

OR sixty years the wartime correspondence between Franklin Roosevelt and Joseph Stalin has languished in obscurity. The correspondence was secret at the time—its existence known only to Roosevelt, Stalin, and their closest advisers—and it was extensive: just over three hundred messages. The messages were sent by cable and often paraphrased to ensure secrecy, although occasionally one of the world leaders would choose an important official such as Harry Hopkins to present a message to the other in person.

No accurate and complete record of this correspondence has ever been published. In 1957 the Soviet Ministry of Foreign Affairs issued *Stalin's Correspondence with Attlee, Churchill, Roosevelt, and Truman*, based on texts of documents in Soviet archives, and this has been reproduced, either under the original title or as *Stalin's Correspondence with Roosevelt and Truman*. But key Roosevelt messages are missing, others are represented only by paraphrases of the messages Roosevelt wrote, all are dated according to when they were received in the Kremlin rather than when they were sent.

My Dear Mr. Stalin is the first book to include all the messages as Roosevelt wrote them, and all Stalin's messages, in the form Roosevelt read them.

The subjects discussed include U.S. armament shipments, the armaments needs of the Soviet Union, strategic decisions to be taken in the war against Hitler and his allies, many messages on the progress of the war and the date of the cross-Channel invasion, the fate of Poland, of intense interest to both men, the terms of surrender, the role and authority of the Security Council, and the composition of the General Assembly. Franklin Roosevelt sent the first message in July 1941. The messages continued until Roosevelt's sudden death in April 1945.

The backgrounds of the two leaders could not have been more different. Roosevelt was born into one of America's first families, brought up in New York in a world of wealth and culture, a coddled only child, educated at Groton, Harvard College, and Columbia University. He married his distant cousin Eleanor Roosevelt, the niece of President Theodore Roosevelt, and rose steadily in state and national politics by virtue of his magnetic personality and intelligence and in spite of the affliction of polio. Stalin, whose mother was a peasant and whose father was a cobbler who drank and who died in a brawl, was born and brought up in Georgia, the republic that formed the southern rim of the USSR. As a child he contracted smallpox, which marked his face; suffered a trauma, probably septicemia, which withered his left arm; and had a form of clubfoot that made him walk with a noticeable rolling gait. A scholarship seminary student noted for his phenomenal memory, he became a revolutionary, was expelled from school, survived prison and exile, helped found and edit *Pravda*, caught Lenin's eye, and became general secretary in 1922. In 1924, when Lenin died, he was one of the seven members of the Politburo. Later four were executed after being forced to confess to treason in the so-called show trials and one committed suicide; the last to die was Leon Trotsky, murdered in Mexico in 1940. By 1941 Stalin had ruled the Soviet Union for twelve years. During that time he forced the collectivization and the industrialization of the USSR that turned it into a superpower, methodically eliminating everyone who stood in his way, as well as those of his friends who had grown too powerful. He could be disarmingly pleasant, but he ruled through fear.

Roosevelt was a man who operated by persuasion and charm and a certain attitude of laissez-faire. He sought ideas and advisers, enjoyed the competition among them, and made up his own mind.

He was a master at bringing people around to his own point of view. The president was determined to break through an arms-length relationship, get to know his man, and make Stalin trust him. To a great extent he succeeded: these letters are the record of the lengths he went to. Roosevelt's messages reveal how he went about shaping the postwar world, how meticulous was the planning that turned the united nations that were fighting Germany and Japan into the United Nations (it was Roosevelt who dreamed up the name) that would keep the peace. Stalin's messages reveal his fears of a strong Germany, his insistence on a subservient Poland, his acceptance of but reservations about the United Nations, and his latent fear that Roosevelt and Churchill might betray him, as Hitler had done, that they might sign a separate peace with Germany.

It might have been expected that the complete communications of these two world leaders would have been published before now, but following Roosevelt's death the Cold War was upon the world, and the last thing anyone wanted to read about was how Roosevelt had helped the Soviet Union beat Germany.

Joseph E. Davies, U.S. ambassador to the Soviet Union from 1936 to 1938, advising Roosevelt as Hitler marched across Europe, predicted in June 1939, that if British Prime Minister Neville Chamberlain continued to appease Germany, "the old Bear will get tired of being cuffed around and make peace on his own terms possibly with Germany."[1] Exactly that happened in August; Germany and Russia signed the Nazi-Soviet pact. Thus protected, Stalin was sure Russia was safe from Hitler. In the spring of 1941, as German forces began assembling for an attack, Stalin refused to believe what was plain to everyone else. From various trusted intelligence sources around the world, as well as from agents inside Germany, came warnings that German forces were massing along the Soviet border and that war was imminent. Nevertheless, on June 14 Stalin ordered *Tass* to publish a statement that "Germany is observing the terms of the non-aggression Pact as scrupulously as the USSR, and therefore rumors of Germany's intention to violate the Pact and attack the USSR are groundless."[2] On the night of June 21, 1941, a report from German defectors who had risked their lives crossing into Russia was placed on Stalin's table with information that the invasion was set for the next day: still Stalin didn't react. Operation Barbarossa commenced at dawn, totally stunning the self-styled strongman (he had changed his name from Djugashvili to Stalin, which meant man of steel).

By the end of July, 3.6 million of Hitler's soldiers had crossed through Poland and were rolling across Russia. Hitler had already conquered Czechoslovakia, Poland, Holland, Belgium, France, Greece, Yugoslavia, Denmark, and Norway. Opinion in the United States and in Great Britain was divided as to whether the Soviet Union would survive. Secretary of War Henry Stimson wrote Roosevelt the day after the invasion that the undisputed consensus of the Army Chiefs of Staff, with which he concurred, was that "Germany will be thoroughly occupied in beating Russia for a minimum of one month and a possible maximum of three months."[3] Roosevelt thereupon requested army and navy planners to map out the probable theaters of war and the manpower that the United States would need to fight Germany. The resulting Victory Program, as the War Plans Division called its blueprint for mobilization, assumed that Russia would be out of the war by 1943. William C. Bullitt, who had served as first U.S. ambassador to Soviet Russia from 1933 to 1936, agreed. "I know no man in Washington who believes that the Soviet Army can defeat the German Army," he told the American Legion in August. Roosevelt was more optimistic. He asked the Soviet ambassador in Washington, Constantin Oumansky, to give him a list of the things that the Soviets most desperately needed to defend their country.[4]

Two days after the invasion Roosevelt released $39 million of frozen Russian assets. Four days later he put his views down on paper for Admiral William Leahy, ambassador to Vichy France; he was clearly hoping that Hitler's commitment was total. "Now comes this Russian diversion. If it is more than just that it will mean the liberation of Europe from Nazi domination—and at the same time I do not think we need worry about any possibility of Russian domination."[5] Five weeks after the invasion Harry Hopkins, Roosevelt's eyes and ears—virtually his alter ego—carried the president's first message to Stalin, assuring him that the United States was coming to the aid of the beleaguered nation. Three months after the invasion, as the German army closed in on Moscow, Roosevelt sent Averell Harriman, who had set up the Lend-Lease program for England, to Moscow with Lord Beaverbrook to draw up an agreement which became known as the Moscow Protocol, which committed the United States to send slightly over $1 billion to the Soviet Union in the following twelve months. He delivered Roosevelt's second message to Stalin.

The correspondence reveals the personalities as well as the policies of Roosevelt and Stalin. We see Roosevelt's awareness of Stalin's mistrust and suspicion of foreigners, a mistrust that permeated Russian society, which Roosevelt spared no effort to overcome. There is a discernable flow to Roosevelt's messages to Stalin. Roosevelt is determinedly friendly. He compliments, flatters, sometimes at Churchill's expense. As the war progresses and he distances himself from Churchill, he soothes Stalin, long-distance. He goes to extraordinary lengths, disregarding the advice of the many government officials who did not approve of his accommodating posture, in his resolve to forge a relationship between the two countries that will survive the war. The interdependence of nations was one of Roosevelt's core beliefs. As he stated well before he was on the national scene, "Our civilization cannot endure unless we, as individuals, realize our personal responsibility to and dependence on the rest of the world."[6]

The correspondence clearly shows that even as Roosevelt was organizing America's entrance into the war he was planning for the peace that would follow. "It was this astounding instinct for the future which above all distinguished Roosevelt," wrote Arthur Schlesinger, Jr., "his extraordinary sensitivity to the emergent tendencies of his age."[7]

It was Roosevelt's deep conviction that when the war was won, the peace should rest with "Four Policemen"—himself, Stalin, Churchill, and Chiang Kai-shek—who would shape and supervise the postwar world by virtue of representing the most powerful (in China's case, potentially powerful) and most populous countries on earth.

The first public clue to Roosevelt's thinking was the care with which he rearranged the order of the signatories of the Associated Powers Declaration (which he renamed the United Nations Declaration on the last day of 1941), which established the grand coalition of countries fighting the Axis powers. When the representatives of the twenty-six countries gathered at the White House to sign the declaration on New Year's Day, 1942, they signed in the order drawn up in the president's handwriting: the United States, the United Kingdom, the USSR, and China; after them all the other countries are listed alphabetically.

Roosevelt's Four Policemen concept shaped the Map Room, which came into being in the White House shortly after the U.N. Declaration. The Map Room was set up by the president's naval aide, Captain John L. McCrea, to be Roosevelt's military information center and communications office, his war room. The walls were lined with maps and charts updated constantly as battle news came in. It was on the ground floor of the White House, across the hall from the elevator, next to the doctor's office. Roosevelt would wheel himself to the Map Room to see the latest war developments and messages, then visit the doctor's office, typically in the late afternoon. There he sat in the dentist's chair installed for him and had his sinuses treated and his legs massaged.

By his own plan the Map Room was the only place in government that contained the complete file of his communications with Stalin, Churchill, and Chiang and their respective governments, and it contained none of his messages to any other national leader. To ensure that neither the secretary of war, nor the secretary of the navy, nor the secretary of state, nor the Joint Chiefs of Staff were aware of the importance he attached to the concept of the Four Policemen, Roosevelt directed that all cables from him to the three world leaders were sent through Navy Department communications and coding facilities and all replies came in through War Department circuits. (All the messages were sent in code, often paraphrased to better prevent the codes from being broken.) "It was the President's wish to have in the Map Room the only complete file of the personal messages he exchanged with Churchill, Stalin, and Chiang Kai-Shek," according to George M. Elsey, commander in the U.S. Naval Reserve and for many years duty officer in the Map Room.[8]

It must be noted that playing his cards close to the chest was his habitual modus operandi: "You never put them on the table," complained Secretary of the Interior Harold Ickes.[9] Gen. John R. Deane, who had been secretary of the Combined Chiefs of Staff (that is, the Anglo-American chiefs) until 1943, was amazed to discover that the American chiefs of staff didn't always know of decisions taken between Roosevelt and Churchill. "For some reason our President often kept our Chiefs of Staff in the dark on these matters until the die was cast."[10]

Access to the Map Room was limited to Harry Hopkins and Admiral Leahy, who became chief of staff to the president following his return from Vichy France in late spring 1942. Except for the code officers and three army watch officers and three navy watch officers on duty around the clock, no one else came in. The only exception was Prime Minister Churchill, when he was in residence at the White House, and although he could examine the progress of the war laid out on the maps and charts covering the walls, he had no access to the files, which were under lock and key.

The transmittal of messages through army and navy channels not only suited Roosevelt's passion for secrecy, it solved the problem of lax State Department transmittal procedures. As Roosevelt knew only too well, his second message to Stalin in September 1941, which he had entrusted to the State Department to deliver to Harriman in Moscow, had been transmitted in the Brown code, one of the least secret of the department codes, which the Germans had intercepted and broken. On October 25, 1941, the State Department sent another message from the president to Stalin by diplomatic pouch, which was delivered to the Kremlin the following spring. Clearly, the State Department was not up to the job of transmitting messages safely.

Roosevelt articulated the idea of the Four Policemen to Vyacheslav Molotov, commissar for foreign affairs, Stalin's most trusted associate, whom he invited to Washington in June 1942 to discuss the possible opening of a second front. Roosevelt told Molotov of his belief that postwar security should be guaranteed by the four countries—the United States, the Soviet Union, England, and China—pointing out that they had a combined population of more than one billion, making them the natural choices to enforce peace instead of "another League of Nations with 100 different signatories."[11] Not incidentally, the global character of such a coalition would discourage regional agreements.

Roosevelt gave to Secretary of State Cordell Hull the task of making the USSR as well as the United Kingdom accept the plan in fact as well as theory. Hull did so in Moscow the following year at the Conference of Foreign Ministers. For Roosevelt and for Hull, the inclusion of China was very important. As they were both aware, China's population was greater than that of the other three nations combined; China and Russia shared the longest border in the world. China, Roosevelt knew, had to be included from the beginning. Roosevelt was therefore adamant that it be a four-power declaration that would form the basis for a postwar peacekeeping organization in spite of opposition from both his allies. Because China was at war with Japan, the Soviet Union was apprehensive that including the Chinese might unduly provoke Japan. Churchill was also less than enthusiastic about the four-power idea, observing of the Russians, "They do not want to be mixed up in all this rot about China as a great Power, any more than I do," but he went along.[12] Extracting agreement on the four-power declaration from the Russians was, according to General Deane, who was present at the talks, "the crowning achievement of Secretary Hull's career."[13] The declaration, signed by Molotov, Eden, Hull, and Foo Ping-sheung, the Chinese ambassador in Moscow, provided for united action against the enemy and unanimity on terms of surrender, stipulated the necessity of creating an international organization, and included agreement not to employ military force in other states unilaterally.

But for the next step, welding these countries into the international body he had in mind, Roosevelt needed personal contact. He knew that only if he and Stalin met could they begin to discuss what the future world should look like. The President began pressing Stalin for a meeting almost at once. Roosevelt was sure that exposure to his personal charm would influence Stalin to trust him.

Roosevelt was a master, according to his contemporaries, at bringing people around to his point of view. Admirers and detractors alike conceded that after one private visit with Roosevelt most political leaders were putty in his hands. His weapon was his vibrant personality. He was, his speechwriter Sam Rosenman observed, "firmly convinced of his own ability to get along with people and to work out acceptable agreements with them."[14]

Roosevelt made it a point to know as much about Stalin as he could. He was aware that as a young man Stalin "had been given over to robbery and murder, all justified by the Marxian theory that the end justified the means."[15] He knew about and spoke about "the indiscriminate killings of thousands of innocent victims."[16] Still, Roosevelt was determined to break through the arms-length relationship and bring Stalin to the realization that a permanent commitment to a postwar peacekeeping organization was in the best interests of the Soviet Union: that in such a political climate Russia would be able to rebuild its shattered economy and achieve its goal of becoming a functioning industrial society. "I bank on his realism. He must be tired of sitting on bayonets," he said to his personal physician, Vice Admiral Ross McIntire.[17]

Roosevelt's correspondence with Churchill has been published, their relationship analyzed in countless books, but this is partly because Churchill, a brilliant writer, made his relationship with Roosevelt appear closer than it was. As Churchill admitted to President Dwight David Eisenhower, to prepare him for the sixth and final volume of his memoirs, *The History of the Second World War,* "I have therefore gone over the book again in the last few months and have taken great pains to ensure that it contains nothing which might imply that there was in those days any controversy or lack of confidence between us. There was in fact little controversy in those years; but I have been careful to ensure that the few differences of opinion which arose are so described that even ill-disposed people will be unable now to turn them to mischievous account."[18]

Because of the Cold War the Roosevelt-Stalin correspondence, in contrast, dropped out of sight, lessening appreciation for the president's wartime statesmanship and diplomacy; no credit has flowed to Roosevelt for his signal achievement of bringing the Soviet Union into the United Nations.

Roosevelt had planned to open the San Francisco Conference at 4:30 on the afternoon of April 25 with an address at the first plenary session. The speech he was planning was very much on his mind—his secretary was expecting to take down the first draft—

when, a fortnight before the conference, he died. Among other consequences, Roosevelt's death robbed the United Nations of the dramatic start his presence would have ensured. On the other hand, Roosevelt's death so affected Stalin that he changed his mind and sent Foreign Minister Molotov to San Francisco to show Russia's solid support for Roosevelt's organization for world peace.

The question is not why Roosevelt acted as though he believed in Stalin, or how Stalin pulled the wool over his eyes. It is, rather, what other tactic would have worked as well. Roosevelt wanted to win the war; he wanted to win the peace that followed. Peace plans were not in place at the close of World War I, and at Versailles the leaders of the victorious Allies, suffering from lack of preparation, made bad decisions; then the United States withdrew into its isolationist cocoon. Roosevelt was determined neither of those things would happen on his watch; his paramount goal was a world organization that would prevent the world from plunging into war again. How could he have created the United Nations any other way than by making Stalin believe he was safer inside it than outside? How could he have gotten a commitment from Stalin to move his troops across Siberia after Germany was defeated and to declare war against Russia's ancient enemy Japan—a commitment that the Joint Chiefs of Staff insisted would save two hundred thousand American lives—unless the Soviet leader trusted the American president? For to a limited extent—that is, within the confines of his personality—the record shows that Joseph Stalin trusted and admired Franklin Roosevelt as he trusted no other leader in the world.

Roosevelt's attitude of accommodation with the Soviet Union was viewed by many at the time as misguided. It still is so viewed in many quarters. The fact that Roosevelt made possible the delivery of massive war materiél from the United States at a critically early moment, helping to enable Stalin to turn back the German invaders and save his country and our world, was conveniently forgotten. So rapidly did things change after Roosevelt's death and the end of the war that as early as the fall of 1945, it was hard to imagine that Stalin had been on *Time* magazine's cover as Man of the Year for 1942, that the magazine had painted him as the savior of the Western world.

Roosevelt operated on the assumption that England and the United States were safe only as long as the Soviet Union held out, and that therefore the United States had to provide the Soviets with everything it deemed necessary. Unlike most of his contemporaries, he never wavered in this belief.

Roosevelt threw his weight into making sure that the United States fed, clothed, and armed the Soviet Army and supplied the tools and raw materials it needed to rebuild its factories. The U.S. aid to the Soviets was on a huge scale. As Roosevelt wrote to Secretary of War Henry Stimson on August 30, 1941, shortly after Hitler invaded Russia, "I deem it of paramount importance for the safety and security of America that all reasonable munitions help be provided for Russia, not only immediately but as long as she continues to fight the Axis powers effectively."[19]

Many in the army, the navy, and the State Department tried to limit U.S. aid to Russia or attach strings to it; Roosevelt refused to permit restrictions. Stimson, forced to deal with Oumansky in the summer of 1941, characterized the Soviet ambassador as a "crook" and "a slick, clever little beast."[20] Even General George Marshall commented that summer, "I think the President should have it clearly pointed out to him that Mr. Oumansky will take everything we own."[21]

Despite their misgivings, both men did what they were told. Starting in March 1942, when needed equipment wasn't reaching Russia quickly enough because of production and convoy problems, Roosevelt put all U.S. war agencies involved in Lend-Lease on notice that he wanted all supplies promised to the Soviet Union released for shipment and shipped as early as possible, regardless how it affected either U.S. or U.K. war programs. General Deane, whom Ambassador Harriman had brought to Moscow with him in 1943 as head of the military mission to administer the Lend-Lease program, commented that this decision of Roosevelt was correct, "one of the most important decisions of the war and one that was vitally essential when it was taken."[22]

Not only did Roosevelt direct that all Russian orders for equipment must be filled, even at great sacrifice to the U.S. war effort, he directed that aid was never to be used as a lever to extract information either from or about the Soviet Union. General Marshall concurred in this policy, although reluctantly, becoming convinced that a quest for such information not only was unnecessary but would irritate the Russians and make operational collaboration "impossible," that nothing was surer to feed Russian xenophobia than to try to trade arms for information.[23] But there was a second reason that Roosevelt was so insistent on the flow of unstinting aid: it was a means of showing Stalin the incredible productive capacity, the robustness, the industrial might of a democratic society. If he had lived, Roosevelt undoubtedly would have continued the policy of generous aid to Russia, instead of abruptly cutting the flow after V.E. day, May 8, 1945. As he wrote to Secretary of State Edward Stettinius on January 5, 1945, "It is my desire that every effort be made to continue a full and uninterrupted flow of supplies to the U.S.S.R."[24]

Harry Hopkins, who earlier had served as head of the Works Progress Administration and the Federal Emergency Relief Administration, as well as secretary of commerce, was the administrator of Lend-Lease and lived in the White House. To make sure that the State Department, which Roosevelt characterized as populated to a large extent by wealthy Ivy League career officers—"fossilized bureaucrats," he called them, generally biased against the Soviet Union—as well as officers in the War Department, also studded with anti-Soviet personnel, didn't interfere with the flow of goods to Russia, Roosevelt made Hopkins head of the newly created Soviet Protocol Committee, thereby circumventing the sabotage efforts of both the State Department and the entire command structure of the army and navy.[25] The president then personally chose Maj. Gen. James H. Burns, fully as committed as Hopkins to the Russian cause, to administer the agency in Washington under Hopkins. General Burns in turn chose Col. Philip R. Faymonville to head Lend-Lease in Moscow and work out Russian priorities. (Administering Lend-Lease turned out to be too taxing and time consuming for Hopkins, who shortly turned it over to Stettinius, his friend who had reorganized U.S. Steel and was as committed to the program as he.)

Faymonville, a West Point graduate, fluent in Russian, had been military attaché in Moscow from 1934 to 1939. While there he spent time with Russians, as other U.S. personnel never did and considered odd; he made many Soviet friends, including Anastas Mikoyan, later the commissar of foreign trade and the Russian in charge of Lend-Lease. Such conduct was questioned by many in the army, where anti-Soviet feeling ran high. In 1938 the army mounted a concerted attack on Faymonville, determined to have him fired as military attaché, going so far as sending derogatory opinions about him to interested parties in the State Department. "I am confident that all officers in the Department who have been stationed in Moscow in Faymonville's time there would agree that the public interest will be served by his tour of duty there being ended," ran one letter. "The Army authorities on their own had reached the conclusion that Colonel Faymonville's usefulness to them was at an end," read another letter, claiming Faymonville had made derogatory remarks about fellow officers.[26] Joseph E. Davies disagreed; he wrote to Roosevelt in 1939 that Faymonville was so effective that if the United States established a secret liaison for the interchange of military and naval information on east Asia with the Soviet government (which was under consideration), Faymonville should be the Moscow representative. Both Stalin and Molotov, Davies reported, "expressed confidence in the judgment, capacity and fairness of our Military Attaché, Lieutenant Colonel Philip R. Faymonville."[27] The secret liaison never came to pass; instead, the army got its way and sent Faymonville home to San Francisco. He became chief ordnance officer for western defenses. Army brass were horrified when Hopkins announced shortly after his trip to meet Stalin that Faymonville would be in charge of Lend-Lease in Moscow, stunned when he insisted that Faymonville be promoted to general; again they tried to get him out of the Soviet Union. Within a short time the Office of the Chief of Staff of the War Department officially requested of J. Edgar Hoover that the Federal Bureau of Investigation target Faymonville. An extensive "discreet" investigation into every aspect of his past was conducted, with the expectation of uncovering evidence of homosexuality. FBI agents examined his life in his childhood home of San Francisco, his extensive schooling, and how and where he spent his leaves; they interviewed personnel in every post he had been posted to. To the chagrin of the army and the FBI, nothing negative turned up. Everyone interrogated without exception praised him. "This was the opinion of all persons interviewed and no derogatory information as to General Faymonville's moral character was uncovered," ran one letter.[28] Another FBI informant volunteered that Faymonville was well liked by Russian officials and observed that "the subject was very well versed in the customs of the Russian people and he spoke their language fluently."[29] General Deane, who had appointed him, called him "the Army's outstanding student of Russian affairs."[30]

The shipments began in October 1941. The paralyzed Russian factories received American machine tools and raw materials—rubber, aluminum, duralumin, brass, cobalt, steel "of all varieties," lead, tin, rubber, armor plate for tanks—so that they could begin to supply their own needs. The army received supplies—planes, 400 a month; tanks, 500 a month; cars, 5,000 in the next nine months; and in huge quantities antitank guns, antiaircraft guns with spare barrels and ammunition, diesel generators, field telephones, field telephone wire, radios, motorcycles, army cloth, wheat, flour, sugar, 500,000 pairs of surgical gloves, 15,000 amputation saws. In October alone 5,500 trucks were shipped. In November, Stalin acknowledged receipt of 432 planes.[31] But this First Protocol, as it was called, which had been agreed to at the Moscow Supply Conference in early October 1941, was not enough. Roosevelt would add, as he wrote Stalin the end of October, a long list of other items, including 200,000 pairs of boots and a million yards of woolen overcoat cloth every month. As far as Roosevelt was concerned, whatever Stalin needed was what Stalin would get. Three additional protocol agreements followed, each running one year, each readjusting the amounts and requirements. By the time of the Second Protocol, starting in the summer of 1942, the United States agreed, among other things, to supply the Soviet Union every month with 500 Jeeps, 10,000 trucks, and 200,000 machine guns complete with ammunition "in the same proportion as for United States troops."[32]

Trucks and combat vehicles were perhaps the most visible American items on the Russian front: more than 400,000 trucks reached Russia, all very much in evidence, each identifiable by the blue "U.S." and serial number stenciled on the hood. Enough food was sent to Russia to supply each soldier with more than a half-pound of rations per day.

Roosevelt would brook no slowdown in the flow of material even in the summer of 1942, when the Atlantic coastline of the United States was harassed by German submarines. The U.S. Air Force was still short of planes, so civilian pilots who had been organized into the Civil Air Patrol patrolled the east coast—in their own planes. Nevertheless, the Second Protocol, which covered this period, called for the shipment to Russia "at an average rate of 100 pursuits, 100 light bombers, and 12 medium bombers per month."[33]

Ramping up factories to supply the huge requirements of the U.S. military as well as those of the Soviet Union and Great Britain was one part of the challenge. Another was getting the ships through to the Soviet Union. The northern supply route around Norway to Archangel on the Arctic Ocean was the shortest route by far, measuring 4,673 nautical miles from New York, but it was the most dangerous, because German U-boats roamed the North Atlantic, and when Archangel became icebound, the trapped convoys had to be rescued by Soviet icebreakers. The toll was high, even though the merchant ships moved in heavily guarded convoys. In 1942 a quarter of the ships bound for Archangel were sunk, nineteen in the first week in April. The seventeenth convoy to sail in 1943 tells part of the dismal story. Out of thirty-five cargo ships that started out for Archangel, two returned to Iceland for technical reasons, twenty-two were sunk (eleven were only damaged but were abandoned by their crews and sent to the bottom by the convoy itself), and eleven reached Archangel. The southern supply route by way of the Middle East was safer but much longer: only 15 percent of those bound for the Persian Gulf were sunk, but from New York to Cape Town to the head of the Persian Gulf measured 12,010 nautical miles; from San Francisco via Singapore to the Persian Gulf ports was only slightly shorter. And once landed in the Persian Gulf, the supplies then had to be transported across Iran. Planes were often shipped by the southern route, and aviation gasoline and other petroleum products delivered there (360,000 tons in 1943). Besides the great distance by sea, a second limiting factor

was the scarcity of trucks. To address this problem 1,900 steam locomotives, 66 diesel locomotives, 9,920 railroad flatcars, 1,000
railroad dump cars, 120 tank cars, and 35 heavy machinery cars
were ordered, built from scratch to fit the wider Russian railroad
gauge, and successfully delivered. As the war ground on, one hundred ships en route or loading for Russia at any one time was the
norm. When U-boats or bad weather caused shipping to fall behind
and additional ships had to laid on to meet the agreed-upon quotas,
Roosevelt's orders as relayed by Hopkins were unequivocal: "The
President desires that ships be provided to fill our quotas . . . even
though this action necessitates changes in commitments of ships already made to other purposes."[34] In January 1942 Roosevelt wrote
a blistering letter to E. S. Land, chairman of the U.S. Maritime
Commission, advising him that he was "disturbed and dissatisfied"
with the number of ships on their way to Russia and urging him to
do more.[35]

The policy of unquestioned massive aid to the Soviet Union that
Roosevelt and Hopkins laid down was to a great extent based on
information and advice supplied by Davies, who had resigned as
ambassador to the Soviet Union in 1938 for personal reasons. On
the flyleaf of his book *Mission to Moscow,* which Davies had given
the president in December 1941, Roosevelt wrote, "This book will
last."

Roosevelt appreciated Davies's view of the Soviet Union and of
the increasingly dark international scene. Davies had predicted that
Stalin might have to make a pact with Hitler and laid out the reasons. Roosevelt, as a consequence, called Davies in for consultation
within weeks of Operation Barbarossa and several times that fall as
he formulated the aid package finally worked out with Russia.
Whether or not Roosevelt appropriated the seed of the idea of the
Four Policemen from Davies, in 1941 both of them were thinking
along the same lines about the British Empire, the United States (although Davies wrote "the Americas"), the Soviet Union, and
China. Davies called them "the great complementary powers of the
earth," because their resources, manpower, raw materials, industrial production, and potential military and naval strength were so
overwhelming and they could be harnessed "so that all men might
live in a decent world."[36]

Davies is often seen as an apologist for Stalin and for communism. This perception is more a commentary on the pervasive anti-communist sentiment of the time than on anything Davies wrote or said. He was neither an apologist for Stalin nor pro-communist. He thought, as did many astute observers at that time, including Roosevelt, that what Stalin wanted—what he believed the Soviet Union needed—was not war but a world at peace so that it could continue transforming itself from a backward agrarian country into a twentieth-century industrial state.

As ambassador to the Soviet Union from November 1936 to June 1938, Davies had quickly developed good rapport with top-level Russian officials, including Stalin, who admired the verve of the free-spending, extraordinarily wealthy American and his even wealthier wife, Marjorie Merriweather Post. On Roosevelt's request, Davies investigated the military and industrial strength of the country, chartering a private railroad car for a two-thousand-mile trip around the Soviet Union, during which he visited new industrial sites, new factories, new power plants seemingly created overnight, "whole regions of plain converted into extraordinary cities and districts dotted with smoking chimneys where but six or seven years ago it was only prairie or bare hills."[37] He noted that even though it wasn't admitted publicly, to become efficient factories were paying their workers according to their output and ability. He believed that communism was so alien to the human spirit that eventually it would fail.

Davies ignored the embassy staff of Soviet experts. He recommended that George Kennan, who was sick, be transferred back to Washington to occupy the new Russian desk at the State Department. He took none of the embassy staff along with him on his tour of the Soviet Union.

Charles Bohlen, who replaced Kennan, later claimed that Davies "never even faintly understood the purges, going far toward accepting the official Soviet version of the existence of a conspiracy against the state." But early in his career Bohlen, a well-connected Harvard graduate, was insulted by the midwesterner Davies, a businessman who had been head of the Federal Trade Commission and who, Bohlen wrote, "treated the [Embassy] staff as hired help and rarely listened to its views."[38] In fact, Davies, who had been a trial lawyer as well as entrepreneur, was increasingly appalled by the purges. He attended the first of the trials, which were called show trials because the officials being tried had already all admitted to their crimes, a few days after his arrival. He wrote about it to Roosevelt: "This trial is a demonstration of the fact that, unless government provides for and protects constitutional methods for opposition to find an outlet, where there exist honest differences of opinion, human nature, even under autocracy, will inevitably find a way, even through conspiracies that breed terrorism, sabotage, assassinations, and the like."[39] Bohlen, Davies's interpreter at the third trial, thought that Davies was naïve even to consider that a prisoner might be innocent, but upon reflection he had to admit that even he "could not separate fact from fiction at the trial. . . . I knew the trial was a phony, but I could not prove it."[40]

Following the resignation of Davies in 1939, Roosevelt appointed Laurence Steinhardt as U.S. ambassador to the Soviet Union. Steinhardt, who was in Moscow when Hitler mounted Operation Barbarossa, was a wealthy lawyer, banker, and professional diplomat. Steinhardt had been chosen particularly because of his banking background and his close ties to the New York banking community. He was expected to work out the thorny problem of Russia's long-standing debt to the United States, which in 1939 continued to roil the relationship between the two countries. In war-torn Russia, Steinhardt's area of expertise was irrelevant and his jaundiced opinion of the Soviet Union made his exit imperative. Just before the German invasion, Steinhardt mistakenly advised Washington that the Ukrainians would not fight for Russia and that "the Stalinist regime could not survive any invasion."[41] Somehow Stalin heard of the ambassador's opinions, for when Averell Harriman arrived in late September, Stalin told him that Steinhardt was a defeatist chiefly interested in his own safety and, further, that the ambassador had twice panicked during the weeks after Operation Barbarossa had commenced. Steinhardt left in mid-November.

Adm. William H. Standley was the next ambassador. Standley was a former chief of naval operations, delegate to the London Naval Conference of 1935, a member of Averell Harriman's team that worked out the first Lend-Lease arrangements with the Soviet Union in October 1941, and an old friend of the president's. But from the moment he arrived in the Soviet Union it became apparent that his own government did not include him in the highest planning councils; he was therefore gradually excluded from Soviet planning councils as well. He arrived in Moscow on April 11, 1942, the day Stalin received a message from Roosevelt asking him to send Vyacheslav Molotov to Washington to discuss "a very important military proposal."[42] The proposal was the opening of a second front—as far as Stalin was concerned, the only action that would blunt the might of the German Army in Russia and save his country.

The message from Roosevelt that Standley delivered to Stalin on April 23 contained no reference to the second front or to Molotov's visit. Stalin, the hands-on head of the Soviet Army, would immediately have noted as he listened to the message being translated for him paragraph by paragraph that Standley, even if he was an admiral and a personal friend of the president's, was out of the military-planning loop, for neither in the message nor in the discussion that followed was this major undertaking mentioned.

Nor was Standley present during the talks in Moscow that Winston Churchill had with Stalin in August 1942. Rather than Standley, Roosevelt sent Harriman to represent American interests. When Roosevelt wanted to set up a private meeting with Stalin—a meeting of the two of them without Churchill—he sent Davies to Moscow rather than risk having Standley do it.

Wendell Willkie visited the Soviet Union carrying a letter of introduction from Roosevelt to Stalin in September 1942—a tour the president felt he owed the Republican whom he had beaten in 1940. ("You of all people ought to know that we might not have had Lend-Lease or Selective Service or a lot of other things if it hadn't been for Wendell Willkie," he once reprimanded Harry Hopkins, who had said something slighting about Willkie.)[43] Willkie not only bypassed the ambassador but, as Standley later wrote, was rude to him: "His actions and attitudes toward me personally on a number of occasions were openly deprecatory and even hostile."[44]

Yet another situation irked Standley: General Faymonville, the Moscow head of Lend-Lease, did not report to him. He tried to change this state of affairs, but Faymonville was an old Russian hand by the time Standley came on the scene: he had his orders from Roosevelt and Hopkins, and his orders did not include reporting to the ambassador. He politely refused.

Shortly after Willkie's visit Standley requested permission to return to the United States to deliver "a very important message" from Stalin. Roosevelt thought it might be a policy matter of grave importance, given the enormous pressure Stalin was under: the German Army was besieging Stalingrad, battling meter by meter toward the Volga through the ruined city under cover of German planes making three thousand sorties a day compared with the Soviet Union's three hundred; on top of that, German U-boats were wreaking havoc with the convoys so that the supplies were not getting through.[45] Stalin's message, however, was a detailed analysis of the Soviet Union's most imperative armament needs—more fighter planes to combat German air superiority—for which they would forsake the delivery of tanks and artillery, as well more trucks, more wheat, fats, meats. Because of U.S. and British convoy losses, Stalin also suggested shipping at least the foodstuffs on Soviet ships via Vladivostock. But he had already mentioned these things to Wendell Willkie, Stalin noted.

Admiral Standley in fact had traveled a long way in wartime merely to present in person a list of grievances to official Washington. At his meeting with the president, he told Roosevelt that he would return to the Soviet Union only if the State Department made it clear to the Kremlin that he should not be ignored. "I resented such actions as the Soviet Foreign Office had countenanced and facilitated in permitting Mr. Willkie repeatedly to by-pass me," he said. He stipulated also, "If I were to return to my post in Moscow, it would have to be with positive evidence of continued confidence in me and increased prestige." And finally, Standley insisted that he wouldn't return to Moscow until it was made clear that General Faymonville would report to him.[46]

Roosevelt and Hopkins had made it clear that "it was not in the interest of the United States to make aid contingent upon full information."[47] Faymonville provided the Russians with information about U.S. policies, if it seemed appropriate and facilitated Lend-Lease. But the military and naval attachés in Moscow and Admiral Standley disagreed with this policy, arguing that in return for aid the Russians should be giving them complete and accurate answers to the multitude of questions they submitted; Standley and the attachés also disagreed in principle with the open-handed U.S. aid policy.

When Standley demanded that Faymonville report to him, the president was noncommittal (and Hopkins, who was present, was silent). "We'll see what we can do, Bill," Roosevelt finally offered, but on November 20 Roosevelt met with Joseph E. Davies at the White House and offered him the ambassadorship. When Davies declined on the grounds of ill health, the White House decided to make the best of a bad situation, offering palliatives to Standley and sending him back to the Soviet Union. Orders for him were drawn, the last sentence of which read, "The Chief of the Supply Mission will report to the Chief of the Democratic Mission, USSR."[48] Standley returned to his post. But this was a case of a situation being literally papered over: nothing changed in Moscow, indeed, no one except Standley expected anything to change. General Burns proceeded to ignore the orders, as did Faymonville.

Admiral Standley finally wrote his own finis as ambassador with an act of amazing ineptitude. As Congress was beginning the overview of the Second Russian Lend-Lease Protocol in the spring of 1943, Standley held a press conference in Moscow. He announced to reporters that the Russians were not letting their people know of—were in fact covering up—the great amount of aid America was sending them. He also commented, "Apparently they want their people to believe that the Red Army is fighting alone."[49]

The ambassador's intemperate remarks were resented by the Russians. Reaction was swift. The Soviet ambassador in Washington, in defense of the Soviet media, paid a visit to Undersecretary of State Sumner Welles armed with a long list of articles from the Moscow press detailing the amounts and substance of U.S. assistance.

In May the admiral submitted his resignation. On June 14, Congress passed the Soviet Protocol; there had been no problem getting the Lend-Lease appropriation on which it depended. Still, Standley's action had been particularly ill-timed: he might have upset the Russian Lend-Lease applecart.

Averell Harriman was the next ambassador. Not only was he

the obvious choice, as far as Secretary of State Cordell Hull was concerned, he was the *only* choice. As he and the president talked in June, Hull advised Roosevelt, "I have no other name to suggest at this time."[50]

Harriman, a fellow Grotonian, was one of Roosevelt's most trusted confidants and emissaries. Because the Soviet press had covered his negotiation of the first Lend-Lease terms right after the Nazi invasion, Harriman was almost as well known and almost as well liked in Russia as Roosevelt.

Arriving with the new ambassador in October was Gen. John Deane, former U.S. secretary of the Combined Chiefs of Staff (of Great Britain and the United States), infinitely more powerful and better connected than General Faymonville, to replace that dedicated champion of aid to the Soviet Union. He would work under Harriman to weld the political and military representation into a coordinated team with a unified purpose. There would be no more infighting between the military and naval attachés and Lend-Lease officials: all would report to General Deane. Those who thought that the policy of open-handed aid to Russia would cease with Faymonville's departure were disappointed: Deane, so much a part of the establishment, just did it more deftly.

Roosevelt had recognized Soviet Russia and established diplomatic and trade relations with the Communist government in November 1933. Many Americans both inside and outside the government thought such engagement unwise. Not unusual is this assessment by George Kennan: "Never—neither then or at any later date—did I consider the Soviet Union a fit ally, or associate, actual or potential, for this country."[51]

In return for recognition Roosevelt laid down certain conditions: religious freedom for all Americans in the USSR, cessation of Comintern activities in the United States, assurances for public trial and notice of arrest, and agreement that the Soviet government, to settle the debts incurred by the Kerensky government, would pay a sum of not less than $75 million to the United States. Litvinov, meeting with Secretary of State Hull and William Bullitt, whom Roosevelt would appoint as the first U.S. ambassador to the USSR, resisted these conditions during two days of talks. Following the failure of Hull and Bullitt, it took Roosevelt one hour's conversation to bring Litvinov around to agree to these terms.

Stalin admired Roosevelt. In a remarkable interview in 1934 he had told H. G. Wells that although he didn't think a planned economy such as the New Deal could exist under the conditions of capitalism, "I do not in the least desire to belittle the outstanding personal qualities of Roosevelt, his initiative, courage and determination. Undoubtedly Roosevelt stands out as one of the strongest figures among all the captains of the contemporary capitalist world." (He added, however, that "if the circumstances are unfavorable, the most talented captain cannot reach the goal.")[52] Stalin told Nikita Khrushchev that Roosevelt was a clever politician, one he could do business with.[53] Years later his opinion was that "Roosevelt was a great statesman, a clever, educated, far-sighted, and liberal leader who prolonged the life of capitalism."[54]

In 1934, when Roosevelt learned that Stalin was toying with the idea of signing a nonaggression pact with Germany, he called in the Soviet ambassador in Washington, Constantin Oumansky, to tell him that he "wished to make it clear, that this Government was viewing the present situation in an objective manner," that he viewed an Axis victory as a state that would "inevitably" and materially affect the position of the United States and the Soviet Union. Further, the president had told Oumansky that he "could not help but feel that if a satisfactory agreement against aggression on the part of other European powers [France and England] were reached, it would prove to have a decidedly stabilizing effect in the interest of world peace."[55]

Stalin overestimated Roosevelt's power to govern because he didn't understand that the checks and balances of the American government were real. Thus, his translator later wrote, "I heard Stalin say to Molotov on different occasions, 'Roosevelt is talking about Congress again. He thinks I will believe that he is truly afraid of Congress and that is why he is unable to make concessions. . . . He is using Congress as an excuse. . . . He is their military leader and commander in chief. It is just convenient for him to hide behind Congress.'"[56]

Roosevelt's views on Stalin were clear. Even as the president sought authorization to help Russia, he restated his views: "The principles and doctrines of communist dictatorship are as intolerable and alien to American beliefs as are the principles and doctrines of Nazi dictatorship."

In the years when they corresponded, Stalin did more than pay attention to what was important to Roosevelt; he followed his lead and made a significant change in Russian society. In September 1941, seeking to allay American opposition to aid to the Soviet Union, Roosevelt declared in a press conference that article 124 of the Soviet Constitution granted freedom of conscience and of religion—as well as freedom to propagandize against religion. Roosevelt asked that this be noted in the Russian press, and it was. Two years later Stalin reestablished the Russian Orthodox Church. Two years after that, even though he and other members of the government took no part, he allowed the church again to become an accepted part of Russian life.

Stalin honored the commitment he had made to draw off German troops following D-day: within days of the Normandy invasion of June 6, 1944, the Red Army launched the major offensive Stalin had promised; for every German soldier facing the Allies in France there were four still fighting the Russians in the east.

Roosevelt knew that an important part of establishing a good relationship with Stalin rested on treating the Soviet Union as an equal partner with the United States, a strategy Churchill, who never trusted Stalin, was dedicated to upsetting. Churchill began the war closely allied with Roosevelt. He wanted to maintain that close relationship, emerge from the war as much an equal as possible, and keep Stalin in the outer circle. To that end Churchill attempted to keep Roosevelt and Stalin from meeting unless he was present, pushed for exclusionary bilateral rather than trilateral decisions, and worked to keep the Soviet Union uninformed. He believed that Stalin's insistence in 1942 on a cross-Channel invasion was calculated to keep the United States and England occupied while he seized the Balkans. Churchill's mistrust of Stalin shows clearly in his letter to his foreign secretary, Anthony Eden, on January 4, 1944, "Of course once we get on to the Continent with a large commitment, they will have the means of blackmail, which they have not at present, by refusing to advance beyond a certain point, or even tipping the wink to the Germans that they can move more troops into the West."[57] By the end of 1943 it was Churchill who was in the outer circle, as was evident to all present at Tehran, where the first meeting of the so-called Big Three took place, a meeting that Roosevelt clearly dominated, according to Charles Bohlen, first secretary of the Moscow embassy, who had become Roosevelt's translator. Roosevelt threw Churchill off balance at the start by artfully arranging to stay in a house on the grounds of the Russian embassy. The British and Russian embassies in Tehran backed on to each other, while the American embassy was at some distance. Driving through the crowded streets of the city was something all wished to avoid. Roosevelt had queried Stalin the week before the conference, "Where do you think we should live?" Stalin in response had undertaken to refit one of the houses on the Soviet embassy grounds for him. Churchill had assumed the president would stay with him, and even wrote Stalin, "It seems therefore best for the President to stay in the British Legation."[58] But the last thing Roosevelt wanted was for Stalin to feel that Great Britain and America were acting in concert. Roosevelt compounded Churchill's discomfiture by refusing to meet with him alone until he had met with Stalin. During the conference, when Stalin needled Churchill, which according to Bohlen he often did, Roosevelt sided with Stalin. As Bohlen and General Deane, another member of the American contingent, observed, the job was made easier because Roosevelt was arguing on the same side as Stalin, which made Churchill odd man out. Roosevelt and Stalin and the American Chiefs of Staff were united in their support of Operation Overlord, the cross-Channel invasion which Churchill had been trying to postpone, as well as in their distaste for colonialism. As far as Iran itself was concerned, Roosevelt, mistrusting both his allies, made them agree to sign a three-power declaration respecting its future independence and territorial integrity. When Stalin made a heavy-handed joke one evening to the effect that he was in favor of liquidating fifty thousand German officers, Churchill was outraged and angrily said he would never approve. Roosevelt, aware of Stalin's mindset, knew that he made the remark, in Bohlen's words, "in quasi-jocular fashion, with a sardonic smile and wave of the hand, . . . meant . . . as a gibe at Churchill." The president casually offered a compromise: only forty-nine thousand should be liquidated.[59] Once, according to Deane, after Churchill had made a long speech, Stalin asked, "How long is this conference going to last?" Stalin had appeared at the conference with a skeleton delegation: two members of the Politburo—Molotov, commissar of foreign affairs, and Marshal Kliment E. Voroshilov, hero of the Civil War, vice president of the Council of People's Commissars, and one of the few surviving original members of the Communist Party. (Lavrenti Beria was also there but did not take part in the proceedings.) It was noted that Stalin rarely conferred with Molotov or Voroshilov. "There could be no doubt that he was the Soviet supreme authority as there was never the slightest indication that he would have to consult his Government on decisions reached," observed General Deane.[60]

In a clear indication of Stalin's lack of knowledge of customs outside his own country, the one British delegate he did confer with was A. H. Birse, the interpreter seated at his left at the dinner Churchill gave to celebrate his sixty-ninth birthday. Birse later remembered that the marshal "sat uncomfortably on the edge of his chair, looked with anxiety at the display of different-sized knives and forks before him, turned to me and said, 'This is a fine collection of cutlery. It is a problem which to use. You will have to tell me, and also when I can begin to eat. I am unused to your customs.'"[61]

The last night of the conference Stalin toasted the industrial might of the United States, which made victory certain. He stood in awe of American industrial output, "particularly of engines. Neither Russia nor England could produce so many engines."[62]

Back in the United States sometime after Tehran, Roosevelt commented to his speechwriter, Sam Rosenman, "Winston has developed a tendency to make long speeches which are repetitious of long speeches which he has made before."[63]

Twice Stalin brought Roosevelt up short with abrupt, angry messages. In the darkest days of 1941, as the German Army drove ever closer to Moscow, Stalin had voiced the idea that a treaty should be drawn up between the Soviet Union, the United States, and England declaring that their alliance should be not only for the war but for the postwar period and stipulating that there should be no separate peace.[64] Stalin's need for that reassurance surfaced when he felt threatened; two of his angry messages reflect a conviction that his fears are being realized and his allies are leaving him out of peace negotiations. One came after Churchill and Roosevelt had met in Quebec to work out the surrender of Italy; Stalin wrote, in October 1943, "the Soviet Government has not been kept informed of the Anglo-American negotiations with the Italians." A garbled and incomplete cable was found to be largely responsible for Stalin's annoyance, and he was readily reassured when the missing information reached him.

The second rift was more serious. In March 1945 Allen Dulles, head of the Office of Strategic Services (OSS) in Switzerland, met with Gen. Karl Wolff, the ranking SS officer in Italy, who wanted to negotiate the surrender of the German Army in Italy. Molotov was informed of the negotiations and requested Soviet representation at the discussions; the request was refused on the grounds that the discussions concerned a military surrender on an Anglo-American front, not a national capitulation. Stalin didn't believe it. Responding to Roosevelt's assurance that no negotiations were taking place, Stalin wrote, "It may be assumed that you have not been fully informed." He included, as evidence of the inaccuracy of much of what the highest level of the Allied command "knew," a letter from the Red Army chief of staff to General Marshall pointing out that the information on German troop movement Marshall had given them was false. Roosevelt was so taken aback by Stalin's accusation this time that he commented to Anna Rosenberg, "We can't do business with Stalin. He has broken every one of the promises he made at Yalta."[65] But a few weeks later he recovered his equilibrium, on April 8, 1945, admonishing Churchill for suggesting a bilateral economic commission in Greece because it would "look as though we for our part, were disregarding the Yalta decision of tripartite action in liberated areas."[66]

It is like a drumbeat, Roosevelt's insistence to Churchill that he include and inform Stalin in all matters, his insistence to his own diplomatic corps that Soviet requests be honored. Roosevelt's hope for world peace rested on Stalin's friendship and on Stalin's willingness to commit the Soviet Union to his vision of a postwar world. The last three messages Roosevelt sent, one to Churchill, one to

Stalin, and one to Harriman, all within forty-eight hours of his death, all have to do with preserving and protecting the feeling of trust between Stalin and himself, and to preserving the Yalta agreements.

At Yalta, Roosevelt succeeded in his supreme objective: bringing the Soviet Union into the United Nations and largely on his own terms. He made Stalin concede that the veto in the Security Council did not extend to setting the agenda: that any nation could bring up any subject for discussion. Although Stalin wavered, he honored this commitment. In return, Roosevelt agreed that the Soviet Union could have two extra nation members in the General Assembly: Byelorussia and the Ukraine, a position that Churchill, knowing that Great Britain could count on the five votes of its dominions (and relying on the concurrence of Canada and Australia as well), strongly supported. (Churchill's supreme objective was to preserve the British Empire: he went along with Roosevelt's dreams for the United Nations but as late as Yalta didn't even bother, according to Bohlen and Stettinius, to read the U.S. position paper dealing with it and so didn't understand the voting procedures formula.)[67]

At Yalta, as insurance against a possible uproar in Congress, Roosevelt secured Stalin's agreement to support a demand for two additional votes for the United States in the General Assembly, if requested. As Roosevelt knew at the time, whether the Soviet Union had one vote or three votes in the General Assembly would make no difference in terms of world power. Roosevelt even got Stalin to withdraw two objectionable amendments that Molotov had proposed to the Declaration on Liberated Europe and prevailed on Stalin to sign the final version of the declaration, which established "the right of all peoples to choose the form of government under which they will live—the restoration of sovereign rights and self-government." He was too much of a realist to believe that Stalin would abide by everything he agreed to at Yalta, but he got his signature on the agreements, and thereby set the standard by which Stalin could be measured.

The sticking point at Yalta was the agreement on Poland. Stalin was insistent that Russia be the dominant voice in Poland. Roosevelt and Stalin raised the use of ambiguous negotiation to an art on this subject, guided by the knowledge that a general agreement was necessary as the first step, expecting that each would come to an accommodation later. That was taken to mean, as agreed at Yalta, that the United States would allow Russia to have majority control of the new Polish government formed in Lublin, and that the London Poles, still officially the Polish government in exile, would have a token minority. As Stalin wrote to Roosevelt, "The Soviet Government insists on this as blood of the Soviet troops abundantly shed for the liberation of Poland and the fact that in the course of the last 30 years the territory of Poland has been used by the enemy twice for attack upon Russia,—all this obliges the Soviet Government to strive that the relations between the Soviet Union and Poland be friendly."[68]

As cooler heads in the United States at the time of Yalta realized, and as Roosevelt was forced to admit, American soldiers would be going home when the war was over; the isolationist United States would not fight for Poland: the Soviet Union, with an army of ten million, carried the field. Roosevelt said to Admiral Leahy, "It's the best I can do for Poland at this time."[69] Concluded Bohlen, the only American who, as Roosevelt's translator, heard every word uttered by Roosevelt and Stalin at Yalta, "Stalin held all the cards and played them well. Eventually, we had to throw in our hand."[70]

Roosevelt's health was visibly deteriorating during the winter of 1944–45. He rarely put on the heavy steel braces he needed to stand. He used them to deliver his inaugural address in January, but that had been a scant five-minute speech. His physician, Admiral McIntire, was worried about him, although his latest checkup before Yalta showed "lungs clear; heart sounds clear and of good quality." McIntire was in favor of the trip to Yalta, feeling that "a sea voyage, at least, would get him away from his desk and give him a week of rest."[71] After his return, when he addressed Congress to explain the agreements, Roosevelt did so sitting down in his wheelchair. When the secret agreement that the Soviets would get two extra votes in the General Assembly became public, many Americans thought the president's poor health had allowed Stalin to outmaneuver him. The truth was more subtle. According to Admiral Leahy, who was present, "Mr. Molotov proposed that the conference agreement to invite two Soviet states to be members of the Assembly of the United Nations Organization be made public, but upon objection by the Prime Minister he withdrew his proposal."[72] Perhaps here one can see how Roosevelt's health might have interfered with his pressing the point. There was nothing wrong, nothing lost, in Roosevelt's agreement to give the Soviet Union extra votes in the General Assembly, but there was a great deal wrong with concealing it. Roosevelt tried to minimize the damage in a press conference at Warm Springs on April 5, telling how it had come about, but his death robbed him of the opportunity to explain his reasons.

The agreement Roosevelt hammered out with Stalin—the Soviet Union would declare war on Japan within three months after Germany surrendered in return for the territory Russia had lost to Japan in 1905—was of major tactical importance to the United States: the long bloody battle for Manila had begun; ahead lay Iwo Jima and Okinawa. Unfortunately for Roosevelt, nothing of the Soviet agreement to declare war on Japan could be divulged until the day the war started. As it turned out, the atomic bomb robbed the agreement of importance. Americans hardly noticed that Stalin's million-man army, which he had moved across Siberia, invaded Manchuria on August 9, because that was the day the United States dropped the second atomic bomb, on Nagasaki. Americans never knew that the Russians took more than a half-million Japanese soldiers prisoner before the surrender was signed in September.

The significance of making Stalin agree to go to war against Japan was twofold. The Joint Chiefs of Staff declared that it was the only way to avoid invading Japan, at a cost of millions of American lives. (At the second Quebec Conference in September 1944, the Chiefs of Staff "took as the target date for the Japanese surrender a time eighteen months after the end of the war with Germany.")[73] But there was another even more compelling reason that no American ever mentioned. As Harriman later stated to the Senate Armed Services and Foreign Relations Committees, "The great danger existed that the Soviet Union would stand by until we had brought Japan to her knees at great cost in American lives, and then the Red Army could march into Manchuria and large areas of Northern China. It would then have been a simple matter for the Soviets to give expression to 'popular demand' by establishing People's Republics of Manchuria and Inner Mongolia."[74]

When Roosevelt died Stalin paid tribute to his fallen comrade by changing his mind and agreeing to send Foreign Minister Molotov to represent the USSR at the San Francisco Conference. Stalin told Ambassador Harriman, "President Roosevelt has died but his cause must live on. . . . Mr. Molotov's trip to the United States, although difficult at this time, [will] be arranged."[75]

Roosevelt's death made a deep impression on the Russian people as well. Russians felt that their country had lost a real friend. And in a most unusual manner, on the day they reported that the president had died, all Soviet newspapers appeared with wide black borders on their front page. Less than a month later, as it became known in Moscow on the morning of May 10 that Germany had surrendered (it had been announced in Great Britain and the United States the day before: Stalin delayed a day, possibly concerned it might be a trick of some sort), huge crowds gravitated to the square in front of the American embassy. The crowds stayed there all day long—"this great crowd," as Kennan remembered, blissfully happy, pushing past the police and pressing against the sides of the building. A Soviet flag was hung next to the Stars and Stripes, which brought forth pleased roars. The crowds stayed well into the evening, cheering, waving, tossing any American who exited the building into the air.[76]

When the war was finally over the tally of Americans killed in action was 405,000. The Soviet Union had lost an estimated 27 million soldiers and civilians, and another 26 million were homeless, their country was in ruins.

Speeches and correspondence of political leaders always present a question of authorship. Roosevelt wrote out, dictated, or authorized all messages bearing his name. When he requested others to draft a message, or to draft a clarification or lay out a specific policy, he edited or approved the result, sometimes in longhand. Harry Hopkins, Admiral Leahy, Edward R. Stettinius after he became Secretary of State in 1944, and Charles Bohlen, the State Department Russian expert who translated for Roosevelt at Tehran and Yalta were those chiefly called upon. Leahy's recollection was that as he and Roosevelt discussed a situation which required an answer, the president would say, "'Bill, suppose you take a shot at this.' I always did, of course, and he always changed it."[77] In the early years Roosevelt marked up the drafts extensively. Later he merely okayed some of them, but by that time Leahy, Hopkins, Stettinius, and Bohlen were perfectly in tune with his thinking. On important matters, his hand is there. As late as three weeks before he died, changes are in his handwriting. He authorized a cable to Stalin containing the soothing words "minor misunderstanding" minutes before he was struck by the cerebral hemorrhage which would prove fatal. Ironically, Roosevelt was by no means sure that Stalin was always the author of his messages. At one point he asked Harriman to check whether a message had actually emanated from Stalin. Harriman did investigate, and found out that indeed Stalin had written the message in question.

Commissar for Foreign Affairs Vyacheslav M. Molotov was the main person upon whom Stalin relied for advice and suggestions, according to Stalin's biographers Gen. Dmitri Volkogonov, head of the Institute of Military History, and Simon Montefiore. Molotov was the only person who was present at all Stalin's meetings, noted Stalin's interpreter, Valentin Berezhkov, who observed that sometimes Stalin even turned to Molotov with a question.[78] It is possible that if ever Stalin had been sick, Molotov would have been in charge, but there is general agreement that Stalin held all the reins of power tightly in his hand: his messages are emphatically his, whether or not they were drafted by someone under his direction. After his years in Russia, General Deane wrote, "No subordinate official in Russia may make a decision on matters in which foreigners are involved without consulting higher authority, and usually this higher authority is Stalin himself, perhaps in consultation with party leaders who move behind the scenes."[79] Harriman agreed, writing, "There can be no doubt that Stalin is the only man to deal with in foreign affairs. Dealing with others without previous instruction from Stalin about the matters under discussion was almost a waste of time."[80]

Correspondence

I N the spring of 1941, as German forces began massing for an attack on his country, Stalin refused to believe the reports confirming Hitler's intention even though messages were pouring in from intelligence sources all over the world and it was plain to everyone else in his immediate circle. Under pressure from his generals he did allow the mobilization of 500,000 reserves in May, but when informed of German reconnaissance flights, he commented, "I'm not sure Hitler knows about those flights."[1] One report that crossed his desk in early June from Richard Sorge, a Soviet spy in Tokyo accredited as a German journalist, even gave the date of the invasion: June 22. Still he refused to believe it would happen. On June 14 he ordered TASS to publish a statement that "Germany is observing the terms of the non-aggression Pact as scrupulously as the USSR, and therefore rumors of Germany's intention to violate the Pact and attack the USSR are groundless."[2] On the night of June 21 reports from German defectors who had risked their lives crossing into Russia were placed on Stalin's table clearly saying that the invasion was set for the next day: still Stalin didn't react. Operation Barbarossa commenced at dawn, as more than 3 million soldiers poured across the border, stunning Stalin. For days, as the news of the collapse of Russia's defenses and the advancement of the German armies continued to pour into the Kremlin, Stalin maintained that "Hitler simply does not know about it," that the invasion was the work of "provocation" by German officers; he would not order resistance.[3] The bulk of the Soviet Air Force—almost 1,000 planes—was destroyed on the ground. Within a week the Germans captured 400,000 soldiers, advanced three hundred miles into Russia, and occupied Minsk; they were clearly marching toward Moscow. Faced with the enormity of the catastrophe that he had so stolidly refused to see, Stalin, reeling, finally faced his self-deception, acknowledging to his immediate circle that he had failed Russia, failed Lenin, and doomed the revolution. "Everything's lost. I give up," he announced. Leaving the Kremlin, he retired to his dacha in Kuntsevo, evidently in the grip of a nervous breakdown. According to Vyacheslav Molotov, Stalin's most trusted associate, he tendered his resignation.[4] Only on July 3, eleven days after the invasion started, after a delegation including Marshal Kliment E. Voroshilov, Molotov, and Lavrenti Beria, the head of the Soviet secret police (NKVD), came to beseech him to return to the Kremlin did he pull himself together, take charge, make a measured, reassuring speech calling on all Russians to defend their country, and again start giving orders. Having survived his own self-doubts, and realizing that even in his moment of weakness he had been unchallenged, Stalin then assumed the titles of commissar of defense and supreme commander in chief.

By mid-July 2 million Russian soldiers had been killed and another 300,000 captured. On July 21 Roosevelt put Maj. Gen. James H. Burns, whom Hopkins called a "doer," in charge of Lend-Lease to Russia. On July 23, upon receipt of a $22 million Russian wish list, Roosevelt directed his appointments secretary Gen. "Pa" Watson to "get the thing through" within two days.[5]

Harry Hopkins was in London in late July 1941 making arrangements for a meeting between the president and Winston Churchill at Argentia Bay in Newfoundland the second week of August. (As the president reminded the prime minister in Newfoundland, they had met once before, at Gray's Inn in London in 1918.) Hopkins knew that a primary purpose of the Argentia meeting was to work out the needs of those countries fighting Hitler, to establish what the United States could do to supply those needs. Everyone's information on Russia was extremely sketchy: could the Soviets hold out against

Hitler long enough for winter to blunt the German attack, or would the Soviet Union have to capitulate? After arranging the details of the conference with Churchill, Hopkins cabled Roosevelt to suggest that he fly to Moscow to learn the answer from Stalin himself. Within twenty-four hours he had Roosevelt's cabled reply:

> July 26, 1941
> [Acting Secretary of State Sumner] Welles and I highly approve Moscow trip and assume you would go in a few days. Possibly you could get back to North America by August 8th. I will send you tonight a message for Stalin.

Roosevelt

· 1 ·

On Monday evening, July 28, Britain's Royal Air Force (RAF) Coastal Command picked up Hopkins in Invergordon, Scotland, in one of the Consolidated Aircraft PBY bombers provided by the United States and flew him to Archangel. Ordinarily the pilots would have waited a day because the weather was so bad, but "a message came from London that the aircraft was ordered to ignore the weather and take off at once."[6] At Archangel, after a brief delay, a Soviet-manned American Douglas Transport flew Hopkins to Moscow.

Hopkins was met by Lawrence Steinhardt, the U.S. ambassador to the Soviet Union, who took him to the official embassy residence, Spaso House, to rest. Steinhardt, who admitted that "it was supremely difficult for any outsider in Moscow to get a clear picture of what was really going on," was extremely pessimistic about the Soviet Union's future. He had advised Washington in late June that the nation would not survive the Nazi invasion.[7]

At 6:30 P.M. on July 30 Hopkins met with Stalin in the Kremlin. Hopkins was enormously impressed by Stalin:

> No man could forget the picture of the dictator of Russia—an austere, rugged, determined figure in boots that shone like mirrors, stout baggy trousers, and a snug-fitting blouse. He wore no ornament, military or civilian. He's built close to the ground, like a football coach's dream of a tackle. He's about five feet six,

about a hundred and ninety pounds. His hands are huge, as hard as his mind. His voice is harsh but ever under control. What he says is all the accent and inflection his words need.[8]

Hopkins delivered the following message from Roosevelt, which Sumner Welles had cabled to him in London.

July 26, 1941

Mr. Hopkins is in Moscow at my request for discussions with you personally and with such other officials as you may designate on the vitally important question of how we can expeditiously and effectively make available the assistance which the United States can render to your country in its magnificent resistance to the treacherous aggression by Hitlerite Germany. I have already informed your Ambassador, Mr. Oumansky, that all possible aid will be given by the United States Government in obtaining munitions, armaments and other supplies needed to meet your most urgent requirements and which can be made available for actual use in the coming two months in your country. We shall promptly settle the details of these questions with the mission headed by General Golikov which is now in Washington, The visit now being made by Mr. Hopkins to Moscow will, I feel, be invaluable by clarifying for us here in the United States your most urgent requirements so that we can reach the most practicable decisions to simplify the mechanics of delivery and speed them up. We shall be able to complete during the next winter a great amount of materiél which your Government wishes to obtain in this country. I therefore think that the immediate concern of both governments should be to concentrate on the materiél which can reach Russia within the next three months.

I ask you to treat Mr. Hopkins with the identical confidence you would feel if you were talking directly to me. He will communicate directly to me the views that you express to him and will tell me what you consider are the most pressing individual problems on which we could be of aid.

May I express, in conclusion, the great admiration all of us in the United States feel for the superb bravery displayed by the Russian people in the defense of their liberty and in their fight for the independence of Russia. The success of your people and all other people in opposing Hitler's aggression and his plans for world conquest has been heartening to the American people.

Hopkins sent the following report to Roosevelt of his first meeting with Stalin:

I told Mr. Stalin that I came as personal representative of the President. The President considered Hitler the enemy of mankind and that he therefore wished to aid the Soviet Union in its fight against Germany.

I told him that my mission was not a diplomatic one in the sense that I did not propose any formal understanding of any kind or character.

I expressed to him the President's belief that the most important thing to be done in the world today was to defeat Hitler and Hitlerism. I impressed upon him the determination of the President and our Government to extend all possible aid to the Soviet Union at the earliest possible time.

I told Mr. Stalin that I had certain personal messages from the President and explained my relationship to the Administration in Washington. I told him further that I just left Mr. Churchill in London who wished me to convey to him the sentiments which I had already expressed from the President.

Mr. Stalin said he welcomed me to the Soviet Union; that he had already been informed of my visit.

Describing Hitler and Germany, Mr. Stalin spoke of the necessity of there being a minimum moral standard between all nations and without such a minimum moral standard nations could not co-exist. He stated that the present leaders of Germany knew no such minimum moral standard and that, therefore, they represented an anti-social force in the present world. The Germans were a people, he said, who without a second's thought would sign a treaty today, break it tomorrow and sign a second one the following day. Nations must fulfill their treaty obligations, he said, or international society could not exist.

When he completed his general summary of the Soviet Union's attitude toward Germany he said "therefore our views coincide."

The rest of Hopkins report was a discussion of the immediate and the long-term needs as Stalin saw them: for machine guns, antiaircraft guns, rifles, airplanes. At this meeting and at the meeting next day, also at 6:30 in the evening, Stalin briefed Hopkins on the strength and makeup of the German Army and gave him a detailed description of Soviet armament, soldiers, and production capabilities. Stalin wrote down the supplies he needed in order of importance: 1. light antiaircraft guns, 2. aluminum (needed for planes), 3. fifty-caliber machine guns, and 4. thirty-caliber rifles.

Stalin

· 2 ·

————

Hopkins met with Stalin again the following evening, July 31, from 6:30 to 9:30 P.M., and reported that "after Stalin had completed his review of the military situation, he expressed to me his great thanks to the President for the interest he was showing in their fight against Hitler. He stated that he wanted to give the President the following personal message; that he had considered putting the message in writing but believed it would be more desirable to have the message delivered to the President by me."

Stalin said Hitler's greatest weakness was found in the vast numbers of oppressed people who hated Hitler and the immoral ways of his Government. He believed these people and countless other millions in nations still unconquered could receive the kind of encouragement and moral strength they needed to resist Hitler from only one source, and that was the United States. He stated that the world influence of the President and the Government of the United States was enormous.

Contrary wise, he believes that the morale of the German army and the German people, which he thinks is already pretty low, would be demoralized by an announcement that the United States is going to join in the war against Hitler.

Stalin said that he believed it was inevitable that we should finally come to grips with Hitler on some battlefield. The might of Germany was so great that, even though Russia might defend itself, it would be very difficult for Britain and Russia combined to crush the German military machine. He said that the one thing that could defeat Hitler, and perhaps without ever firing a shot, would be the announcement that the United States was going to war with Germany.

Stalin said that he believed, however, that the war would be bitter and perhaps long; that if we did get in the war he believed the American people would insist on their armies coming to grips with German soldiers; and he wanted me to tell the President that he would welcome the American troops on any part of the Russian front under the complete command of the American Army.

I told Stalin that my mission related entirely to matters of supply and the matter of our joining in the war would be decided largely by Hitler himself and his encroachment upon our fundamental interests. I told him that I doubted that our Government, in event of war would want an American army in Russia but that I would give his message to the President.

He repeatedly said that the President and the United States had more influence with the common people of the world today than any other force.

Finally, he asked me to tell the President that, while he was confident that the Russian Army could withstand the German Army, the problem of supply by next spring would be a serious one and that he needed our help.

In spite of his directives to his appointments secretary and Major General Burns, Roosevelt fretted that the supplies destined for Russia were mired in bureaucratic limbo and wouldn't reach Russia in time to stem the German advance. He directed the following message to Wayne Coy, one of the most respected administrators in Washington, whom Roosevelt had put in charge of Soviet aid in Harry Hopkins's absence:

August 2, 1941
Personal Memorandum for Wayne Coy
I raised the point in Cabinet on Friday that nearly six weeks have elapsed since the Russian War began and that we have done practically nothing to get any of the materials they asked for on their actual way to delivery in Siberia.

Frankly, if I were a Russian I would feel that I had been given the run-around in the United States

Please get out the list and please, with my full authority, use a heavy hand—act as a burr under the saddle and get things moving. . . .

Step on it![9]

F.D.R.

Stalin

· 3 ·

Intent on moving the Finnish border, only twenty miles from Leningrad, farther away, the Soviets invaded Finland in 1939. The Finns fought fiercely in the so-called Winter War, but in the end agreed to cede the disputed territory and sign a nonaggression pact with the Soviet Union. The resentment toward Russia, however, pushed Finland into the Axis camp. Finland declared war on Russia and joined Hitler in Operation Barbarossa.

The U.S. State Department kept constant diplomatic pressure on Finland beginning in September, informing the Finnish ambassador that the country "would forfeit our friendly support in the future difficulties that would inexorably arise from her course of action." Finland remained an ally of Hitler; the United States finally broke off relations in 1944.[10] Stalin asked Great Britain to declare war on Finland, but the British waited until December 7, 1941—a day after the Finns had declared war on them.

Ambassador Oumansky didn't realize that Roosevelt had left Washington, ostensibly on a vacation but actually to meet Prime Minister Winston Churchill at Argentia Bay in Newfoundland, when he tried to deliver the following message.

Washington, August 5, 1941
My dear Mr. President,

Mr. Stalin has directed me to convey to you urgently the following personal message:

The Soviet Union holds that the question of restoring the neutrality of Finland and of detaching her from Nazi-Germany is of utmost importance. The Soviet Government is in possession of most reliable information showing that the breaking off of relations between Great Britain and Finland and the blockade of by Great Britain have not failed to produce desirable results and have caused conflicts within the governing circles of Finland. There are now voices audible in those circles in favor of Finnish neutrality and reconciliation with the Soviet Union.

Mr. Stalin is convinced that, should the Government of the United States consider it opportune to impress upon the Finnish Government the danger of a break of relations by the United States—the Finnish Government would become more resolute and acquire more courage in detaching itself from Nazi-Germany.

In this event the Soviet Government would be willing to make to Finland certain territorial concessions so as to facilitate her transition to a peaceful policy and the Soviet Government would be willing to conclude with Finland a new Peace Treaty. . . .

C. Oumansky

Roosevelt and Churchill

· 4 ·

———

Following their meeting at Argentia Bay, Roosevelt and Churchill issued a joint statement on August 14, known as the Atlantic Charter. The principles set forth resonated through the corridors of power throughout the war and helped shape the peace as Roosevelt particularly had hoped and planned. He believed that the goals would galvanize and inspire those countries already engaged as well as those—like the United States—threatened by the war. To that end the charter declared that the signatories renounced aggrandizement, "territorial or other," desired that there be no territorial changes "that do not accord with the freely expressed wishes of the people concerned," voiced respect for the right of everyone "to choose the form of government under which they will live," and declared that "they hope[d] to see established a peace which will afford to all nations the means of dwelling in safety within their own boundaries."

At the same time Roosevelt and Churchill framed a message to Stalin, which Roosevelt instructed the State Department to send.

Two days earlier, by the perilous margin of one vote, the U.S. House of Representatives had passed the extension of the Selective Service Act.

August 14, 1941

Joint message to Stalin. Please have it cabled to our Embassy in Moscow and ask [Ambassador] Steinhardt to arrange with [Ambassador] Cripps so that the text is delivered by both of them simultaneously. I have also agreed to have the text of this message given to the press for the Saturday morning papers. Please see that this is done in Washington. The text of the message is as follows.

We have taken the opportunity afforded by the consideration of the report of Mr. Harry Hopkins on his return from Moscow to consult together as to how best our two countries can help your country in the splendid defense that you are making against the Nazi attack. We are at the moment cooperating to provide you with the very maximum of supplies that you most urgently need. Already many shiploads have left our shores and more will leave in the immediate future.

We must now turn our minds to the consideration of a more long-term policy, since there is still a long and hard path to be traversed before there can be won that complete victory without which our efforts and sacrifices would be wasted.

The war goes on upon many fronts and before it is over there may be yet further fighting fronts that will be developed. Our resources though immense are limited, and it must become a question of where and when those resources can best be used to further to the greatest extent our common effort. This applies equally to manufactured war supplies and to war materials.

The needs and demands of your and our armed services can only be determined in the light of the full knowledge of the many facts which must be taken into consideration in the decisions that we make. In order that all of us may be in a position to arrive at speedy decisions as to the apportionment of our joint resources, we suggest that we prepare a meeting which should be held at Moscow, to which we would send high representatives who could discuss these matters directly with you. If this conference appeals to you, we want you to know that pending the decisions of that conference we shall continue to send supplies and material as rapidly as possible.

We realize fully how vitally important to the defeat of Hitlerism is the brave and steadfast resistance of the Soviet Union and we feel therefore that we must not in any circumstances fail to act quickly and immediately in this matter of planning the program for the future allocation of our joint resources.

Franklin D. Roosevelt
Winston S. Churchill

Roosevelt

· 5 ·

The German Army, stretching from the Baltic in the north to the Black Sea in the south, continued its march toward Moscow. On August 20 the siege of Leningrad began. Within three weeks the German Army had surrounded and cut off the city, planning on starving into submission the 2.2 million people trapped there. The trickle of foodstuffs that came in over icebound Lake Ladoga was all that reached the city for nine hundred days.

To ward off the prejudice against aid to Russia "among large groups in this country who exercise great political power," Roosevelt suggested to Ambassador Oumansky, whom he saw on September 11, that any publicity Moscow might generate regarding the freedom of religion granted under the Constitution of 1936 "might have a very fine educational effect before the next lend-lease bill comes up in Congress."[11]

To set up the supply machinery Roosevelt appointed his fellow Grotonian Averell Harriman, the chairman of the Union Pacific Railroad, and Churchill appointed Lord Beaverbrook, the English minister of supply, to head their respective countries' Moscow missions. Harriman and Beaverbrook were to begin by meeting with Stalin to work out the logistics of long-term aid to his beleaguered country. (Beaverbrook's mission was twofold. As Churchill told him, "Your function will be not only to aid in the forming of the plans to aid Russia, but to make sure we are not bled white in the process.")[12] Mission members under Harriman were Adm. William H. Standley; Maj. Gen. James Burns, the Lend-Lease official in charge of aid to Russia; and the Russian expert Col. Philip R. Faymonville acting as secretary. Roosevelt wrote a letter of introduction for Harriman, then in London, to give Stalin, but the message went to London via a B-24 bomber in the Ferry Command, and Harriman had left for Moscow before the message arrived. Worried intelligence officers burned the letter rather than risk sending it to Moscow in a plane that might be shot down over German territory. The State Department subsequently radioed it to the American embassy in Moscow in the nonconfidential Brown code, and the Germans intercepted it. Germany released a deliberately garbled version, quoting Roosevelt as starting the letter "My Dear Friend Stalin" and closing with "In cordial friendship." Drew Pearson, a popular Sunday night radio broadcaster, announced to the American public that the Germans had intercepted the letter.[13] The president's message follows.

For Harriman from the President.
September 29, 1941

My letter of September 17 delayed in transit, later destroyed.

Will you please deliver following personal message from me to his

Excellency the President of the Soviet of People's Commissars of the USSR:

My dear Mr. Stalin,

This note will be presented to you by my friend Averell Harriman, whom I have asked to be head of our delegation to Moscow.

Mr. Harriman is well aware of the strategic importance of your front and will, I know, do everything he can to bring the negotiations in Moscow to a successful conclusion.

Harry Hopkins has told me in great detail of his encouraging and satisfactory visits with you. I can't tell you how thrilled all of us are because of the gallant defense of the Soviet armies.

I am very sure that Hitler made a profound strategic mistake when he attacked your country. I am confident that ways will be found to provide the material and supplies necessary to fight him on all fronts, including your own.

I want particularly to take this occasion to express my great confidence that your armies will ultimately prevail over Hitler and to assure you of our great determination to be of every possible material assistance.

Yours very sincerely
Franklin D. Roosevelt

Stalin

· 6 ·

In mid-September the Wehrmacht encircled Kiev, the capital of the Ukraine, and captured an estimated 400,000 Russian troops. When the Anglo-American mission arrived in Moscow on September 28, the Germans were so close, Harriman said, that "We could see the flash of the Russian anti-aircraft guns at night."[14] Harriman and Beaverbrook were invited to the Kremlin to meet Stalin at 9:00 P.M. This was the first of three evening meetings. The last evening the Russians laid on a lavish banquet in the eighteenth-century Kremlin Palace of Catherine the Great, but it was obvious that Stalin's mind was on the war. "Stalin was very restless, walking about and smoking continuously, and appeared to both of us to be under an intense strain," observed Beaverbrook.[15]

On October 1 Harriman and Beaverbrook signed the Moscow Protocol, setting forth the aid that Great Britain and America would send to Russia.

Moscow, Kremlin
October 3, 1941
My dear Mr. Roosevelt,

Your letter has been presented to me by Mr. Harriman. I avail myself of the opportunity to express to you the deep gratitude of the Soviet government for having put at the head of the American Delegation such an authority, as Mr. Harriman, whose participation the proceedings of the Moscow Conference of the three powers has been so effective.

I have no doubt, that you will do everything necessary to ensure the carrying out of the decisions of the Moscow Conference as speedily and as completely as possible, particularly in view of the fact that the Hitlerites will certainly try to take advantage of prewinter months to exert every possible pressure on the front against the USSR.

Like you I have no doubt that final victory over Hitler will be won by those countries, which are uniting now their efforts in order to speed up the annihilation of bloody Hitlerism—a task, for the sake of which the Soviet Union now makes so great and so heavy sacrifices.

Sincerely yours,
J. Stalin

Roosevelt

· 7 ·

Orel, 220 miles south of Moscow, and Kalinin, 100 miles to the northwest, fell to the Germans. The losses prompted Maj. Ivan Yeaton, U.S. military attaché in Moscow, to cable Washington on October 10 that the German onslaught was such that the end of Soviet resistance was in sight. Hopkins was annoyed, writing Secretary of War Henry Stimson that Major Yeaton, whom he had spoken to in Moscow in July, was incapable of forming an intelligent opinion because he had hardly any contact with Russians. "I can not see how any Military Attaché could get any reasonable expression of opinion from commuters or the general public which would be worthwhile."[16] The better-informed Lieutenant Colonel Faymonville, in Moscow to organize aid for Russia, cabled the following day that the Soviet General Staff believed that with adequate reserves the Soviet Army could prevent the encirclement of Moscow, and that all planned shipments of war matériel should be exceeded if possible.[17] Within the month, at Hopkins insistence, the army promoted Faymonville to brigadier general and put him officially in charge of Lend-Lease. Roosevelt specifically instructed Faymonville not to use or allow Lend-Lease to be used by others as a lever to seek information about Russian armaments or military plans. An indication of the extreme pressure Russia was under is that there is no record of this message in Soviet archives.

For Stalin from the President
October 13, 1941

We are shipping October 94 light tanks and 72 medium 32-ton tanks with spare parts and ammunition. Most of these will leave the United States by October 15.

We are shipping 100 bombers and 100 of our newest fighter planes with spare parts and ammunition. These will be placed on ships during the next ten days.

We are shipping 5,500 trucks during October and large amounts of barbed wire. All other military supplies we promised for October are being swiftly assembled to be placed on ships.

Three ships left the United States yesterday for Russian ports. Every effort being made to rush other supplies.

F.D.R.

Roosevelt

· 8 ·

By mid-October the German Army had broken through the Russian lines and was within seventy miles of Moscow. On October 10 large-scale industrial evacuation of the city was begun. (It was to continue for months: 498 companies and 210,000 workers were moved to the east.) On October 15 things looked so hopeless that Stalin decided to evacuate the government to Kuibyshev, the ancient city of Samara, six hundred miles away. Plans were implemented to dynamite the main buildings and the bridges around Moscow. Most government officials and records left for Kuibyshev. Vyacheslav Molotov, commissar for foreign affairs, ordered the diplomatic corps loaded onto a special train bound for Kuibyshev. Both Ambassador Steinhardt and the British ambassador, Sir Stafford Cripps, protested; both asked Molotov for permission to stay in Moscow as long as Molotov and Stalin stayed. Molotov was firm, however, and said that he and Stalin would join them. The special train carrying the diplomats, which was equipped with neither dining car nor drinking water, took five days and four nights to cover the distance.

Stalin's library and personal papers were transferred to Kuibyshev. A secret train waited near his dacha; his Douglas aircraft waited at a nearby airfield; his dacha was booby-trapped. Richard Sorge, who had proved so right about Operation Barbarossa, had reported that Japan was not at that time planning to attack Russia. Gambling that Sorge was right again, Stalin had ordered his Far Eastern Army to make haste to Moscow. The question was whether the fresh troops, tanks, and planes secretly en route to Moscow would reach the city in time. He, as well as most of the Politburo, decided to wait in Moscow.[18]

The Soviet Union paid for the first supplies sent by the United States by the sale of gold and by treasury loans. But almost immediately the Soviets found it impossible to continue funding the armaments and materiél the United States was sending. On October 24 Congress voted to include Russia in the Lend-Lease program.

Roosevelt wrote the following message the next day. Unaccountably, it was lost and not received by the Kremlin until March 16, 1942, somehow caught up in the turmoil engulfing the country as the Germans continued their advance. The U.S. Embassy advised the Russian embassy that the message had originally been sent by the State Department by diplomatic pouch via Tehran, then had been further delayed en route; it was finally delivered to Kuibyshev on March 15.[19] In any case Roosevelt sent a message a few days later that explained in great detail the aid that the United States planned to provide.

October 25, 1941, Franklin D. Roosevelt
My Dear Mr. Stalin,

Mr. Harriman has handed me your kind note dated October 3, 1941. I appreciate very much hearing from you.

A cable has already gone to you advising you that we can include the Soviet Union under our Lend-Lease arrangements.

I want to take this opportunity to assure you again that we are going to bend every possible effort to move these supplies to your battle lines.

The determination of your armies and people to defeat Hitlerism is an inspiration to the free people of all the world.

Very sincerely yours,

Roosevelt

· 9 ·

"This telegram," Harry Hopkins noted, "represents the President's decision to put the Russians under Lend-Lease. . . . There has been an endless amount of discussion. . . . It has become more and more clear that this is the only technique to finance their purchases."[20]

Steinhardt delivered a paraphrase of the telegram to Deputy Foreign Minister Andrei Vishinsky in Kuibyshev to give to Stalin—not the original, which Vishinsky requested—because, as Steinhardt explained to Secretary of State Cordell Hull, "I did not feel justified in complying with his request as to have done so would have compromised our Navy Department Code." Following is the message as written.[21]

Mr. Stalin;
October 30, 1941

I have seen the Protocol of the Conference held in Moscow and discussed the data contained therein with the members of our Mission.

I have approved all of the items of military equipment and munitions and have directed that the utmost expedition be used to provide so far as possible the raw materials. I have ordered that the deliveries begin at once and be maintaining in the greatest possible volume.

In order to remove any financial obstacles I have also directed that arrangements be effected immediately whereby shipments up to the value of one billion dollars may be made under the Lend Lease act.

I propose, subject to the approval of the Government of the USSR, that no interest be charged on the indebtedness incurred as a result of these shipments and that the payments on such indebtedness by the Government of the USSR begin only five years after conclusion of the war and completed over a period of ten years thereafter.

I hope that your Government can arrange to make special efforts to sell the United States such commodities and raw materials as may be available and of which the United States may be in urgent need. The proceeds of such sales to the Government of the United States to be credited to the account of the Soviet Government.

I want to take this opportunity to express the appreciation of this government for the expeditious way in which the supply conference in Moscow was handled by you and your associates and to assure you that all of the implications of that conference will be carried out to the limit.

I trust you will not hesitate to get in touch with me directly should the occasion require it.

Roosevelt

Roosevelt

· 10 ·

October 31, 1941

For Stalin from the President

1. It was agreed in the Confidential Protocol of the Moscow Supply Conference that the possibility of supply of a number of items you requested was to be investigated.

Investigation shows that in addition to the items definitely offered in the Protocol the following items can be made available as requested and I have so directed.

Item 7, Field Telephone Apparatus
Item 8, Field Telephone Cable
Item 9, Underwater Telegraph Cable
Item 10, Submarine Cable
Item 11, Aluminum and Duraluminum

Item 18, Rolled Brass

Item 22, Tubes and other manufactures of copper

Item 31, Hot-Rolled Steel

Item 32, Steel Billets

Item 33, Cold-Rolled Steel Strip

Item 34, Cold-Rolled Steel Sheet

Item 35, Tinplate

Item 36, Steel-Wire

Item 37, Steel-Wire-Ropes

Item 41, Barbed Wire

Item 45, Petroleum-Products

Item 46, Ethylene Glycol

Item 47, Sodium Bromide

Item 48, Phosphorus

Item 52, Colloxylin

Item 58, Abrasives

Item 59, graphitized Electrodes

Item 64, Sole Leather

2. The items listed below can be made available in part or require further mutual study:

Item 6, Trucks, 5,600 immediately and 10,000 monthly thereafter. Difficulty will be shipping.

Item 14, Nickel, the full amount of this item will be supplied jointly by United States and Great Britain in equal amounts for the next three months; further amounts to be subject to later considerations.

Item 19, Magnesium Alloys. Cannot be supplied from the United States at the present time. Study of the possibilities will be continued.

Item 20, Electrolytic Zinc, the full amount of this item will be supplied jointly by the United States and Great Britain as follows: Great Britain will supply the full amount for October, the United States will supply the full amount for November and each will supply 750 tons monthly thereafter.

Item 21, Bimetal, requires further study of possibilities of supply.

Item 23, Ferrosilicon, 300 tons monthly.

Item 24, Ferrochrome, 200 tons monthly. Immediate study will be given to possibilities for further expansion of American production of Ferrosilicon and Ferrochrome with a view to increasing monthly amounts if possible.

Item 25, Armor Plate, 1,000 tons monthly for the present. It may be possible to increase monthly supplies of this item later as capacity is enlarged.

Item 26, Hard alloys and cutting tools, 100,000 dollars monthly.

Item 28, High-Speed Steel, 100 tons monthly for the present. Further study will be given to possible increases in monthly amounts.

Item 29, Tool Steel, 500 tons monthly.

Item 30, Calibrated Steel, requires further study as to possibilities of fabrication.

Item 38, Steel Alloy Tubes, 200 tons monthly.

Item 39, Stainless Steel Wire, 20 tons monthly.

Item 40, Nickel Chrome Wire, 20 tons monthly.

Item 42, Toluel, 2,000 tons monthly and 10,000 tons of TNT as soon as possible.

Item 43, Nitroglycerine Powder. Powder of the chemical composition specified is not manufactured in this country. Studies are being given by representatives Amtorg and U.S. Army to the possibility of using a comparable powder manufactured in this country.

Item 44, Phenol, 400 tons before the end of the year and 750 tons monthly thereafter.

Item 49, Dibutil-Phtalate, 400 tons before the end of year and 300 tons monthly thereafter.

Item 50, Dimethylaniline, 100 tons monthly beginning November, 200 tons monthly beginning March 1942.

Item 51, Diphenylamine, 100 tons monthly.

Item 53, Metal cutting machine tools, is receiving further joint study by Great Britain, United States and Amtorg.

Item 54, Electric Furnaces, 140 pieces definitely, further amounts dependent upon specifications.

Item 55, Forgings and Press Equipment, 627 pieces definitely, further amounts dependent upon specifications.

Item 56, Various Industrial Equipment, every assistance practicable will be given, satisfaction or particular requisitions being dependent upon specifications.

Item 66, Army Boots, at least 200,000 pairs monthly available and already offered to Amtorg.

Item 67, Army Cloth, amounts available dependent upon specifications but one million yards woolen overcoat cloth will be available upon requisition over next four months.

3. Further Communications will be sent shortly on navy and medical supply lists.

Roosevelt

Stalin

· 11 ·

November 4, 1941
Mr. President,

Although I have not yet received the text of your message, Mr. Steinhardt, the Ambassador of the United States of America, on November 2, 1941, transmitted to me, through Mr. Vishinsky, an aide-mémoire setting forth the contents of your message to me.

In this connection permit me first of all to express complete agreement with your evaluation of the work of the conference of the three powers in Moscow which is to be attributed in the greatest degree to the services of Mr. Harriman and also Mr. Beaverbrook who did everything possible for the successful conclusion of the work of the conference in the shortest time. The Soviet Government expresses its deep gratitude for your statement that the decisions of the conference will be carried out to the maximum extent.

Mr. President, the Soviet Government accepts with sincere gratitude your decision to grant to the Soviet Union a non-interest bearing loan in the sum of one billion dollars to pay for supplies of armaments and raw materials for the Soviet Union, as exceptionally substantial assistance to the Soviet Union in its great and difficult struggle with our common enemy, blood-thirsty Hitlerism. On behalf of the Government of the USSR, I express complete agreement with the conditions set forth by you concerning the granting of this loan to the Soviet Union payments on which shall commence five years after the termination of the war and be made during the ten years after the expiration of this five year period.

The Government of the USSR is prepared to do everything possible in order to furnish the United States of America those goods and raw materials which are at its disposal and which the United States may need.

With respect to your proposal, Mr. President, that personal direct contact should be immediately established between you and me, should circumstances require this, I share your desire with satisfaction and am prepared to do everything necessary to make this possible.

With sincere respects,
J. Stalin

Roosevelt

· 12 ·

Roosevelt sent Steinhardt a cable November 5, 1941, advising him that he was being replaced by "someone who is fully acquainted with detailed problems of American production and supply."[22] During the conference discussions Stalin had asked Harriman what he thought of the Russian ambassador Constantin Oumansky. Harriman had replied that Oumansky "talked too much and ran around the capital creating more irritation than good will."[23] Within weeks Oumansky, too, was gone, replaced by Maxim Litvinov, with whom Roosevelt had negotiated the recognition of the Soviet government. Litvinov, like Oumansky, was Jewish.

On November 7, to reassure the populace, with German guns booming in the background, Stalin held a military parade. "Stalin led the Politburo up the steps to the Mausoleum, just like old times—except it was earlier and everyone was extremely nervous." Generals on white steeds, lines of T-34 tanks, and columns of troops marched past. Stalin delivered a speech meant to rally his people.[24]

Of the medical supplies that Russia had requested, the portion that would go to civilian relief was eligible for Red Cross assistance, with the assent of Congress. Allen Wardwell was a member of the law firm of Davis, Polk, Wardwell, Gardiner and Reed. Sergey Kolesnikov was chairman of the executive committee of the Society of the Red Cross and Red Crescent of the Soviet Union.

November 6, 1941

I am happy to inform you that medical supplies in the list prepared by the Medical Supplies Committee of the Three-Power Conference will be provided as rapidly as these supplies can be purchased and shipped, less such portion thereof as the British may provide. Conditions of American supply and production make impossible the immediate purchase of large amounts of certain items requested, but twenty-five percent of the total list can be provided within 30 to 60 days and the balance in installments during the next 8 months.

The American Red Cross is prepared to provide approximately one-third of the total list at an approximate cost of $5,000,000 as a gift of the American people. Acting on my instructions, the American Red Cross will procure these supplies with funds placed at my disposal by the Congress and also funds contributed by the American people for relief in the Soviet Union. As the American Red Cross must account to Congress and to its contributors for the use of these funds and supplies, Wardwell, the Chairman of the Delegation, outlined in a letter to Mr. Kolesnikov of the Soviet Alliance the kind of cooperative arrangement between Red Cross societies of our respective countries which is desired. The Red Cross is also transmitting a message to Kolesnikov today pointing out the importance of reasonable observation by the American Red Cross representative of the distribution made of its supplies subject, of course to all appropriate military considerations. I would deeply appreciate it if your Government can assure me that the desired arrangements are acceptable. I may point out that the procedures proposed by the American Red Cross are the same which are followed with regard to their assistance in Great Britain and other countries.

On the basis indicated, the American Red Cross is prepared to consider further substantial assistance in the Soviet Union as needs develop and requests are made.

Stalin

· 13 ·

———

This message was hand-delivered to Undersecretary of State Sumner Welles in Washington by the Soviet chargé d'affaires on November 21, with the request that Welles personally deliver it to President Roosevelt.

Text of Personal Message of J. V. Stalin to Mr. F. D. Roosevelt.
November 14, 1941

Your message informing me of the favorable solution of the question in regard to deliveries of medical supplies by the American Red Cross was received by me on November 11, 1941. The Soviet Government has no objections to the establishment of organizational forms of cooperation between the Red Cross Societies of our both countries. It is understood that this cooperation will be organized in accordance with the exchange of letters, the contents of which was agreed upon by representatives of both countries in the beginning of November in Kuibyshev.

Stalin

Roosevelt

· 14 ·

On December 7, 1941, the Japanese bombed Pearl Harbor, sinking or badly damaging eighteen U.S. Navy ships, destroying 180 planes, and killing 2,403 men. On December 8 the U.S. Congress declared war on Japan. On December 9 China declared war on Japan, Germany, and Italy. On December 11 Hitler and Mussolini declared war on the United States, which in turn acknowledged itself at war with Germany and Italy.[25]

Roosevelt noted on the original of this message "Given to Litvinov December 14, 4:30 p.m." Roosevelt sent a similar message to Chiang Kai-shek. At the same time he gave copies of both messages to Viscount Halifax, the British ambassador in Washington, requesting, "I hope you will ask London if they will go ahead with the holding of the Singapore conference and also instruct your people in Chungking and Moscow to take part in the proposed meetings as soon as they are held by Chiang Kai-shek and Stalin. I assume, of course, that Australia and New Zealand will be represented in Singapore."[26]

A supreme war council had been set up by the Allies too late to be effective in World War I. The idea behind this last-minute message was to avoid a similar mistake. Events, however, were moving too fast for the proposed conference to take place. A Pacific war council was established in London in February.[27]

FROM THE PRESIDENT TO MR. STALIN
December 14, 1941

In my judgment it is of the utmost importance that immediate steps be taken to prepare the way for common action not merely for the next few weeks but also for the permanent defeat of Hitlerism. I very much wish that you and I could meet to talk this over personally. But because that is impossible at the moment I am seeking to initiate three preliminary moves which I hope will be preparatory to a more permanent joint planning.

First, I am suggesting to Generalissimo Chiang Kai-shek that he call a conference immediately in Chungking consisting of Chinese, Soviet, British, Dutch and American representatives. This group would meet not later than December seventeenth and report to their respective Governments in the greatest confidence by Saturday, December twentieth. This would give us the preliminary picture of the joint problem from the angle of Chungking.

Second, I am asking the British to assemble a military-naval conference in Singapore, reporting by Saturday the twentieth principally from the operational angle in the Southern zone.

Third, I would be very happy if you personally would talk with American, British and Chinese representatives in Moscow and let me have your suggestions as to the whole picture by Saturday, the twentieth.

Fourth, I am during this coming week covering the same ground with British Missions here and will send you the general picture from this end.

I have had a good talk with Litvinov and I fully appreciate all of your immediate problems.

Again I want to tell you of the real enthusiasm through the United States for the progress your armies are making in the defense of your great nation.

I venture to hope that the preliminary conferences I have outlined for this coming week may lead to the establishment of a more permanent organization to plan our efforts.

Hopkins and I send our warm personal regards.

Franklin D. Roosevelt

Stalin

· 15 ·

TO THE PRESIDENT FROM J. STALIN

December 17, 1941

I received your message on the 16th of December. As there was no mention of the object of the suggested conferences in Chungking and Moscow, and that there was only one day left before their opening, I thought I might be able, in conversation with Mr. [Anthony] Eden [the British foreign secretary], who has just arrived in Moscow, to elucidate the question of the objects of the conferences, and to find out whether they could be postponed for some time. It transpired, however, that Mr. Eden has no information on this point, either. In view of the above, I should be glad to receive from you the necessary details, to ensure that the participation of representatives of the Union of Soviet Socialist Republics in these conferences should bring results. Allow me to thank you for the feelings you express with regard to the successes of the Soviet army. I wish you all success in your struggle against the aggression in the Pacific. I send you and Mr. Hopkins my warm personal greetings.

Roosevelt

· 16 ·

There was strong opposition among Catholics to the idea of U.S. aid for the Soviet Union. For this reason Roosevelt had sent Myron Taylor, special ambassador to Pope Pius XII, to Rome in late September to inform the pope about the imminent Harriman-Beaverbrook mission to Moscow. Roosevelt did not send the following message, scribbling "not sent" at the top and crossing out his signature, probably realizing that the pope's antipathy to the Soviet Union was so well known that the letter was pointless.

not sent
January 28, 1942
His Excellency Joseph Stalin, President of the Soviet of People's Commissars of the Union of Soviet Socialist Republics.
Dear Mr. Stalin:

When Myron Taylor returned from Vatican City last month he informed me of the earnest desire of the Pope to obtain for the prisoners of war held by the Soviet Government and for their families the comfort of an exchange of news. It was suggested only that some information of a general and innocuous nature regarding prisoners held by your authorities might be made available. The Pope has undertaken to interest himself assiduously in the welfare of Soviet prisoners in the hands of our enemies. I have been turning over in my mind the best method of bringing this to the attention of the appropriate authorities of your Government and have determined to approach you directly.

I have every confidence that the assurances of the Pope to alleviate the suffering of and obtain information concerning Soviet prisoners may be relied upon. In view of the benefit to your solders and their families I hope that you will feel than an arrangement of this nature can be worked out. If I can be of any assistance to you in the matter, you know that you are free to call upon me.

Very sincerely yours
~~Franklin D. Roosevelt~~

Roosevelt

· 17 ·

In late January the Japanese invaded and secured the Solomon Islands. On February 2 they invaded Java in the Dutch East Indies. On February 8 they invaded Singapore, capturing eighty-five thousand British soldiers; seven days later the city was theirs.

Washington, February 9, 1942
Personal from the President to Stalin.

Our shipments for January and February have included and will include 244 fighter planes, 24 B-25s, 233 A-20s, 408 medium tanks and 449 light tanks.

The reports here indicate you are getting on well in pushing the Nazis back.

While we are having our immediate troubles in the Far East, I believe we will have that area reinforced in the near future to such an extent that we can stop the Japs but we are prepared for some further setbacks.

I realize the importance of getting our supplies to you at the earliest possible date and every effort is being made to get shipments off.

Roosevelt

Roosevelt

· 18 ·

Since his years as assistant secretary of the navy Roosevelt, who always loved the sea, thought of himself as a navy man. He felt particularly comfortable among other navy men and chose a navy man whenever he had the chance. His personal physician, Ross McIntire, was a naval officer, a navy man was always in charge of the Map Room, Admiral Leahy was his chief of staff, and his valet was navy petty officer Arthur Prettyman. Indeed, he associated so closely with the navy that it took Gen. George Marshall considerable effort to persuade Roosevelt not to refer to the navy as "we" and the army as "they."[28]

Roosevelt appointed Adm. William H. Standley as ambassador

to the Soviet Union in February. Standley had been line commander of navy vessels from monitor to battleship, chief of naval operations from 1933 to 1937, and the naval member of the Moscow mission. Roosevelt told Molotov that he had chosen Admiral Standley to replace Steinhardt "because he was direct, frank, and simple," a statement with which Molotov agreed.[29]

For Standley, however, about to turn sixty-nine, it was a hardship post for which he was unsuited.

Washington, February 12, 1942
Personal for [Walter] Thurston [chargé d'affaires in Soviet Union]
Please transmit to Stalin the following message from the President:

I am much pleased that your Government has expressed its willingness to receive as the Ambassador the United States my old and trusted friend, Admiral Standley. The Ambassador and I have been closely associated for many years. I have complete confidence in him and recommend him to you not only as a man of energy and integrity but also as one who is appreciative of and an admirer of the accomplishments of the Soviet Union, which, you will recall, he visited with Mr. Harriman last year. Since his return from Moscow Admiral Standley has already done much to further understanding in the United States of the situation in the Soviet Union and with his rich background and his knowledge of the problems which are facing our respective countries I am sure that with your cooperation he will meet with success in his efforts to bring them still more closely together.

It has just been brought to my attention that the Soviet Government has placed with us requisitions for munitions and supplies of a value which will exceed the billion dollars which last autumn were placed at its disposal under the Lend-Lease Act following an exchange of letters between us. I propose, therefore, that under this same Act a second billion dollars be placed at the disposal of your Government upon the same conditions as those upon which the first billion were allocated. In case you have any counter-suggestions to offer with regard to the terms under which the second billion dollars should be made available, you may be sure that they will be given careful and sympathetic consideration. In any event it may prove mutually desirable later, in order to meet changing conditions, to review such financial arrangements as we may enter into now.

Roosevelt

Stalin

· 19 ·

The President of the Council of People's Commissars of the Soviet Union (Stalin) to President Roosevelt.
February 18, 1942

I have received your message informing me of consignments of armaments from the United States for January and February.

I would like to emphasize the fact that at the present moment, when the peoples of the Soviet Union and its army are exerting all their powers to thrust back, by their determined offensive, Hitler's troops, the fulfillment of American deliveries, including tanks and aeroplanes, is of the utmost importance for our common cause, for our further successes.

Stalin

· 20 ·

The President of the Council of People's Commissars of the Soviet Union (Stalin) to President Roosevelt
February 20, 1942
My Dear Mr. President:

Acknowledging the receipt of your message of 13th February, I would like first to say that I share your confidence that the efforts of the newly-appointed Ambassador of the United States to the Union of Soviet Socialist Republics, Admiral Standley, of whom you speak so highly and in such warm terms, to bring our two countries still closer to one another, will be crowned with success.

Your decision, Mr. President, to place at the disposal of the Soviet Government another billion dollars, in accordance with the law of the supply of armaments under the Lend-Lease Act, on the same conditions which applied to the first billion, is accepted by the Soviet Government with sincere gratitude. With regard to your inquiry I have to inform you that, at the present moment, in order not to delay matters, the Soviet Government is not raising the question of the modification of the conditions attaching to the granting by your Cabinet of the above-mentioned second billion dollars or of taking into consideration the extremely strained state of the resources of the USSR in the war against our common foe. At the same time I entirely agree with you and should like to express the hope that at a later date we shall be able jointly to fix a time when it will appear desirable to both of us to revise the financial agreements now concluded in order to pay special attention to the above-mentioned circumstances.

I should like to take this opportunity to draw your attention to the fact that the Soviet organizations when realizing the loan granted to the USSR are at present experiencing great difficulties with regard to the transport of armaments and materials purchased in the United States to USSR ports. We would consider the most suitable arrangement for the transport of armaments from America, in the circumstances, would be that which is successfully adopted for the transport of armaments from England to Archangel, but which heretofore has not been possible to apply to deliveries from the United States. According to this arrangement, the British military authorities delivering armaments and materials, designate the ships themselves, as well as organizing their loading in the port, and their convoy to the port of destination. The Soviet Government would be extremely grateful if the same arrangements for the delivery of armaments and the convoying of ships to the USSR ports, could be adopted by the United States Government also.

> With sincere respect, I remain,
> J. Stalin

Roosevelt

· 21 ·

After receiving Stalin's February 20 cable, Roosevelt was particularly concerned because deliveries to Russia were still disappointingly slow. On March 7 the president wrote to all U.S. war agencies that he "wished all material promised to the Soviet Union on Protocol to be released for shipping and shipped at the earliest possible date regardless of the effect of these shipments on any other part of the war program."[30]

The "further news" Roosevelt alludes to was that Soviet armies had succeeded in driving the Germans from Moscow province, as well as from Kalinin and Tula, freeing literally hundreds of villages. As the Germans retreated, however, they robbed and killed and burned every house to the ground.

From the President to Stalin
February 23, 1942

This will acknowledge your message of February 20.

I want you to know that at the appropriate time we shall be glad to reconsider with you our agreement relative to the funds we are advancing under the Lend-Lease Act. At the moment the all important problem is to get the supplies to you.

I am having canvassed at once your suggestion relative to centralizing control here of munitions being sent to Russia.

The further news of the successes of your Army heartens us very much.

I wish to send you my warm congratulations on the Twenty-fourth Anniversary of the founding of the Red Army.

Roosevelt

· 22 ·
———

Stalin had been pressing British Foreign Secretary Eden and Churchill to agree to recognition of Russia's enlarged boundaries as of 1941, which included the Baltic states, parts of Finland and Romania, and part of Poland, moving Poland's eastern boundary to the Curzon line, named for the British foreign secretary, Lord Curzon, who had proposed it in 1919. As far as Roosevelt was concerned, however, all territorial considerations were contrary to the Atlantic Charter, a matter to be settled only when the war was over and the victors sat down at the peace table. At their meeting in January in Washington, Churchill had specifically agreed with the president on this point, reiterating to Roosevelt that to grant Stalin's territorial demands "would be contrary to all the principles for which we were fighting."[31] Although this was an article of faith for Roosevelt, however, for Churchill, now so sorely pressed, it was just a bargaining chip. Driven by fear that Stalin was again contemplating throwing in his lot with Hitler, Churchill tried six weeks later to persuade Roosevelt to abrogate the agreement and permit him to agree to Stalin's territorial demands. (Stalin was equally unsure of Churchill: he had said to Beaverbrook in October 1941 that an agreement proscribing any separate peace with Germany "should be extended to a treaty, an alliance not only for war but for postwar as well.")[32]

But Roosevelt would have nothing to do with Churchill's plea. His assessment was that Stalin was firmly in the Allied camp, that he trusted Roosevelt because Roosevelt had never let him down, that he relied on the United States to come through, and that he would continue to do so even though the war was going badly. On the other hand, as Roosevelt commented to Secretary of the Treasury Henry Morgenthau, he thought Stalin had good cause not to trust Churchill, because "every promise the English have made to the Russians, they have fallen down on. . . . The only reason we stand so well with the Russians is that up to date we have kept our promises."[33]

In the interests of his friend, however, he was more circumspect, writing Churchill, "I know you will not mind my being brutally frank when I tell you that I think I can personally handle Stalin better than either your Foreign Office or my State Department. Stalin hates the guts of all your top people, He thinks he likes me better, and I hope he will continue to do so."[34]

Roosevelt then diverted Stalin's attention from postwar borders with a huge carrot: an invitation to discuss the opening in 1942 of a second front, which he believed the United States should champion. For this purpose Roosevelt proceeded to invite Molotov to Washington. For Stalin, who was gearing up his forces to repel the next Wehrmacht offensive as his armies were desperately defending Leningrad and protecting factories in the south, nothing was more important.[35] In the United States planning for the second front had been going on for months. Secretary of War Stimson, General Marshall, and the War Plans Division had developed the logistics to attack France with a force of 48 divisions and 5,800 planes about April 1, 1943, crossing the Channel at its narrowest point, between Calais and Le Havre. Roosevelt felt that a smaller invasion force, which became code-named SLEDGEHAMMER, could be ready to go in the fall of 1942 if it became necessary to divert German divisions away from the Soviet Union to avoid its defeat. Churchill was against the idea of a cross-Channel invasion, but Roosevelt sent Marshall and Harry Hopkins to London with the invasion plans to change his mind, and Churchill, aware of Roosevelt's insistence, reluctantly agreed to go along. Roosevelt stated the matter plainly: the Soviets were in need of succor, as everyone, including Stalin, could plainly see; further, as the president wrote Churchill on April 3, "Your people and mine demand the establishment of a front to draw off pressure on the Russians, and these peoples are wise enough to see that the Russians are today killing more Germans and destroying more equipment than you and I put together."[36] Hopkins and Marshall took off for London at 4:30 A.M. April 4 and plunged into talks with Churchill and the British General Staff, finally bringing them around.

Having lined up Great Britain, Roosevelt proceeded with his invitation for Molotov. Roosevelt originally wrote this message to Stalin on April 1 but then held on to it, changing it in his own hand and finally noting, "Copy of message given to Commissar of Russian Embassy April 11, 12 noon."

Personal from the President to Mr. Stalin
April 11, 1942

It is unfortunate that geographical distance makes it practically impossible for you and me to meet at this time. Such a meeting of minds in personal conversation would be greatly useful to the conduct of the war against Hitlerism. Perhaps if things go as well as we hope, you and I could spend a few ~~hours~~ *days* together next Summer near our common border ~~of~~ off Alaska. But, in the meantime, I regard it as of the utmost military importance that *we have the nearest possible approach to ~~the~~ an exchange of views.*

I have in mind a very important military proposal involving the utilization of our armed forces in a manner to relieve your critical western front. This objective carries great weight with me.

Therefore, I wish you would consider sending Mr. Molotov and a General upon whom you rely to Washington in the immediate future. Time is of the essence if we are to help in an important way. We will furnish them with a good transport plane so that they should be able to make the round trip in two weeks.

I do not want by such a trip to go over the head of my friend, Mr. Litvinov, in any way, as he will understand, but we can gain time by the visit I propose.

I suggest this procedure not only because of the secrecy, which is so essential, but because I need your advice before we determine with finality the strategic course of our common military action.

I have sent Hopkins to London relative to this proposal.

The American people are thrilled by the magnificent fighting of your armed forces and we want to help you in the destruction of Hitler's armies and material more than we are doing now.

I send you my sincere regards.

Franklin D. Roosevelt

Stalin

· 23 ·

———

On April 15 Harry Hopkins exultantly cabled Roosevelt that the British government had agreed to the cross-Channel invasion; Marshall cabled Secretary of War Stimson, "The British Government now intended to proceed immediately and energetically with all necessary preparations for the major operation."[37]

J. V. Stalin to F. Roosevelt
April 20, 1942

Let me thank you for the message which I received in Moscow the other day.

The Soviet Government agrees that it is necessary to arrange a meeting between V. M. Molotov and yourself for an exchange of opinions on the organization of a second front in Europe in the immediate future. V. M. Molotov can come to Washington with a competent military representative not later than May 10 to 15.

It goes without saying that Molotov will also stop in London for an exchange of opinions with the British Government.

I have no doubt that it will be possible to arrange a personal meeting between you and myself. I attach great importance to it, particularly in view of the important tasks facing our countries in connection with the organization of victory against Hitlerism.

Please accept my sincere regards and wishes of success in the fight against the enemies of the United States of America.

J. Stalin

Roosevelt

· 24 ·

The following message from President Roosevelt to Marshal Stalin was presented in person by Admiral Standley on the occasion of his first meeting with Stalin. Standley reported that it was translated, several paragraphs at a time, by V. N. Pavlov. After the passage urging Stalin to meet with Roosevelt "somewhere in Alaskan or Siberian waters" was translated, Stalin interrupted, saying, "I am grateful to President Roosevelt for his greetings and kind message. The question of a meeting between us has been the subject of an exchange of notes. I still have hopes that it can be brought about."[38]

April 23, 1942

I am the bearer of special greetings of friendship from President Roosevelt, Marshal Stalin. The President wishes me to express to you his admiration for the magnificent courage, fortitude, and resourcefulness shown by the Red Army and the Russian people in meeting the Nazi attack and turning it back, an admiration shared not only by the American people but by all liberty-loving people of the world.

The President also asked me to tell you that there was good reason for the traditional friendship between our two peoples, even before America became a nation. This reason is found in the character of the two peoples. We both realize that the misunderstandings which sometimes arise are due to the great distances which separate us and the lack of rapid communications. The President told me that he was sure that if the two of you could sit down together and talk matters over, there would never be any lack of understanding between our countries. To this end, and as may be entirely practicable, President Roosevelt wishes me to urge you to meet with him somewhere in Alaskan or Siberian waters during the next summer to discuss the entire problem of world affairs.

The President regrets the delays which have occurred in the delivery of Lend-Lease supplies and fully hopes and believes that the United States will be able to live up to the established schedules by the end of this month. He realizes the vital necessity of the united effort of all the United Nations and he is determined, and has issued instructions, that the highest priority be given to the production of supplies for Russia. Any obstacles in the way of the flow of these supplies for Russia must be removed.

Roosevelt

· 25 ·

———

The need for ships, Harry Hopkins had notified the President in April, "is going to be desperate."[39] From January to April the shipping losses just in the western part of the Atlantic totaled 1.2 million tons, and as April turned into May the situation only got worse. The lack of U.S. patrol planes allowed German Adm. Karl Donitz's submarines to prowl off the American coast and boldly pick off tankers: Americans in New Jersey shore towns, in Virginia Beach, and up and down the Florida coast could see ships burning out at sea. The convoys headed for the northern route to Archangel on the White Sea and to Murmansk on the Barents Sea, connected to Archangel by rail, were being preyed upon by Donitz's U-boats as well as by German planes and destroyers at a greater rate as well, in part because the German Navy had added another wheel to its Enigma machines, and English code breakers no longer could read their messages.

The following note in the president's handwriting accompanied this message: "Dear M. Litvinov: would you be kind enough to send this to Mr. Stalin? Thanks—F.D.R."

May 4, 1942
For Mr. Stalin:

We are having grave difficulties with the Northern convoy route and have informed Litvinov of the complications. You may be sure, however, that no effort will be omitted to get as many ships off as possible.

I have heard of Admiral Standley's cordial reception by you and wish to express my appreciation.

I am looking forward to seeing Molotov and the moment I hear of the route we shall make preparations to provide immediate transportation. I do hope Molotov can stay with me in the White House while he is in Washington but we can make a private home nearby available if that is desired.

Roosevelt

Stalin

· 26 ·

———

In the months of April, May, and June eighty-four ships left U.S. ports for Murmansk. Forty-four got through; seventeen were forced to unload their cargoes in Scotland, and twenty-three were destroyed.

Roosevelt had charged Hopkins to ask Churchill whether the size of the convoys could be increased to make up for the shipping losses. Churchill had answered evasively, avoiding any mention of making up for shipping losses. Roosevelt immediately reacted, writing Churchill on April 26, "I have seen your cable to Harry relative to the shipments to Russia. I am greatly disturbed by this because I fear not only the political repercussions in Russia but even more the fact that our supplies will not reach them promptly. We have made such a tremendous effort."[40]

May 15, 1942

I thank you for the message conveyed through Ambassador Litvinov. I have already requested Prime Minister Churchill to contribute to the speediest overcoming of certain difficulties in connection with the transportation and convoying of ships to the USSR. Since the delivery of materials in May from the USA and England is of the utmost urgency, I make a similar request to yourself, Mr. President.

The journey of Mr. Molotov to the USA and England must be postponed for a few days owing to uncertain weather conditions. It appears that this journey can be made on a Soviet airplane both to England and to the USA. I would at the same time add that the Soviet Government considers that Mr. Molotov's journey should be accomplished without any publicity whatever till the return of Mr. Molotov to Moscow, as was done when Mr. Eden visited Moscow in December last.

In regard to the place of residence of Mr. Molotov during his sojourn in Washington, Mr. Molotov and I thank you for your kind suggestions.

Roosevelt

· 27 ·

Foreign Minister Vyacheslav Molotov was the second-most-powerful man in the Soviet Union. He was an old Bolshevik who had changed his name from Skriabin to Molotov, which means "hammer." His relationship to Stalin dated back to 1912 when they both worked on *Pravda*. He had been a member of the Politburo since 1924, had been president of the Soviet of People's Commissars until Stalin took it over in 1941, and was the minister whom Stalin trusted more than any other. Molotov arrived at the White House on Friday, May 29. He met first with the president, Secretary of State Cordell Hull, Hopkins, Ambassador Litvinov, General Marshall, and Adm. Ernest King. Molotov had no effort convincing Roosevelt and the Joint Chiefs of Staff that it was imperative to mount the second front that summer. The invasion, all agreed, had to be of sufficient strength to draw off forty German divisions to prevent Hitler from dealing the Soviet Union a crushing blow from which it could not recover. Molotov argued that if the United States postponed the decision, "You will have eventually to bear the brunt of the war, and if Hitler becomes the undisputed master of the continent, next year will unquestionably be tougher than this one." After confirmation from General Marshall that a second front could be created, the president, according to Hopkins, "then authorized Mr. Molotov to inform Mr. Stalin that we expect the formation of a Second Front this year." Accordingly, Molotov issued a public statement June 11 to that effect, saying, "In the course of the conversations full understanding was reached with regard to the urgent tasks of creating a Second Front in Europe in 1942."[41] The code name given for the 1942 assault on France was SLEDGEHAMMER.

Roosevelt was particularly pleased with Molotov's visit, calling it "a real success because we have got on a personal footing of candor. . . . I was greatly pleased by the visit. . . . He warmed up far more than I expected."[42] Molotov stayed at the White House for the first few days of his visit. When Roosevelt left for Hyde Park on Monday, June 1, Molotov moved to Blair House.

On June 6 the decisive Battle of Midway took place; U.S. dive bombers sank four of Japan's six fleet-class carriers and sent three hundred Japanese planes down in flames. The battle marked the end of the Japanese offensive and the first naval defeat the Japanese had suffered in 350 years. It was not until the evening, however, that the outcome was known, by which time this message was on its way.

To: *Mr.* Stalin
From the President
June 6, 1942

I appreciate every so much your sending Mr. Molotov to see me. We had a very satisfactory visit and I shall await anxiously the news of his safe arrival.

Roosevelt

Stalin

· 28 ·

June 12, 1942

The Soviet Government shares your view, Mr. President, as to the satisfactory results of Mr. V. M. Molotov's visit to the United States.

I take this opportunity to thank you, Mr. President, on behalf of the Soviet Government, for the cordial hospitality offered to Mr. Molotov and his staff during their sojourn in the United States.

Mr. V. M. Molotov has safely returned to Moscow today.

Molotov himself wrote Roosevelt the following letter.

Before returning to my country I allow myself once more to express to you, Mr. President, the great satisfaction I feel in having reached a full understanding concerning the urgent tasks connected with the creation of a second front in Europe in 1942 for speeding up the rout of Hitlerite Germany and concerning cooperation of our countries in the post-war period in the interests of all freedom-loving peoples.

Please accept my sincere gratitude for the cordial reception and hospitality offered to us by you, Mr. President, and the Government of the United States of America, and my best wishes to you personally and to the people of the United States of America.

Vyacheslav Molotov

Roosevelt

· 29 ·

On June 7 the Germans launched a massive infantry and tank attack on Sevastopol, a seaport on the Black Sea which they had besieged and started bombing eight months earlier.

On June 10 the Germans announced that they had leveled the village of Lidice in Czechoslovakia, killed all its inhabitants and extinguished its name, in return for the killing in Prague of Reinhard Heydrich, deputy chief of the Gestapo. The German Army continued its policy of killing and committing atrocities as it marched across Russia.

On June 11 the master Lend-Lease agreement between the United States and the Soviet Union, nearly identical to the agreement between the United States and Great Britain worked out on February 23, was signed by Secretary of State Hull and Soviet Ambassador Litvinov.

The U.S. Navy, reporting that Japanese troops had seized the islands of Kiska and Attu, was predicting a possible move against the whole chain of Aleutian Islands.[43]

The Soviet Union desperately needed fighter planes to repel the expected spring and summer German offensives. The obvious solution was to fly the planes from the aircraft factories scattered over the United States directly to Fairbanks, Alaska, and then on to landing fields in Siberia. But although the Soviets agreed "in principle" to this, and the War Department worked out the logistics, the Russians, ever suspicious of foreigners, delayed implementation of the plan for months. Only Stalin could approve of landing fields for U.S. planes on Russian soil.

Ambassador Standley presented the following message to Stalin on June 19.

To: Mr. Stalin
From: President Roosevelt
June 17, 1942

The development of the situation in the North Pacific and Alaskan area presents tangible evidence that the Japanese may be preparing to conduct operations against the Maritime Provinces of the Soviet Union. In the event of such an attack we are prepared to come to your assistance with our air power, provided suitable landing fields are available in Siberia.

In order that such an operation can be promptly carried out, the efforts of the United States and the Soviet Union must be carefully coordinated.

I was very happy to learn through [Litvinov] that you have approved of the movements of our planes from Alaska through Northern Russia to your western battlefront. In order to meet this new danger in the Pacific area, I believe that an immediate exchange of detailed information pertaining to existing establishments in the Siberia and Alaska areas and the initiation of secret staff conversations between our joint Army, Navy, and Air representatives are essential to our common interests. I consider this matter of such urgency that our conferees should be empowered to make definite plans and initiate action. I propose that you and I designate such representatives and that they meet in Washington and Moscow immediately.

Roosevelt

Roosevelt

· 30 ·

June 23, 1942
To: Ambassador Standley for Mr. Stalin
From: President Roosevelt

Supplementing my radiogram to you of June seventeenth it is desired to emphasize the great savings in time that would be effected in the delivery of aircraft to the Soviet Union if deliveries could be accomplished through Alaska and Siberia as we are now doing. Also a ferry route through Siberia would permit the ferrying of short range aircraft which are now being shipped by water. I am prepared to have our ferrying crews deliver airplanes to you at Lake Baikal provided landing fields, weather and navigational facilities can be established to connect with our own airways at Nome. Such an airway in Siberia could also be easily connected with landing fields leading into the Vladivostok area. This would enable us to rapidly move our air units into that area to assist you in the event the Japanese should initiate operation against your maritime provinces. As a result of my study of the problem of establishing an air route through Siberia to Lake Baikal it is evident that bulk supplies, such as gasoline and machinery to develop landing fields would have to be moved into Eastern

Siberia via water over certain rivers emptying into the Arctic Ocean. This water movement would have to be accomplished within the next few weeks while these rivers are ice free. The necessity for initiating action at an early date has dictated my communicating with you before receiving an answer to my radiogram of June seventeenth. To expedite the development of this air route, if you agree with its importance and urgency, it is requested that you authorize a survey and exploratory flight of one of my airplanes from Alaska over the proposed route to determine the supplies and equipment necessary in the construction of the essential landing fields and navigational aids. The personnel making such flight would wear civilian clothes and take all necessary action to insure that they would not be identified in any respect with the military service. They would, in fact, make the flight as personnel of a commercial agency. The survey flight would not be in lieu of the conversations by our joint Army, Navy and Air representatives which I recommended in my telegram of June seventeenth, but would be conducted for the sole purpose of enabling those representatives to commence their discussions with a more definite and detailed information of the problems involved than would otherwise be the case. We could of course take on one or two of your officers or officials at Nome, Alaska.

Roosevelt

Stalin

· 31 ·

In late June the Germans began a major offensive against the Caucasian oilfields and grain in the south. The German Sixth Army under Gen. Friedrich Paulus, 300,000 strong, the army that had conquered Paris in 1940, led the charge. Stalin, who had concentrated Russian troops in the north expecting an assault on Moscow, was caught completely off guard.

On June 30, after a defense of 250 days, Sevastopol fell to the Germans.

Moscow, July 1, 1942

In connection with your recent messages I consider it advisable to state that I share in full your opinion regarding the expediency of the air route for the delivery of aircraft from the United States via Alaska and Siberia to the Western front. Having taken this into consideration the Soviet Government has already given the necessary orders regarding the completion of the work in the immediate future undertaken in Siberia in connection with the preparation for the reception of aircraft; that is, work on the fitting out of the existing air fields and their appropriate installations. With regard to whose aviators shall deliver the aircraft from Alaska it appears to me that this matter may be entrusted as the State Department proposed at one time to Soviet aviators, who would be sent to Nome or any other feasible place at an agreed-upon time. The carrying out of the survey flight suggested by you may also be entrusted to an appropriate group of these aviators. Completely to insure the reception of these planes we would like to know at this time the number of planes which the United States of America intends to deliver to the Western Front by this route.

With regard to your proposal concerning the meeting of representatives of the Army and Navy of the United States of America and the Soviet Union for the purpose of exchanging information so far as this will be necessary, the Soviet Government is agreeable to the organization of such a meeting and proposes that it should take place in Moscow.

Telegram No. 231
From: Ambassador Standley in Moscow
July 2, 1942

Accompanied by my Military Attaché, I talked with Stalin today, and in confirmation of the President's statement regarding Japan's aggressive attitude in the northern Pacific, I repeated the information furnished by telegram No. 174 [not reproduced here] from the Department. I then brought up the differences between the terms contained in the President's messages and those in Stalin's reply. The following were discussed specifically:

First. To my mention of the lack of any reference to heavy freight movement via northern rivers, Stalin replied that this route could not be used as during this season only one more navigation month remained. I was assured, however, that the Siberian area air fields were completely equipped and prepared to receive American planes.

Second. With regard to the suggestion of the President that representatives of the Soviet Union might participate in the proposed American planes survey flight, Stalin stated that it would be "entirely agreeable" for American representatives to accompany the Soviet plane on its test flight.

Third. With reference to the proposal by Mr. Stalin that American and Soviet representatives organize a meeting in Moscow for the exchange of information regarding the proposed route, and to the President's thought that meetings take place both in Moscow and Washington, I stated that it would be necessary to bring an American air expert to Moscow from Washington as there were none here, and suggested that a Soviet expert who is already in Washington might be named by the Soviet Government to confer with the appropriate American officials, adding that the American and Soviet experts could then return here to act as the President proposed and Stalin seconded. The latter replied that he saw no need of any additional discussions in Washington as it was obviously only a question of the monthly number of planes that could be delivered.

Fourth. Nome or other feasible point in Alaska then Semchan, then Yakutsk, then Kirensk and then Krasnoyarsk is the course that Stalin stated the route would follow.

Roosevelt

· 32 ·

This cable was delivered on July 6. On that day Voronezh in south central Russia fell to the Germans.

The British stronghold at Tobruk, gateway to Libya, fell to the Germans on June 21, when thirty-three thousand British troops surrendered to an inferior German force; Field Marshal Erwin Rommel, the "Desert Fox," began his drive into Egypt on June 24, and on the 30th engaged the British Eighth Army at El Alemain.

Priority
July 5, 1942
From President Roosevelt for J. V. Stalin

The crisis in Egypt with its threat to the supply route to Russia has led Prime Minister Churchill to send me an urgent message asking whether forty A twenty bombers destined for Russia and now in Iraq can be transferred to the battle in Egypt. It is impossible for me to express a judgment on this matter because of limited information here. I am therefore asking that you make the decision in the interest of total war effort.

Roosevelt

Stalin

· 33 ·

J. V. Stalin to F. Roosevelt.
July 7, 1942

In view of the situation in which the Allied forces find themselves in Egypt I have no objection to forty of the A 20 bombers now in Iraq en route to the USSR being transferred to the Egyptian front.

Roosevelt

· 34 ·

July 6, 1942

I am designating Major General Follett Bradley, Colonel [Joseph] Michela and our Naval attaché, Captain [Jack] Duncan, to represent this country at the conferences to be held in Moscow which were suggested in my cable to you of June 17.

General Bradley will be the only representative that will be sent to Moscow from this country.

We are prepared to have an American four engine plane at Nome within the next few days to make the survey trip, three or four Soviet officers to accompany it. On the other hand, we would be very happy to have American officers accompany a Soviet plane.

General Bradley will come to Moscow fully prepared and authorized to discuss all plans in relation to the conference.

Roosevelt

Roosevelt

· 35 ·

Deliver to Joseph Stalin and inform Standley
July 9, 1942

I deeply appreciate your reply authorizing transfer to Egypt of forty bombers. I am arranging to ship to you at once one hundred and fifteen additional medium tanks with ammunition and spare parts. These tanks will be in addition to all tanks going forward as provided in July protocol.

Roosevelt

Stalin

· 36 ·

___

For the President from Stalin
July 18, 1942

Your message about the assignment of Maj. Gen. F. Bradley, Capt. Duncan and Col. Michela as American representatives to the Conference has been received by me. As American representatives they will receive all the cooperation necessary for the accomplishment of the mission assigned them. Representing the USSR at the Conference will be Major General Sterligov, Colonel Kabanov and Colonel Levandovich.

As to the survey flight it would be possible to send within a few days from Krasnoyark to Nome one plane (having in mind an American two motored plane) which could bring back the American officers on the return trip.

I use this opportunity to express to you my appreciation for the information about the additional 115 tanks being sent to the USSR.

I consider it a duty to advise you that, which our specialists confirm, the American tanks catch on fire very easily from projectiles of anti-tank weapons striking the rear or sides. This results from the fact that high grade gasoline used in American tanks forms a heavy layer of gas vapors creating favorable conditions for catching fire.

German tanks also operate on gasoline but their gasoline is of low grade which gives off little vapor in view of which they are less vulnerable to fire.

Our specialists consider that the diesel motor is most suitable for tanks.

Roosevelt

· 37 ·

___

This message was written because there had been no reply to Roosevelt's July 6 message. Stalin's preceding message, when finally received, made this message redundant, however, and it was not sent.

July 20, 1942
Dear Mr. Stalin:

It is still a matter of deep regret to me that thus far the pressure of events has rendered it impossible for us to meet and personally discuss various matters vitally affecting the common interests of the United States and the Soviet Union.

As you are already aware I feel that one of the most important of our problems is that of finding ways for speeding up the delivery of airplanes to the Soviet Union. Your decision that the route across Alaska and Siberia should be utilized for the delivery of planes will, I am convinced greatly aid our efforts to solve this particular problem.

In accordance with our understanding that there should be a meeting of the representatives of the Army and Navy of the Soviet Union and of the United States of America for exchanging such information as might be necessary in order that the most effective use should be made of the Alaskan-Siberian route, I am sending to the Soviet Union as my representative to conduct these conversations Major General Follett Bradley of the United States Air Corps with the personal rank of Minister.

Relying as I do upon the discretion and judgment of General Bradley, I recommend him to you as one of the most able officers of the United States Army and hope that you and officers of the armed forces of the Soviet Union will find it possible to discuss with him various matters relating to the establishment of the new air route with the same degree of frankness as that which I have charged him to discuss these matters with you.

Very sincerely yours,
Franklin D. Roosevelt

Roosevelt

· 38 ·

July 22, 1942
Deliver to Joseph Stalin and inform Standley

Your message concerning the arrangements for the Moscow Conference and proposed survey flight from Alaska has been received by me.

Members of the survey flight will be ready to depart from Alaska August 1st. In this connection a four engined bomber will be available at Nome in event it is required.

Your report on the difficulties with American tanks at the front is much appreciated. This information will be most helpful to our tank experts in eradicating the trouble with this model. Future models, however, will operate on a lower octane and the fire hazard therefore reduced.

Roosevelt

Stalin

· 39 ·

On July 27 German forces crossed the Don and occupied Rostov.

August 2, 1942

Your plane B-25 will arrive Nome between 8 and 10 August and will carry 3 American participants on survey flight.

Roosevelt

· 40 ·

Churchill had journeyed to Washington and Hyde Park in late June to present the case against SLEDGEHAMMER, the cross-Channel invasion scheduled for October, to Roosevelt. He was strongly against the project, warning the president that the Channel would turn into "a river of blood."[44] The prime minister also handed Roosevelt a paper stating that the British government was sure such an operation "would lead to disaster."[45] Faced with this strong British reaction, reluctantly agreeing that the time was not yet ripe, and urgently desirous of having American troops engage the Germans in battle before the year was out, Roosevelt tentatively agreed to an invasion of North Africa (Operation TORCH, previously called GYMNAST) to take place in October.

The Joint Chiefs of Staff, however, were only partially committed to this change of plans. General Marshall, in particular, had personally assured Molotov that SLEDGEHAMMER was going to happen and still thought it the wisest course.

On July 16 General Marshall, Admiral King, and Harry Hopkins flew to London at Roosevelt's request to try again to push

SLEDGEHAMMER, which, the president told the men, he believed "might be the turning point which would save Russia this year. SLEDGEHAMMER is of such grave importance that every reason calls for accomplishment of it. . . . The principal objective of SLEDGE-HAMMER is the positive diversion of German Air Forces from the Russian front."[46] The British military once more refused to go ahead with the plans, however, and cast doubt among the U.S. Navy officers as to the advisability of landing on the northern French coast pointing out that it became a "lee shore" in October; finally the 1942 cross-Channel invasion was irrevocably abandoned.

Roosevelt's instructions emphasized to his three emissaries that it was "of the highest importance that U.S. ground troops be brought into action against the enemy in 1942." Hopkins took this as Roosevelt's "most important" point.[47]

While Roosevelt settled for the invasion of North Africa, it might have been his fallback plan all along. Someone had to tell Stalin of the change of plans. Since Stalin, deeply involved in the day-to-day military planning, couldn't leave Moscow, Churchill flew to Moscow to deliver the bad news.

August 5, 1942
For Mr. Stalin from the President inform Standley
I have information which I believe to be definitely authentic that the Japanese government has decided not to undertake military operations against the Soviet Union at this time. I think this means postponement of any attack on Siberia until next spring. Will you be good enough to impart this to your visitor [Churchill]?
Roosevelt

Roosevelt

· 41 ·

Churchill asked Roosevelt to allow Harriman to accompany him to Moscow to show Stalin that the change in plans was a joint U.S.–U.K. decision. "I feel that things would be easier if we all seemed to be together."[48]

For Stalin from the President inform Standley
August 5, 1942

I am asking Harriman to proceed Moscow to be at disposal of yourself and your visitor to help in any possible way.

Roosevelt

Roosevelt

· 42 ·

————

For the President and the Secretary of State
August 6, 1942

I called upon Molotov upon my arrival today and delivered the President's recent messages to Stalin. Molotov stated that of course he would deliver the messages but added that he failed to understand the message to the effect the Japanese would not attack the Soviet Union until the spring of 1943 for the reason that Litvinov had reported to the Foreign office that the President had advised him late in July that his information at the time was to the effect that the Japanese would definitely attack the Soviet Union during the first ten days of August 1942. I agreed to report this to the President for possible reconciliation.

Standley

For delivery to Ambassador Standley
August 7, 1942

Please tell Mr. Molotov my recent message to Mr. Stalin in regard to Japan was based on last minute information which has been subsequently strengthened.

Roosevelt

Stalin

· 43 ·

————

Stalin to President
August 7, 1942

I have received your message of August 5th.

I express my appreciation for the advice concerning the forthcoming arrival of Mr. Harriman in Moscow.

As to your information regarding Japan I have learned of it with interest and of course I too shall not fail to transmit it to the visitor.

Roosevelt

· 44 ·

Wendell Willkie had been Roosevelt's Republican opponent in the previous presidential election. Roosevelt appreciated his help in legitimizing his foreign policy in the face of opposition from the isolationist wing of the Republican Party. He participated in setting up Willkie's tour, writing to him, "It is my thought that you could do the Middle East and that Russia and China could be subject to developments which you and I can talk over. General Marshall and General [Henry Harley "Hap"] Arnold will have the details."[49] He sent Willkie on a government plane and sent the following message to Stalin.

Admiral Standley
Kuibyshev
August 8, 1942
Please convey the following message to Mr. Stalin for me.

I should like to have your frank opinion on the following plan which I think may be useful:

I am sending Mr. Wendell Willkie to visit the Governments in Egypt, Saudi Arabia, Syria, Turkey, Iraq and Iran for the primary purpose of explaining to the Governments of these smaller countries the danger they run in a German victory and that their greatest hope for the future lies in the defeat of Nazi domination of the places of the Near East and Middle East.

Mr. Willkie much wants to visit the Soviet Union for a wholly different purpose. He wants to know more about the wonderful progress made by the Russian people, in addition to seeing for himself the undying unity of thought in repelling the invader and the great sacrifices all of you are making.

He is, as you know, my recent opponent in the 1940 elections and is the head of the minority party today. He is greatly helping in war work and is heart and soul with my Administration in our foreign policy of opposition to Nazism *and real friendship with your government.*

Personally I think that for the sake of the present and the future a visit by him to the Soviet Union would be a good thing. He would fly to Russia in the first half of September.

Please tell me confidentially and frankly if you would care to have him come for a very short visit.

Roosevelt

Stalin

· 45 ·

Stalin to Roosevelt
August 12, 1942

Your message of August 9 to hand. The Soviet Government takes a favorable view of Mr. Wendell Willkie's visit to the USSR and I can assure you that he will be most cordially entertained.

Roosevelt

· 46 ·

Churchill arrived in Moscow on August 12 for three days of talks. Accompanied by Harriman, he met with Stalin less than three hours after his arrival. After initial problems caused by Stalin's visible disappointment at the postponement of the second front (Churchill promised a much larger and stronger offensive in 1943, when more soldiers, more landing craft, and a million American troops would be available), Churchill and Stalin, according to Harriman, began in their talks to find common interests. When Churchill told Stalin about the U.S. bombing campaign against Germany which was just starting, Stalin said that homes as well as factories should be targeted. "Now there began an easing of the tension and an increasing understanding of common purpose. Stalin and Churchill, between them, soon had destroyed most of Germany's important industrial centers," reported an amused Harriman.[50]

When Churchill told Stalin of the U.S.–British military plans to land troops in North Africa at Casablanca, Oran, and Algiers in October, Harriman recalled, Stalin suddenly said, "May God prosper this undertaking." The remark sounded strange coming from the leader of a party that rejected religion, but in fact it simply reflected Stalin's early seminary training. Although Stalin was angry over the postponement of the second front, by the end of Churchill's visit, he had come to appreciate the pluses for Russia in Operation TORCH, the invasion of French North Africa. As he told Harriman, TORCH would take the German enemy in the rear, provoke French and Germans to fight each other, knock Italy out of the war, and encourage Spain to remain neutral.[51]

Averell Harriman took the opportunity at the final banquet to tell Stalin that Roosevelt wanted to meet with him. Stalin replied that he too believed a meeting was "of great importance," suggesting to Harriman that the meeting take place in the winter, when "I am not so preoccupied. . . . Perhaps Iceland in December." When Harriman commented to Stalin that that was a long dangerous flight, Stalin replied that the flight didn't worry him, that he had good planes.[52] As it turned out, Stalin was reluctant to fly; he had never been in a plane.

On August 7 the U.S. Marines landed on Guadalcanal, Tulagi, and Florida islands in the Solomon Islands.

To: Stalin
From: The President
August 18, 1942

I am sorry that I could not have joined with you and the Prime Minister in the Moscow Conferences. I am well aware of the urgent necessities of the military situation, particularly as it relates to the situation on the Russian front.

I believe we have a toehold in the southwest Pacific from which it will be very difficult for the Japanese to dislodge us. Our naval losses there were substantial but it was worth it to gain the advantage which we have. We are going to press them hard.

On the other hand, I know *very well* that our real enemy is Germany and that our force and power must be brought against Hitler at the earliest possible moment. You can be sure that this will be done, *just as soon as it is humanly possible to put together the transportation.*

In the meantime, over 1,000 tanks will leave the United States in August for Russia, and other critical supplies, including airplanes, are going forward.

The United States understands that Russia is bearing the brunt of the fighting and the losses this year. We are filled with admiration of your magnificent resistance. Believe me when I tell you that we are coming as strongly and as quickly as we possibly can.

Roosevelt

Stalin

· 47 ·

At 6:00 P.M. on August 23, the day after Stalin wrote the following message to Roosevelt, six hundred German planes began dropping incendiary bombs on Stalingrad. Soviet reinforcements were on their way to the threatened city, but they had not yet arrived. Soviet air cover was nonexistent; the Germans had the sky to themselves. The bombs killed an estimated forty thousand civilians that day. Stalin cabled his Stalingrad commanders:

> The enemy has broken through your front in small numbers. You have sufficient opportunity to smash him. Assemble the aircraft of both fronts and use them against the enemy. Mobilize the armoured trains and put them on the circular track around Stalingrad. . . . Once again, by his incompetence and inefficiency, Lopatin has let down the Stalingrad front. Put some effective supervision over him and organize a second line behind his army. Most important, don't panic, don't be afraid of this audacious enemy and keep faith in our success.[53]

Stalin to Roosevelt

August 22, 1942

I have your message of August 18. I also regret that you could not have participated in the conversations I recently had with Mr. Churchill.

In connection your remarks regarding the shipment from the United States during August of tanks and war materials, I would like to emphasize our special interest at present time in receiving from US aircraft and other types of armaments, and also trucks, in greatest possible quantity. Furthermore I hope all measures will be taken to guarantee most expeditious delivery of goods to Soviet Union, especially by northern sea route.

Roosevelt

· 48 ·

August 22, 1942

Dear Mr. Stalin

Mr. Wendell Willkie, the titular leader of the opposition party in the United States, about whom I have already telegraphed you, ought to get to Moscow about the fifteenth or twentieth of September. I am delighted that you will receive him and I think it will be of real benefit to both of our countries if he can get a firsthand impression of the splendid unity of Russia and the great defense you are conducting.

According to our present plans, and in accordance with my suggestion, he will proceed to Chungking in order to see the Generalissimo and to tell him that the United States is thoroughly alive to the necessity of China's victory in the war against Japan.

From there he wants to return to the United States via Eastern Siberia and Alaska, as this is much the quickest route and because he wants to be back by October fifteenth.

My very warm regards,

Very sincerely yours,

Stalin

· 49 ·

On September 1 Averell Harriman gave a briefing on the battle for Stalingrad to the Joint Chiefs of Staff, during which he stated, according to Admiral Leahy, that "he believed Russia would continue to fight, but the tone of his remarks left some doubt as to how long."[54]

Lopatin was relieved of command, but by September 13 columns of German tanks and motorized infantry were rolling into the center of the city and approaching the Volga. For days Stalin did not leave his office in the Kremlin, ordering his bodyguard to wake him every two hours. On the night of September 14 the first Russian reinforcements, ten thousand strong, crossed the Volga into the city. For weeks the battle seesawed between the Germans and the Russians. The casualties were enormous on both sides.

Willkie arrived in Moscow in late September. He did "an enormous amount of good," according to Hopkins. The Russians applauded his call for establishing a Second Front. On his return home, he reported the Russian bitterness about the seventeen American merchant ships bound for Murmansk that, faced with almost certain German U-boat attack, had unloaded their cargoes in Scotland; the Kremlin suspected the British had "stolen" Lend-Lease material belonging to the Soviet Union.[55]

Only Russian ships could sail to Vladivostok, the eastern terminus of the Trans-Siberian railway, because of the three countries involved in Lend-Lease, only the Soviet Union was not at war with Japan.

October 7, 1942

Availing myself of the opportunity to send you a personal message afforded by Mr. Standley proceeding to Washington, I would like to express a few considerations on the military supplies from the United States to the USSR. It is reported that the difficulties with supplies are caused primarily by the shortage of shipping. In order to ease the shipping situation, the Soviet Government would agree to a certain cuts in the American supplies of armaments to the Soviet Union. We should be prepared temporarily to have discontinued the supplies of tanks, artillery, ammunition, revolvers and such like. At the same time we are in extreme need of an increase in the supply of fighter planes of modern types (such as for instance Airacobras) and in getting under all circumstances certain kinds of other supplies. It should be born in mind that Kitty Hawk planes are not up to the mark in the fight against modern German fighter planes.

It would be good, if the USA could in any case insure our getting every month the following supplies:

500 fighter planes
8 to 10 thousand trucks
5,000 tons of aluminum
4 to 5 thousand tons of explosives.

In addition to this it is important to get the supply during the 12 months of two million tons of grain (wheat) and also as much as possible of fats, food concentrates and canned meat. A considerable amount of these foodstuffs could be shipped via Vladivostok on Soviet ships, if the US consented to concede to the USSR at least 20 to 30 ships. I have already spoken to Mr. Willkie about all this and am sure that he will communicate it to you.

As regards the situation at the front, you are of course aware that during the last few months the situation grew worse in the south, especially in the Stalingrad sector, due to the shortage of planes, particularly fighter planes. The Germans turned out to have a large reserve of planes. In the South the Germans have at least a double supremacy in the air, which prevents us from giving our troops cover. The practice of the war has shown that the most gallant troops become powerless if they are not shielded from the air.

Roosevelt

· 50 ·

To: *Mr.* Stalin
From: The President
October 8, 1942

The Prime Minister has sent me copy of his message to you.

We are going to move as rapidly as possible to place an Air Force under your strategic command in the Caucasus. I am now trying to find additional planes for you immediately and will advise you soon.

I am also trying to arrange to have some of our merchant ships transferred to your flag to increase your flow of materials in the Pacific.

I have just ordered an automobile tire plant to be made available to you.

We are sending very substantial reinforcements to the Persian Gulf to increase the flow of supplies over that route and are confident that this can be done. We are sending a large number of engines and other equipment, as well as personnel.

I am confident that our contemplated operation will be successful.

Everyone in America is thrilled by the gallant defense of Stalingrad and we are confident that it will succeed.

Roosevelt

Roosevelt

· 51 ·

___

From Roosevelt to Stalin
October 11, 1942

Every possibility of increasing the number of fighter planes to be sent to Russia is being examined by me. The fact of the matter is that all the Airacobra production is now going to fighting fronts immediately. While these urgent combat requirements make it impossible to increase the number of Airacobras for you at the moment nevertheless I am hoping to increase our production of this type at the expense of other types in order to give you more planes. Also if our forthcoming operations which you know about turn out as successfully as they promise, we would then be in a position to release fighters. Our heavy bombardment group has been ordered mobilized immediately for the purpose of operating on your southern flank. These planes and sufficient transports will go to the Caucasus at an early date. This movement will not be contingent on any other operation or commitment. Twenty merchant ships for use in the Pacific are also being made available to you. In October we will ship to you two seven six combat planes and everything possible is being done to expedite these deliveries. I shall telegraph you in a day or so in reference to explosives, aluminum and trucks.

Roosevelt

Roosevelt

· 52 ·

___

From the President for Mr. Stalin. Show Bradley and Faymonville.
October 14, 1942

In response to your request I am glad to inform you that the items involved can be made available for shipment as follow:

Trucks—8,000 to 10,000 per month

Explosives—4,000 short tons in November and 5,000 tons per month thereafter

Wheat—2,000,000 short tons during the remainder of the protocol year at approximately equal monthly rates.

Canned Meats—10,000 tons per month.

Meat—15,000 tons per month.

Lard—12,000 tons per month.

Vegetable oil—10,000 tons per month.

Soap stock—5,000 tons per month.

I have directed that every effort be made to keep our routes fully supplied with ships and with cargo in conformity with your desires as to priorities on the commitments we have made to you.

I am still exploring the aluminum shipments and will advise you of these at an early date.

Roosevelt

Stalin

· 53 ·

Memorandum for the President from Harry Hopkins

Ambassador Litvinov has transmitted the following message to you from Stalin:

October 15, 1942

I am in receipt of your message of October 12 and thank you for your communication.

J. Stalin

Stalin

· 54 ·

General Chuikov, commander of the Soviet army at Stalingrad, described October 14, when the Germans attacked with five new infantry divisions and two tank divisions, supported by masses of infantry and planes, as "the bloodiest and most ferocious day in the whole battle." Under the steady drum of shots and explosions that caused vibrations in the dugouts sufficient to shatter tumblers, the Germans pushed the Russians back, according to Chuikov, only one and a half kilometers and sustained such heavy losses that they could not continue further.[56]

October 19, 1942
From Premier Stalin to President Roosevelt

I have received your message of October 16. My answer has been delayed because matters connected with the front have diverted my attention. The whole business now entirely a matter of your cargoes reaching the Soviet Union within the time stated.

Roosevelt

· 55 ·

From the President to Premier Stalin notify chargé d'affaires
October 24, 1942

Admiral Standley has handed me your personal note copy of which you had previously sent me. Our ambassador has given me a very full report of the situation in Russia as he sees it. He confirms reports we have already had of the strength and fighting qualities of your army and the urgent need of supplies indicated by you. I fully recognize these needs.

Roosevelt

Stalin

· 56 ·

(For the President) This acknowledgement phoned to White House previous to write up.
October 28, 1942

Your message of October 24 received. I thank you for the information.

Roosevelt

· 57 ·

Roosevelt sent Maj. Gen. Patrick Hurley, minister to New Zealand, to visit Stalin armed with a letter explaining his views on the future of the war. Although the letter is dated October 5, Hurley presented the letter to Stalin only on November 14, while Standley was absent from Moscow. Stalin was particularly pleased with

Hurley's visit, although Andrei Vishinsky in Washington had not been, telling Hurley "that Mr. Willkie, Ambassador Standley, the Military Attaché and the Naval Attaché to Moscow were all coming home and wondering why, with all this wealth of reporting imminent, anyone else should have to go to Russia."[57]

October 5, 1942
My dear Mr. Stalin,

I am giving this letter of presentation to you to General Patrick J. Hurley, former Secretary of War and at present United States Minister to New Zealand.

General Hurley is returning to his post in New Zealand and I have felt it to be of the highest importance that, prior to his return, he should be afforded the opportunity of visiting Moscow and of learning, so far as may be possible, through his own eyes the most significant aspects of our present world strategy. I wish him in this way as a result of his personal experiences to be able to assure the Government of New Zealand and likewise the Government of Australia that the most effective manner in which the United Nations can join in defeating Hitler is through the rendering of all possible assistance to the gallant Russian armies, who have so brilliantly withstood the attacks of Hitler's armies.

I have requested General Hurley likewise to visit Egypt, as well as Iran and Iraq, in order that he might thus personally familiarize himself with that portion of the Middle East and see for himself the campaign which is being carried on in that area.

As you know, the Governments of Australia and of New Zealand have been inclined to believe that it was imperative that an immediate and all-out attack should be made by the United Nations against Japan. What I wish General Hurley to be able to say to those two Governments after his visit to the Soviet Union is that the best strategy for the United Nations to pursue is for them first to join in making possible the defeat of Hitler and that this is the best and surest way of insuring the defeat of Japan.

I send you my heartiest congratulations on the magnificent achievements of the Soviet Armies and my best wishes for your continued welfare.

Believe me,

Yours very sincerely,
Franklin D. Roosevelt

Stalin

· 58 ·

Roosevelt considered Operation TORCH, the invasion of North Africa, of paramount importance for the morale of both the United States and Russia—it was, after all, the only way to strike against Germany in 1942—and crucial also from a tactical point of view. Knowing that the invasion would strike a chord with voters, Roosevelt hoped that it would take place October 30, before the congressional elections. "Please," he had said to General Marshall, "make it before election day."[58] Circumstances didn't permit it, and the Republicans gained forty-seven seats in the House, whittling the Democratic majority down to nine, as well as gaining ten seats in the Senate.

On November 8 General Eisenhower landed Allied soldiers at Casablanca in Morocco and at Oran, Algiers, and Bone in Algeria. The soldiers found themselves under attack by Vichy French troops. Eisenhower cast about for a high-ranking French official with whom he could negotiate a cease-fire, settling on the commander in chief of the French fleet, Adm. Jean-François Darlan, who happened to be in Algiers visiting his sick son. Eisenhower agreed to recognize Darlan as the authority in French North Africa in exchange for an immediate cease-fire. The deal saved untold American lives, but it was unpopular in the United States and throughout the world because Darlan was despised as a former collaborator with Germany.[59]

TO PRESIDENT ROOSEVELT FROM PREMIER STALIN
November 14, 1942
Dear Mr. President:

I am very grateful to you for your letter which General Hurley has handed in today. General Hurley and I had a long talk on strategy. It seems to me that he has understood me and is satisfied that the strategy which is now being followed by the Allies is correct. He asked to be allowed to see one of our fronts and, in particular, to go to the Caucasus. He will be afforded an opportunity to do so.

There were no major changes on the Soviet-German front during the last week. We expect to begin our winter campaign in the nearest future.

Preparations for it are now going on. I shall keep you informed as to the progress of this campaign.

We here are all highly gratified by the brilliant successes of American and British armed forces in North Africa. Allow me to congratulate you upon this victory. With all my heart I wish you further successes.

With sincere respect,

Stalin

Roosevelt

· 59 ·

On November 15, 1942, General Hurley sent the following long cable to Roosevelt.

1. Stalin expressed his understanding of the desire for an all out attack against Japan now. He definitely disapproved that strategy at this time as it would divert matériel and force from this theater. he denied Japan's ability to exploit within the ensuing year or 18 months the war resources of the territories she has occupied.

2. Stalin stressed the paramount importance of the defeat of Hitler first, and maintained that the defeat of Japan would be logical consequence. He completely agreed with strategy indicated in your letter and amplified by me.

3. Stalin made clear the necessity of accumulating in Russia as quickly as possible the matériel essential to enable Russia to assume the offensive. Such an offensive, he considered, a proper implementation of the strategy outlined by you.

4. Stalin stated that eventually we would need an additional front in Asia from which to attack Japan simultaneously with an attack from the Pacific.

5. Stalin repeated his commendation already expressed through the press of the operations in North Africa.

6. Stalin agreed to afford me the means of a complete understanding of Russian strategy in Russia. He proposed that this be done through contact with proper military authorities and personal reconnaissance of the vital fighting front.

My discussion with Stalin of the foregoing subjects began at 11 p.m. on November 14 and continued to 12:30 a.m. on November 15. Molotov, whom I had visited several days before, but with whom I had not discussed the purpose of my mission, sat through the entire conference. He did not participate in the discussions. Pavlov interpreted.

I opened the conference by extending your greetings and expressing your admiration for the fortitude and the intelligence with which Russia is conducting her great fight. I then assured Stalin that any statement he might make to me would be transmitted directly and secretly to President Roosevelt alone. I handed him your letter of October 5 addressed to him. On his direction it was read and interpreted to him at once. Before commenting on the letter he asked if I had anything to say in regard to the subject matter or if I wished to amplify the contents.

I reviewed briefly my recent service in the Pacific area, explained the present situation in that theater, and presented the argument that has heretofore been made by Australians, New Zealanders, and some Americans—including myself—to the effect that we should attack, defeat and destroy the autocracy of Japan before she had time to exploit the great resources of the territory she had occupied. I concluded by pointing out that the defeat of Japan would remove a formidable enemy from our rear and would permit the full utilization of our resources in the Western theater; that likewise, the defeat of Japan would release the war resources of Russia now in the Asiatic area. This would enable the United States and Russia to bring their full force to bear on the paramount objective—the defeat of Hitler.

I then told him that contrary to these views you had decided that the most effective plan in which the United Nations could join for defeating Hitler was through rendering all possible support to the Russian armies and that the defeat of Japan would naturally follow the defeat of Germany. I told Stalin that it was now my purpose to help make your strategy effective.

Mr. Stalin then began talking—slowly, quietly, deliberately. He expressed his greetings to you and his appreciation of your splendid leadership. His first sentence on the subject under discussion was to the effect that you had adopted the correct and the most effective strategy. He stressed the imperative need of creating a reserve in Russia to justify Russia in assuming the offensive. He referred again to the necessity for a second front in Europe eventually, but agreed fully on the effectiveness of the opening of what he referred to as another front in Africa.

Up to this time he had made no reference to Japan. I then referred to his recent anniversary address and expressed appreciation for his outline of the objectives of the Soviet-American-Anglo coalition. I referred with commendation to his letter to

Mr. Cassidy of the Associated Press on the American-British achievements in North Africa. I then started to suggest that in all his public discussion he had made no mention of the Eastern theater. Before I completed the sentence he laughed and interrupted me to say, "I know. You are going to say that I failed to mention your enemy—Japan."

In this statement I cheerfully acquiesced. He then began a clear analysis of what he termed the war in Asia. His first comment was that I had placed too much stress on Japan's ability to exploit the war resources now in his line. He said that Japan had only such tooling as she had received from the United States before the war and was now receiving from Germany. He described this as absolutely insufficient.

He said that Japan did not possess trained workers in sufficient numbers in Japan or in the area she occupied. His whole argument on this subject led to the conclusion that there was no danger whatever of Japan being able exploit the captured resources to any appreciable extent within the next year or 18 months. At one point this discussion indicated that Russia intended in due course to cooperate in the establishment of a mainland front against Japan, but further discussion of that subject so modified his statement that it should not be taken as a commitment.

I asked him if it were not a fact that Japan's role was not that of a selfish opportunist, watching Germany's progress and holding herself in position to take advantage of any success that might come to Germany in the Western theater. This he answered in the negative. He said that the cooperation between Japan and Germany was complete. He knew that recently Japan had made increased demands on Germany for surface ships and airplane engines. He said that Japan was incapable of constructing first class airplanes without the aid of Germany. Great traffic was taking place between Germany and Japan at the present.

The surface craft and the airplanes which Japan had lost were irreplaceable by Japan alone. The number of Japanese sea craft sunk by the United States and airplanes destroyed had greatly increased Japan's demands upon Germany. He was positive in his conclusion that Japan would be unable to sustain herself in the war without the aid of Germany.

All of this led him to agree completely with you that the defeat of Japan would be a logical consequence of the defeat of Germany.

At this point Stalin stopped me to ask if he had made clear

his position on all the questions I had presented. I told him he had, but he had not yet given me a clear statement of Russia's strategy in Russia and that I would like to know, for instance, what Russia now had between her enemy and her oil, how much matériel Russia would require before she could take the offensive, and where, how, and when she contemplated the offensive. Here I expected to be thrown out of the Kremlin.

He replied that heretofore he had steadfastly declined to permit any but Russians to have the opportunity of seeing and understanding Russia's manner of contact with the enemy and her present and future strategy. Much to my surprise he then said it would take about 3 days for him to make arrangements for proper officers to consult with me on strategy, and a personal reconnaissance trip by me to the vital fighting areas.

Stalin's attitude was uniformly good-natured, his expressions were always clear, direct and concise. His attitude toward you and the United States was always friendly and respectful. [Hurley]

THE WHITE HOUSE

WASHINGTON

From the President to Premier Stalin Inform Chargé D'Affaires

November 19, 1942

Dear Mr. Stalin:

I am glad you have been so kind to General Hurley.

As you can well recognize, I have had a problem in persuading the people of Australia and New Zealand that the menace of Japan can be most effectively met by destroying the Nazis first. General Hurley will be able to tell then at firsthand how you and Churchill and I are in complete agreement on this. Our recent battles in the Southwest Pacific make the position there more secure even though we have not yet eliminated attempts by the Japanese to extend their southward drive.

The American and British Staffs are now studying further moves in the event that we secure the whole south shore of the Mediterranean from Gibraltar to Syria. Before any further step is taken, both Churchill and I want to consult with you and your Staff because whatever we do next in the Mediterranean will have a definite bearing on your magnificent campaign and your proposed moves this coming Winter.

I do not have to tell you to keep up the good work. You are doing that and I honestly feel that things everywhere look brighter.

With warm regards.

Roosevelt

Stalin

· 60 ·

By the beginning of November, Hitler thought that he had all but taken Stalingrad. On November 8 he had announced, "I wanted to reach the Volga . . . at a particular city. By chance it bore the name of Stalin himself. . . . I wanted to capture it and . . . we have as good as got it."[60] In some places German soldiers were within one hundred yards of the river. But neither Hitler nor General Paulus knew that Stalin was about to unleash one million new soldiers against him. The preparations for the counteroffensive had begun in August. On November 19 the two Russian armies—one of which had been moving stealthily into Stalingrad, mostly at night, transporting huge numbers of troops and equipment across the Volga in pontoons and ferries, the other north of the Don—began the Russian counterattack, catching the German army completely by surprise. The two wings, one striking out southward, the other toward the northwest, began a drive to encircle the Germans and cut them off from their supplies. Within five days they had closed the "ring."

November 20, 1942
Private message of Premier Stalin to President Roosevelt

Offensive operations in the district have begun in the South and Northwest sectors. The first stage of these offensive operations aims at seizing the Stalingrad-Likhaya railroad line and at destroying the communications of the Stalingrad group of the German troops. In the northwest sector a breach 22 kilometers long has been made in the German front, in the South sector—12 kilometers long. The progress of the operation is not bad.

Roosevelt

· 61 ·

U.S. Adm. William Halsey, as a result of learning from American cryptanalysts that Adm. Isoroku Yamamoto was planning to send a large convoy with a battleship and cruiser escort to Guadalcanal to aid and resupply Japanese troops, unexpectedly sent the carrier *Enterprise,* being repaired at Pearl Harbor, plus battleships, to do battle. The U.S. fleet decimated the Japanese fleet, and within weeks the Japanese evacuated all their forces from Guadalcanal. But the damaged *Enterprise* was the navy's only aircraft carrier in the Pacific.

November 25, 1942
From: The President for Mr. Stalin.

I want you to know that we have hit the Japs very hard in the Solomons. There is a probability that we have broken the backbone of the strength of their fleet, although they still have too many aircraft carriers to suit me, but we may well get some more of them soon.

We are in the Southwest Pacific with very heavy forces by air, land and sea and we do not intend to play a waiting game. We are going to press our advantages.

I am sure we are sinking far more Jap ships and destroying more airplanes than they can build.

I am hopeful that we are going to drive the Germans out of Africa soon and then we will give the Italians a taste of some real bombing and I am quite sure they will never stand up under that kind of pressure.

The news from the Stalingrad area is most encouraging and I send you my warmest congratulations.

Roosevelt

Stalin

· 62 ·

———

PERSONAL MESSAGE FROM PREMIER STALIN TO PRESIDENT ROOSEVELT
November 27, 1942

I thank you for your message received by me on November 21. I fully understand your desire to make the present military situation clear to the people of Australia and New Zealand, and the need for attention to operations in the south-west Pacific.

As regards operations in the Mediterranean, which are developing so favorably, and may influence the whole military situation in Europe, I share your view that appropriate consultations between the Staffs of the

United States of America, Great Britain and the USSR have become desirable.

Greetings and my best wishes for new successes in further offensives.

Stalin

· 63 ·

B-24 bombers based in North Africa were scheduled to begin bombing Italy on December 4.

The German Army tried but failed to break through and rescue its men trapped in Stalingrad in the last days of November. Wrote a United Press correspondent permitted to tour Stalingrad a few days later, "10,000 horses had been killed during the Russian breakthrough. The whole steppe was strewn with these dead horses and wrecked gun-carriages and tanks and guns ... and no end of corpses, Rumanian and German."[61]

PERSONAL MESSAGE FROM PREMIER STALIN TO PRESIDENT ROOSEVELT
November 28, 1942

Thank you for your message which I received on November 27. I rejoice at your successes around the Solomon Islands and at the rapid growth of your forces in the south-west part of the Pacific.

Being sure that the Germans will soon be driven out of North Africa, I hope the intensive bombings of Italy planned by you will, of course, be of importance.

In the course of the Stalingrad operations certain successes have been achieved by us. Facilitated considerably by snowfall and fogs which prevented the German aviation from fully using its forces.

We have decided to undertake an operation at the central front as well, in order to prevent the enemy from moving his forces southward.

Please accept my cordial greetings to yourself and my best wishes to the American armed forces.

Roosevelt

· 64 ·

_____

The White House
Washington
December 2, 1942
From Roosevelt for Stalin.

The more I consider our mutual military situation and the necessity for reaching early strategic decisions the more persuaded I am that you, Churchill and I should have an early meeting.

It seems to me that a conference of our military leaders alone will not be sufficient, first because they could come to no ultimate decisions without our approval and secondly because I think we should come to some tentative understanding about the procedures which should be adopted in event of a German collapse.

My most compelling reason is that I am very anxious to have a talk with you. My suggestion would be that we meet secretly in some secure place in Africa that is convenient to all three of us. The time, about January fifteenth to twentieth. We would each of us bring a very small staff of our top Army, Air and Naval commanders.

I do hope that you will consider this proposal favorably because I can see no other way of reaching the vital strategic decisions which should be made soon by all of us together. If the right decision is reached, we may and I believe will knock Germany out of the war much sooner than we anticipated.

I can readily fly, but I consider Iceland or Alaska out of the question at this time of the year. Some place can, I think, be found in southern Algeria or at or near Khartoum where all visitors and press can be kept out. As a mere suggestion as to date what would you think of sometime around January 15?

Roosevelt

Stalin

· 65 ·

_____

The converging Russian armies succeeded in closing the net, trapping the German Sixth Army and the Fourth Panzer Division—

300,000 men—in a ring thirty-five miles wide by twenty miles long. Stalin had telephoned the Russian chief of staff, Marshal Alexander Vasilevsky, on November 27 urging "top priority for the liquidation of the German Stalingrad forces."[62] The battle raged on, but in the first days of December the German soldiers fought back fiercely and the Red Army was unable to force a resolution, so the Soviet command had to throw in new units from the Stavka Reserve. The United Press correspondent Henry Shapiro, allowed in for a few days after the ring was closed, noted that "a fairly high proportion of the food was American—especially lard, sugar and spam," but that he saw only an occasional American jeep or tank.[63]

December 6, 1942
Private message from Premier Stalin to President Roosevelt
I received your message on December 5, I welcome the idea of a meeting of the leaders of the Governments of the three countries to determine a common line of military strategy. However, to my great regret, I shall not be able to leave the Soviet Union. I must say that we are having now such a strenuous time that I cannot go away even for a day. Just at this time serious operations of our winter campaign are in the process of developing and in January they will not weaken. It is more likely that the contrary will be the case.

Round Stalingrad, as well as at the central front, the battles are developing. Round Stalingrad we are keeping encircled a group of German troops and hope to finish them off.

Roosevelt

· 66 ·

December 8, 1942
I am deeply disappointed that you feel you cannot get away for a conference with me in January. There are many matters of vital importance to be discussed between us. These relate not only to vital strategic decisions but also to things we should talk over in a tentative way in regard to emergency policies we should be ready with if and when conditions in Germany permit.

These would include also other matters relating to future policies about North Africa and the Far East which cannot be discussed by our military people alone.

I fully realize your strenuous situation now and in the immediate future and the necessity of your presence close to the fighting front.

Therefore, I want to suggest that we set a tentative date for meeting in North Africa about March first.

Roosevelt

Stalin

· 67 ·

Criticism of Eisenhower's deal with Darlan received extensive press in the United States. "If we will make a deal with a Darlan in French territory, then presumably we will make one with a Goering in Germany or with a Matsuoka in Japan," editorialized one newspaper.[64]

The issue faded from public dialogue when Darlan was assassinated on Christmas Eve. Pierre Boisson was governor of Dakar. Gen. Henri-Honoré Giraud had recently escaped from Nazi imprisonment and would have been ideal, but he insisted on being supreme commander.

December 14, 1942
Private message of Premier Stalin to President Roosevelt

I too must express my deep regret that it is impossible for me to leave the Soviet Union either in the near future or even at the beginning of March. Front business absolutely prevents it, demanding my constant presence near our troops.

So far I do not know what exactly are the problems which you, Mr. President, and Mr. Churchill intended to discuss at our joint conference. I wonder whether it would not be possible to discuss these problems by way of correspondence between us, as long as there is no chance of arranging our meeting? I admit that there will be no disagreement between us.

Allow me also to express my confidence that the time is not being lost and that the promises about the opening of a second front in Europe given by you, Mr. President, and by Mr. Churchill in regard of 1942 and in any case in regard of the spring of 1943, will be fulfilled, and that a second front in Europe will be actually opened by the joint forces of

Great Britain and the United States of America in the spring of the next year.

In view of all sorts of rumors about the attitude of the Union of Soviet Socialist Republics toward the use made of Darlan and of other men like him, it may not be unnecessary for me to tell you that, in my opinion, as well as in that of my colleagues, Eisenhower's policy with regard to Darlan, Boisson, Giraud and others is perfectly correct. I think it a great achievement that you succeeded in bringing Darlan and others into the waterway of the Allies fighting Hitler. Some time ago I made this known also to Mr. Churchill.

Roosevelt

· 68 ·

—————

December 16, 1942
From the President to *Mr.* Stalin

I am not clear as to just what has happened in regard to our offer of American air assistance in the Caucasus.

I am fully willing to send units ~~large or small~~ with American pilots and crews. I think they should operate by units under their American Commanders but each group would *of course* be under overall Russian command as to tactical objectives.

Please *let me know* ~~inform me by dispatch as to~~ your desires in this matter *as soon as possible, as I truly want to help all I can. Pursuit plane program would of course not be affected. What I refer to is essentially the bombing plane type which can be flown to the Caucasus.*

Roosevelt

Stalin

· 69 ·

—————

December 18, 1942
Private message of Premier Stalin to President Roosevelt.

I am very grateful to you for your readiness to help us. As to Anglo-American air-squadrons with personnel, at the present moment the necessity of having them sent to Transcaucasia has passed. Now the major battles are and will be developing at the central front and in the Voronezh area. I shall be very grateful to you, if you expedite the delivery of planes, especially fighter planes—without the personnel which is now extremely necessary to yourself—to be used in the above-mentioned areas.

The peculiar state of Soviet aviation is that we have more than enough fliers, but not enough planes.

Roosevelt

· 70 ·

December 21, 1942
For Mr. Stalin from the President
Am very sorry that arrangements for conference could not be made but I can well understand your position.

This will acknowledge your note about the Anglo-American squadrons. We will expedite delivery of planes to the utmost. I have arranged to get you ten transport planes in January. I am writing you in regard to certain post war matters.

Roosevelt

Roosevelt

· 71 ·

On the last day the House was in session, December 16, 1942, Congressman Martin J. Kennedy offered and the House passed Joint Resolution 371.

Resolved
That the Congress of the United States, on behalf of the American people, and with a deep and abiding sense of gratitude, does hereby convey to the members of our armed forces and auxiliary services, and those of our Allies on land, on sea, and in the air its best wishes and greetings of the season to them and to their families and its fervent hope and prayer for a speedy and complete victory and a lasting peace.

And be it further resolved
That the Congress of the United States does hereby respectfully request that the Commander in Chief of our armed forces, President Franklin Delano Roosevelt, transmit these greetings

through the proper and official channels to the armies through-out the world.

The message Roosevelt sent, received by the Kremlin on December 28, follows.

Struggling side by side against powerful foes, thousands upon thousands of soldiers of those nations, large and small, which are united in defense of freedom and justice and human rights face the holiday season far from home, across oceans or continents, in fields of desert sand or winter snow, in jungles, forests, on warships or merchant vessels, on island ramparts from Iceland to the Solomons, in the old and new worlds.

They strive to the limits of their strength, without regard for the clock or the calendar, to hold the enemy in check and to push him back. They strike mighty blows and receive blows in return. They fight the good fight in order that they may win victory which will bring to the world peace, freedom, and the advancement of human welfare.

With a deep and abiding sense of gratitude the Congress of the United States has by a joint resolution asked me to transmit on behalf of the people of the United States to the armed forces and auxiliary services of our Allies on land, on sea, and in the air, the best wishes and greetings of the season to them and to their families and a fervent hope and prayer for a speedy and complete victory and a lasting peace.

Accordingly, I shall be grateful to you if you will convey to your armed forces and auxiliary services, in the name of the Congress of the United States, in my own name, and in the name of the people of the United States, the cordial wishes and greetings and the hope and prayer expressed in the joint resolution.

Roosevelt

· 72 ·

December 30, 1942
For Mr. Stalin from the President

I note in a radio news report from Tokyo that a Japanese submarine sank an Allied nation submarine in the Pacific on October 12.

This report appears to refer to your submarine L-16 sunk by enemy action on October 11 while en route to the United States from Alaska and I am sending to you this expression of regret for the loss of your ship with its gallant crew and of my appreciation of the part your Navy is also contributing to the Allied cause in addition to the heroic accomplishments of your Army.

Roosevelt

Roosevelt

· 73 ·

Maj. Gen. Follett Bradley had been in Moscow since August 1942 as leader of a special air mission.

December 30, 1942
For Mr. Stalin from the President

In the event that Japan should attack Russia in the Far East, I am prepared to assist you in that theater with an American Air Force of approximately 100 four-engined bombardment airplanes as early as practicable, provided that certain items of supply and equipment are furnished by Soviet authorities and that suitable operation facilities are prepared in advance. Supply of our units must be entirely by air transport, hence it will be necessary for Soviet Government to furnish such items as bombs, fuel, lubricants, transportation, shelter, heat, and other minor items to be determined.

Although we have no positive information that Japan will attack Russia, it does appear to be an eventual probability. Therefore, in order that we may be prepared for this contingency, I propose that the survey of air force facilities in the Far East, authorized by you to General Bradley on October 6, be made now, and that the discussions initiated on November 11 on your authority between General Bradley and General Korolenko be continued.

It is my intention to appoint General Bradley, who has my full confidence to continue these discussions for the United States if you so agree. He will be empowered to explore for the United States every phase of combined Russo-American operations in the Far East Theater and, based upon his survey, to recommend the composition and strength of our air forces which will be allocated to assist you should the necessity arise. He will also determine the extent of advance preparations practicable and necessary to ensure effective participation of our units promptly on initiation of hostilities. His party will not exceed twenty persons to fly into Russia in two American Douglas DC-3 type airplanes.

If this meets with your approval, I would suggest that they proceed from Alaska along the ferry route into Siberia; thence under Russian direction to the Headquarters of the Soviet Armies in the Far East, and thence to such other places in Russia as may be necessary to make the required surveys, and discuss operating plans.

It would be very helpful if an English-speaking Russian officer, such as Captain Valdimirov now in Washington or Captain Smolyarov in Moscow, is detailed to accompany General Bradley as adjutant and liaison officer.

I seize this opportunity of expressing my admiration for the courage, stamina, and military prowess of your great Russian Armies as reported to me by General Bradley and as reflected in your great victories of the past month.

Roosevelt

Stalin

· 74 ·

———

Stalin to Roosevelt
December 31, 1942
I beg you, Mr. President, to accept my thanks for the cordial greetings and good wishes sent on behalf of the American people to the armed forces of the Soviet Union and to transmit same to the Congress of the United States.

Joseph Stalin

Stalin

· 75 ·

———

January 5, 1943
Marshal Stalin to President Roosevelt
I have received your message concerning the Far East. Please accept my appreciation of your willingness to send 100 bombers for the Soviet Union to the Far East. However, I must say that at the present time we want aid in airplanes, not at the Far East, where the USSR is not engaged in war, but at the front of the fiercest war against the Germans, i.e., at the Soviet-German front. The arrival of these airplanes, without fliers (we have enough

fliers of our own), at the south-western or the central front would play an enormous role on the most important sectors of our struggle against Hitler.

Roosevelt

· 76 ·

January 8, 1943
From the President to Premier Stalin

After reading your reply to my radio concerning the Far East I am afraid I did not make myself clear.

As I previously explained reference South Caucasus, it is not practicable to send heavy bombers to Russia at this time other than in existing organized units.

Our proposal regarding the 100 planes referred to a situation *which would occur* ~~where~~ *if hostilities were* ~~had~~ *actually to break* ~~broken~~ out between Japan and Russia. Under such conditions we calculated that by regrouping our air units in the Pacific theater 100 planes in organized units could be concentrated in Eastern Siberia because their action as well as your battle there would enable us to reduce our air strength elsewhere in the Pacific theater.

My radio was intended to be in the nature of anticipatory *protective* planning *against a possibility only.* The only immediate action recommended was in reference to the survey and discussions by General Bradley with Soviet officials. Only by such preliminary survey and advance planning will it be possible to render reasonably prompt assistance in the event of an outbreak of hostilities ties in Siberia.

I should like to send General Marshall to Moscow for a visit in the very near future and if this can be arranged I hope that you will be able to discuss this matter with him at that time. He will be able to tell you about the current situation in Africa and also about planned operations for balance of this year in all war theaters. I think this will be very helpful and he will have the latest news. Meanwhile I would appreciate an early reply to my proposal of December 30 that General Bradley and his party proceed without delay to the Far East for survey and staff discussions.

My deep appreciation for the continuing advances of your armies. The principle of attrition of the enemy forces on all fronts is beginning to work.

Roosevelt

Roosevelt

· 77 ·

———

January 9, 1943
To Premier Stalin from the President.

I have arranged that two hundred C-47 transport planes be assigned to you in January. Your mission here is being advised of the dates of delivery by months. I am going to do everything I can to give you another one hundred but you can definitely count on the two hundred.

FDR

Stalin

· 78 ·

———

Roosevelt had suggested that Marshall visit Moscow to explain to Stalin the principal factors influencing American military decisions, particularly important on the eve of his meeting with Churchill at Casablanca. Harriman had lunch with Ivan M. Maisky, the Soviet ambassador to Great Britain, to find out why, in the message that follows, Stalin suggests that he will refuse to receive General Marshall in Moscow. He reported back to Hopkins that "Maisky . . . indicated Stalin had misunderstood the President's offer to send U.S. bomber groups to Siberia as indicating desire on our part to embroil them with Japan at a time when their information indicated no imminent prospect of Japanese attack. It was for this reason Stalin answered so curtly Marshall's proposed visit."[65]

Eisenhower's invasion of Tunisia started off badly. This was his first taste of war, and neither he nor his green American troops were at first able to cope with Field Marshal Rommel's tactics or his vastly superior German tanks. In February a German panzer division routed American forces at Kasserine Pass in Algeria.

Private message of Premier Stalin to President Roosevelt
January 13, 1943

I wish to express my gratitude for your decision to send 200 transport planes to the Soviet Union.

As regards sending bombing avio-units to the Far East, I made it clear in my previous messages that what we want is not avio-units, but airplanes without fliers, as we have more than enough fliers of our own.

This is in the first place.

In the second place, we want your aid in airplanes not in the Far East, where the USSR is not in a state of war, but at the Soviet German front, where the need for aviation aid is particularly acute.

I do not quite understand your suggestion that General Bradley should inspect Russian military objects in the Far East and in other parts of the USSR. It would seem obvious that Russian military objects can be inspected only by Russian inspectors, just as American military objects can be inspected only by American inspectors. In this respect must be no misunderstanding.

As regards General Marshall's journey to the USSR, I must say that his mission is not quite clear to me. I would ask for elucidation as to the purpose and aims of this journey, so that I could consider this question in full consciousness of what it entails, before giving my answer.

My colleagues are concerned over the slowing down of operations in North Africa and, moreover, as it is said, not for a short time, but for a long period. May I have some information from you on this point?

Roosevelt and Churchill

· 79 ·

Roosevelt and Churchill met in Casablanca on January 14 with their chiefs of staff. Roosevelt chose Africa, according to Hopkins, because he wanted to get away and liked the drama of the trip. The president and his party flew from Miami to North Africa in a Pan American Boeing clipper.

At the conference, Churchill's plan that the next military offensive after the North African campaign would take place in the Mediterranean won out over Roosevelt and Marshall's plan for a cross-Channel invasion. However, this information was withheld from Stalin for several weeks. More pleasing to Stalin was Roosevelt's surprise announcement that the United States was calling for unconditional surrender of Germany, Japan, and Italy. Given no choice, Churchill grudgingly went along with the idea. (Secretary of State Hull, too, was surprised, admitting, "Originally this principle had not formed part of the State Department's thinking. We were as much surprised as Mr. Churchill when the President stated it suddenly to a press conference. . . . I was told that the Prime Minister was dumbfounded.")[66]

The Japanese had captured Rabaul, the capital of the Australian territory of New Guinea, on January 23.

[Marrakech] January 25, 1943
President Roosevelt and Prime Minister Churchill to Premier Stalin

1. We have been in conference with our Military Advisers and we have decided the operations which are to be undertaken by American and British forces in the first nine months of 1943. We wish to inform you of our intentions at once. We believe these operations, together with your powerful offensive, may well bring Germany to her knees in 1943. Every effort must be made to accomplish this purpose.

2. We are in no doubt that our correct strategy is to concentrate on the defeat of Germany, with a view to achieving early and decisive victory in the European theatre. At the same time, we must maintain sufficient pressure on Japan to retain the initiative in the Pacific and Far East, sustain China, and prevent the Japanese from extending their aggression to other theatres such as your Maritime Provinces.

3. Our main desire has been to divert strong German land and air forces from the Russian front and to send to Russia the maximum flow of supplies. We shall spare no exertion to send you material assistance by every available route.

4. Our immediate intention is to clear the Axis out of North Africa and set up the naval and air installations to open:

(1) An effective passage through the Mediterranean for military traffic, and

(2) An intensive bombardment of important Axis targets in Southern Europe.

5. We have made the decision to launch large scale amphibious operations in the Mediterranean at the earliest possible moment. The preparation for these operations is now under way and will involve a considerable concentration of forces, including landing craft and shipping in Egyptian and North African ports. In addition we shall concentrate in the United Kingdom a strong American land and air force. These, combined with the British forces in the United Kingdom, will prepare themselves to re-enter the Continent of Europe as soon as practicable. These concentrations will certainly be known to our enemies, but they will not know where or when,

or on what scale we propose to strike. They will, therefore be compelled to divert both land and air forces to all the shores of France, the Low Countries, Corsica, Sardinia, Sicily, the heel of Italy, Yugoslavia, Greece, Crete and the Dodecanese.

6. In Europe we shall increase the Allied Bomber offensive from the U.K. against Germany at a rapid rate and, by midsummer, it should be more than double its present strength. Our experiences to date have shown that the day bombing attacks result in destruction and damage to large numbers of German Fighter Aircraft. We believe that an increased tempo and weight of daylight and night attacks will lead to greatly increased material and morale damage in Germany and rapidly deplete German fighter strength. As you are aware, we are already containing more than half the German Air Force in Western Europe and the Mediterranean. We have no doubt that our intensified and diversified bombing offensive, together with the other operations which we are undertaking, will compel further withdrawals of German air and other forces from the Russian front.

7. In the Pacific it is our intention to eject the Japanese from Rabaul within the next few months and thereafter to exploit in the general direction of Japan. We also intend to increase the scale of our operations in Burma in order to reopen our channel of supply to China. We intend to increase our air force in China at once. We shall not, however, allow our operations against Japan to jeopardize our capacity to take advantage of every opportunity that may present itself for the decisive defeat of Germany in 1943.

8. Our ruling purpose is to bring to bear upon Germany and Italy the maximum forces by land, sea and air which can be physically applied.

Stalin

· 80 ·

---

30 January 1943
Private message of Premier Stalin
to President Roosevelt and Prime-Minister Churchill.

I received your friendly joint message on January 27. I thank you for the information on the decisions taken in Casablanca regarding operations to be carried out by American and British armed forces in the course of the first nine months of 1943.

As I understand that by the decisions taken regarding Germany you yourselves set the task of crushing it by opening a second front in Europe in 1943, I should be very obliged to you for information on the concrete operations planned in this respect and on the scheduled time of their realization.

As regards the Soviet Union, I can assure you that the armed forces of the USSR will do everything in their power to continue the offensive against Germany and her allies on the Soviet-German front. Circumstances permitting, we intend to wind up our winter campaign in the first half of February of this year. Our troops are tired, they need rest and will hardly be able to continue the offensive beyond that time.

Roosevelt

· 81 ·

Field Marshal Paulus and what remained of his army could have escaped from Stalingrad, but Hitler refused to give the order to retreat. Finally, on January 31, with his men starving to death because there was no food and freezing to death because they were so lightly clothed, Paulus surrendered with the remnants of his army, some 92,000 soldiers. Altogether, 500,000 Russians and 200,000 Germans had died at Stalingrad. Nothing remained of the city but a mass of rubble.

February 4, 1943
His Excellency Joseph V. Stalin,
    Supreme Commander of the Armed Forces
    Of the Union of Soviet Socialist Republics,
        Moscow.
As Commander-in-Chief of the Armed Forces of the United States of America I congratulate you on the brilliant victory at Stalingrad of the armies under your Supreme Command. The one hundred and sixty-two days of epic battle for the city which has for ever honored your name and the decisive result which all Americans are celebrating today will remain one of the proudest chapters in this war of the peoples united against Nazism and its emulators. The commanders and fighters of your armies at the front and the men and women, who have supported them in factory and field, have combined not only to cover with glory their country's arms, but to inspire by their example fresh determination among all the

United Nations to bend every energy to bring about the final defeat and unconditional surrender of the common enemy.

Franklin D. Roosevelt

Stalin

· 82 ·

Moscow, February 5, 1943
Mister Franklin D. Roosevelt
Commander in Chief of the Armed Forces of The United States of America,
White House,
Washington, D.C.

I thank you for the congratulations in connection with the victory of the Soviet armies at Stalingrad. I express confidence that the joint fighting operations of the armed forces of the United States, of Great Britain and of the Soviet Union will soon lead to victory over our common enemy.

J. Stalin

Roosevelt and Churchill

· 83 ·

Roosevelt promised the invasion of Europe to Molotov in Washington in 1942. In his January 7 state of the union message he said, "I cannot prophesy. I cannot tell you when or where the United Nations are going to strike next in Europe. But we are going to strike—and strike hard. I cannot tell you whether we are going to hit them in Norway, or through the Low Countries, or in France, or through Sardinia or Sicily, or through the Balkans, or through Poland—or at several points simultaneously."[67] Then, following the Casablanca conference, reporters heard Roosevelt emphasize that "the conferences between him, Prime Minister Winston Churchill and their respective military advisers had been primarily to make plans for war on land and sea and in the air during 1943." The article these words appeared in, in the *New York Times* of February 3, was headlined "President Implies 1943 Invasion Plan."[68]

Clearly it wasn't just Stalin's impression that the cross-Channel invasion would take place before the year was out: Roosevelt had all but promised it. Stalin was becoming increasingly impatient, and after Stalingrad, more verbal about his disappointment.

Churchill drafted the following message informing Stalin of the latest war plans. Roosevelt changed paragraphs "b" and "d" as indicated, and told Churchill to inform Stalin "that I approve of this message."[69]

February 9, 1943

Prime Minister Churchill to Premier Stalin most secret and personal. Your message of 30 January. I have now consulted the President and the matter has been referred to the Staffs on both sides of the ocean. I am authorized to reply for us both as follows.

(a) There are a quarter of a million Germans and Italians in Eastern Tunisia. We hope to destroy or expel these during April, if not earlier.

(b) ~~When this is accomplished, we intend, in July or earlier if possible, to attack Italy across the Central Mediterranean with the object of promoting an Italian collapse, and establishing contact with Yugoslavia. We expect to meet with serious opposition from German forces. If not, our task will be much easier.~~

(b) When this is accomplished, we intend in July, or earlier if possible, to seize Sicily with the object of clearing the Mediterranean, promoting an Italian collapse with the consequent effect on Greece and Yugoslavia, and wearing down the German Air Force; this is to be closely followed by an operation in the eastern Mediterranean, probably against the Dodecanese.

(c) This operation will involve all the shipping and landing craft we can get together in the Mediterranean and all the troops we can have trained in assault landing in time, and will be of the order of three or four hundred thousand men. We shall press any advantage to the utmost once ports of entry and landing bases have been established.

(d) ~~We are aiming for August for a heavy operation across the Channel, for which between seventeen and twenty British and US divisions will be available, of which four to seven will be US divisions, with a gross strength of fifty thousand each. Here again assault landing craft will be a limiting factor. Weather may, of course, spoil the Channel operation, in which case it will be prepared with stronger forces for September.~~

(d) We are also pushing preparations to the limit of our resources for a cross channel operation in August in which both British and United States units would participate. Here again, shipping and assault landing craft will be limiting factors. If the operation is delayed by weather or other reasons, it will be prepared with stronger forces for September. The timing of this attack must of course be dependent upon the condition of German defensive possibilities across the Channel at that time.

(e) Both the operations will be supported by very large United States and British Air Forces, and that across the channel by the whole Metropolitan Air Force of Great Britain. Together these operations strain to the very utmost the shipping resources of Great Britain and the United States.

(f) The President and I have enjoined upon our Combined Chiefs of Staff the need for the utmost speed and for reinforcing the attacks to the extreme limit that is humanly and physically possible.

Stalin

· 84 ·

After American forces under Gen. Lloyd Fredendall's command were forced to retreat at Kasserine Pass in Tunisia, Eisenhower replaced him with Gen. George S. Patton, who retook the pass the end of February. In March a sick General Rommel gave up command of his army; in May the British Eighth Army, benefiting from General Patton's brilliant tactics, which tied up German troops, broke through and captured 250,000 Axis soldiers.

Stalin sent virtually the same cable to Churchill.

February 16, 1943
STRICTLY AND PERSONAL MESSAGE OF PREMIER STALIN TO PRESIDENT ROOSEVELT

On February 12 I received from Mr. Churchill a message with additional information on the decisions taken by yourself and Mr. Churchill at Casablanca. As Mr. Churchill, informed me that his message is a joint reply expressing your opinion as well, I cannot but put before you certain considerations which I am simultaneously making known to Mr. Churchill.

It is obvious from the above-mentioned message, that the completing of the military operations in Tunisia is now being postponed until April. There is no need to prove at length how undesirable is this postponement of the operations against the Germans and Italians. Precisely at this particular moment when the Soviet troops are still able to continue their wide offensive, the activities of Anglo-American troops in Northern Africa are imperatively essential. Simultaneous pressure brought to bear on Hitler from our front and from yours in Tunisia would be of positive significance to our common cause and would create very serious difficulties for Hitler and Mussolini, and would also expedite the operations planned by you in Sicily and the Eastern part of the Mediterranean.

As regards the opening of a second front in Europe, particularly in France, it appears from your message that it is scheduled only for August or September. It seems to me, however, that the present situation demands that this date should be brought nearer as much as possible, and that the second front in Europe should be opened considerably earlier than the time mentioned. In order to prevent the enemy from recovering, it is highly important, to my opinion, that the blow from the West should not be postponed until the second half of the year, but dealt in the spring or at the beginning of summer.

According to reliable information in our possession, during the period beginning with the end of December, when the activities of the Anglo-American forces in Tunisia for some reason came to a standstill, the Germans transferred to the Soviet-German front 27 divisions, including 5 tank divisions, from France, Belgium, Holland and Germany itself. Thus, instead of rendering assistance to the Soviet Union by diverting German forces from the Soviet-German front, the result was a relief for Hitler, who in view of the slowing-down of Anglo-American operations in Tunisia, obtained an opportunity to move additional troops against the Russians.

All of this should prove that the earlier we jointly make use of the military difficulties created in Hitler's camp, the more grounds there will be to count upon the rout of Hitler in the near future. If we do not take all this into account now and do not avail ourselves of the present moment to further our common interests, it may so happen that the Germans, having obtained a breathing-spell and gathered their forces, will be able to recover. It is clear to both of us that such an undesirable miscalculation should not be allowed.

Roosevelt

· 85 ·

_____

February 22, 1943
Personal from the President to Mr. Stalin.

I have received your message of February 16th in which you present certain considerations that you have communicated to Mr. Churchill in reply to his message to you of February 12th.

I regret equally with you that the Allied effort in North Africa did not proceed in accordance with the schedule which was interrupted by unexpected heavy rains that made the roads extremely difficult for both troops and supplies en route from our landing ports to the front lines *and made the fields and mountains impassable.*

I realize fully the adverse effect of this delay on the common allied effort and I am taking every possible step to begin at the earliest possible moment successful aggressive action against the Axis forces in Africa with the purpose of accomplishing their destruction. You are fully informed in regard to the wide dispersion of America's transportation facilities at the present time and I can assure you that we are making a maximum effort to increase the output of ships to improve our transportation.

I understand the importance of a military effort on the Continent of Europe at the earliest practicable date in order to reduce Axis resistance to your heroic army, and you may be sure that the American effort will be projected onto the Continent of Europe at as early a date subsequent to success in North Africa as transportation facilities can be provided by our maximum effort.

We hope that the success of your heroic army, which is an inspiration to all of us, will continue.

Roosevelt

Roosevelt

· 86 ·

_____

February 22, 1943
Personal to Mr. Stalin from the President

On behalf of the people of the United States, I want to express to the Red Army, on its twenty-fifth anniversary, our profound admiration for its magnificent achievements unsurpassed in all history.

For many months, in spite of tremendous losses in men, supplies, transportation and territory, the Red Army denied victory to a most powerful enemy. It checked him at Leningrad, at Moscow, at Voronezh, in the Caucasus, and finally, at the immortal battle of Stalingrad, the Red Army not only defeated the enemy but launched the great offensive which is still moving forward along the whole front from the Baltic to the Black Sea. The enforced retreat of the enemy is costing him heavily in men, supplies, territory, and especially in morale.

Such achievements can only be accomplished by an army that has skillful leadership, sound organization, adequate training, and above all, the determination to defeat the enemy, no matter what the cost in self-sacrifice.

At the same time, I also wish to pay tribute to the Russian people from whom the Red Army springs, and upon whom it is dependent for its men, women and supplies. They, too, are giving their full efforts to the war and are making the supreme sacrifice.

The Red Army and the Russian people have surely started the Hitler forces on the road to ultimate defeat and have earned the lasting admiration of the people of the United States.

Roosevelt

Stalin

· 87 ·

This message was delivered by Maxim Litvinov, Soviet ambassador to the United States.

February 24, 1943
Message from Premier Stalin to President Roosevelt

Please accept my sincere gratitude for your friendly message on the occasion of the 25th Anniversary of the Red Army and for your high praise of its fighting successes.

I share your confidence that these successes will open the path to the final defeat of our common foe who should and will be crushed by the united might of our countries and or all freedom loving peoples.

J. Stalin

Stalin

· 88 ·

———

March 16, 1943
Most secret and personal message
From Premier Stalin to President Roosevelt

Now that I have Mr. Churchill's reply to my message of February 16, I consider it my duty to answer yours of February 22, which likewise was a reply to mine of February 16.

I learned from Mr. Churchill's message that Anglo-American operations in North Africa, far from being accelerated, are being postponed till the end of April; indeed, even that date is given in rather vague terms. In other words, at the height of the fighting against the Hitler troops—in February and March—the Anglo-American offensive in North Africa, far from having been stepped up, has been called off altogether, and the time fixed for it has been set back. Meanwhile Germany has succeeded in moving from the West 36 divisions, including six armoured, to be used against the Soviet troops. The difficulties that this has created for the Soviet Army and the extent to which it has eased the German position on the Soviet-German front will be readily appreciated.

Mr. Churchill has also informed me that the Anglo-American operation against Sicily is planned for June. For all its importance that operation can by no means replace a second front in France. But I fully welcome, of course, your intention to expedite the carrying out of the operation.

At the same time I consider it my duty to state that the early opening of a second front in France is the most important thing. You will recall that you and Mr. Churchill thought it possible to open a second front early as 1942 or this spring at the latest. The grounds for doing so were weighty enough. Hence it should be obvious why I stressed in my message of February 16 the need for striking in the West not later than this spring or early summer.

The Soviet troops have fought strenuously all winter and are continuing to do so, while Hitler is taking important measures to rehabilitate and reinforce his Army for the spring and summer operations against the USSR; it is therefore particularly essential for us that the blow from the West be no longer delayed, that it be delivered this spring or in early summer.

I appreciate the considerable difficulties caused by a shortage of transport facilities, of which you advised me in your message. Nevertheless, I think I must give a most emphatic warning, in the interest of our common cause, of the grave danger with which further delay in opening a second front in France is fraught. That is why the vagueness of both your reply and Mr. Churchill's to the opening of a second front in France causes me concern, which I cannot help expressing.

Anthony Eden had been in Washington in March discussing plans for the postwar world. After he left, Roosevelt, on March 30, held a press conference sure to reach Stalin's ears, in which he discussed the disarray that had prevailed at Versailles in 1919, asserted that he was determined to avoid such a state of affairs following the Second World War, and expressed his urgent desire to meet with Stalin to iron out general agreement and objectives.

> Questioner: Mr. President, you spoke of plans to have conversations with Russia in the near future. Is there anything more specific we can have on that? This summer, do you plan—
> Roosevelt: No—not today.
> Questioner: Is hope still "springing eternal" about Mr. Stalin?
> Roosevelt: Yes.[70]

Stalin

· 89 ·

In late September 1939, the Red Army took some fifteen thousand Polish soldiers from prisoner-of-war camps and later killed many of the officers. They buried forty-five hundred of the officers in the Katyn Forest near Smolensk. In 1941 and 1942, hearing rumors that the prisoner-of-war camps had been disbanded, the Polish government-in-exile in London sought repeatedly to find out what had happened to the officers. They were stonewalled by the Russians. As the Germans retreated in April 1943, they announced that they had found the bodies of the thousands of Polish officers, all of whom had been shot in the back of the head, and charged that the Russians had killed them in 1940. The Soviet Union countered with charges that the officers had been killed by the Germans in July 1941. The cover-up worked to an extent: a group of Allied war correspondents who were given a tour of selected graves by the

Russians offered the general opinion that the Russian case, based on dated evidence (in hindsight clearly planted by the Soviets), was "convincing."[71] The Polish government-in-exile, however, continued to present convincing evidence of its own, including records of the refusal of the Russian government to answer their repeated queries as to the fate of the officers and the abrupt cessation of letters from the officers to their families after March 1940, which indicated that the Kremlin had done the deed.

Faced with a demand for an investigation by the International Red Cross, an investigation that the Soviets could not control and which would certainly have led to the truth, Stalin severed relations with the Polish government-in-exile. This issue—the killing of the flower of the Polish officer corps, which the Poles knew about and were determined to prove, and which Stalin was equally determined would remain hidden—was a major factor in the Polish government-in-exile's hostility to Stalin.

The killings, according to documents released by the Soviet Union in 1992, were carried out because Beria and Stalin believed that the officers, the cream of the Polish Army, were potential enemies of the Soviet Union.[72] Wladyslaw Sikorski was the premier of the Polish government-in-exile. The president was in Monterrey, Mexico, when he received the following message from Stalin, forwarded by Secretary of State Cordell Hull via the Map Room on 24 April 1943.

April 21, 1943
The recent conduct of the Polish Government towards the Soviet Union is regarded by the Soviet Government as absolutely abnormal and contrary to all rules and standards governing relations between allied countries.

The campaign of calumny against the Soviet Union, initiated by the German fascists regarding the Polish officers they themselves slaughtered in the Smolensk area, on German-occupied territory, was immediately taken up by the Sikorski government and inflated in every possible way by the official Polish press. The Sikorski government, far from taking a stand against the vile fascist slander of the Soviet Union, did not even see fit to ask the Soviet government for information or explanations.

The Hitlerite authorities, after perpetrating an atrocious crime against the Polish officers, are now engaged upon an investigation farce for the staging of which they have enlisted the help of certain pro-fascist Polish elements picked up by them in occupied Poland, where everything is under Hitler's heel and where honest Poles dare not lift their voices in public.

The governments of Sikorski and Hitler have involved in these "investigations" the International Red Cross which is compelled to take part under conditions of a terroristic regime with its gallows and mass extermination of a peaceful population, in this investigation farce, under the stage management of Hitler. It should be clear that such "investigations," carried out, moreover, behind the Soviet Government's back, cannot inspire confidence in persons of any integrity.

The fact that this campaign against the Soviet Union was launched simultaneously in the German and the Polish press, and is being conducted along similar lines, does not leave any room for doubt that there is contact and collusion between Hitler, the enemy of the Allies, and the Sikorski government in the conduct of the campaign.

At a time when the people of the Soviet Union are shedding their blood in the bitter struggle against Hitlerite Germany and straining every effort to rout the common foe of all liberty-loving democratic countries, the government of Mr. Sikorski, pandering to Hitler's tyranny, is dealing a treacherous blow to the Soviet Union.

All these circumstances force the Soviet Government to infer that the present government of Poland, having fallen into the path of collusion with the Hitler government, has actually discontinued relations of alliance with the USSR and assumed a hostile attitude toward the Soviet Union.

In view of these circumstances the Soviet Government has come to the conclusion of the necessity for breaking relations with the present Polish government.

I deem it necessary to inform you of the above and trust that the Government of the United States will realize the inevitability of the step which the Soviet Government has been compelled to take.

END OF STALIN MESSAGE.

The following are remarks of Hull:

> In considering this matter the following are the most important developments with respect to Soviet-Polish relations which have taken place during your absence:
>
> 1. On April 14 the Polish Minister in the absence from Washington of the Ambassador brought to the attention of the Department the charges made by German propaganda agencies to the effect that the Germans had discovered near Smolensk a mass grave containing the bodies of some 10,000 Polish officers executed by the Russians in 1940. The Minister under instruc-

tions while acknowledging that the story might well be a fabrication on the part of the Germans, said that the Polish Government could not fail to take note of the allegations since it had for over a year and one-half been endeavoring to ascertain without success from the Soviet authorities the whereabouts of approximately 8,000 Polish officers known to have been captured by the Red Army in 1939. He also pointed out that in December 1941 the Polish Prime Minister himself had taken up with Stalin and Molotov the whereabouts of the missing Polish officers and advised the Government of the evasive reply received.

2. Lord Halifax on April 21 handed me an *aide mémoire* indicating that because of the recent grave deterioration of Polish-Soviet relations there was a danger of serious trouble among the Polish armed forces abroad particularly those in the Middle East. It stated that Mr. Churchill was considering sending a message to Stalin. The draft text of this message, together with further information on recent developments and on the actions which the British Government would like to take, would be communicated to the United States Government shortly with a view to ascertaining whether we would wish to make a similar approach to the Soviet Government.

The Ambassador said then that the *aide mémoire* was only a preliminary reference and that he expected in a few days to receive a somewhat more elaborate statement from his Government. Lord Halifax has not yet taken up the matter in detail.

3. In connection with the statement in paragraph 4 of Mr. Stalin's messaging indicating that the International Red Cross has been "compelled" to take part in the investigations carried out behind the back of the Soviet Government, it should be pointed out that the American Consul in a telegram from Geneva dated April 22, 6 p.m. stated that he had been informed that the International Red Cross Committee had communicated in April 22 to the Polish and German Governments that the International Red Cross was prepared to propose the designation of neutral experts to conduct an investigation provided "all parties concerned" request it to do so (special reference to the Soviet Union as a party concerned was made therein).

4. The Department of State has thus far had no intimation from any source other than Stalin's message quoted above that the Soviet Government contemplates breaking relations with the Polish Government.

5. I am endeavoring to delay action on the Finnish matter until you return in view of the foregoing developments.

HULL

Roosevelt

· 90 ·

The president drafted a reply, which he sent through the Map Room to Secretary Hull for his opinion, noting to Hull that he should read "long telegram from Churchill to me dated 25th." Churchill had written Roosevelt that as the result of "strong representations" by Anthony Eden, Sikorski had withdrawn his request for an investigation by the Red Cross.

The following cable went out as Roosevelt wrote it, with the excision of the word "stupid" in the second paragraph.

26 April 1943
Mr. Stalin, Moscow.

I have received your telegram while on my Western inspection trip. I can well understand your problem but I hope in present situation you can find means to label your action as a suspension of conversation with the Polish Government in exile rather than a complete severance of diplomatic relations.

It is my view that Sikorski has not acted in any way with Hitler gang, but rather that he made a ~~stupid~~ mistake in taking the matter up with the International Red Cross. Also I am inclined to think that Churchill will find ways and means of getting the Polish Government in London to act with more common sense in the future.

Let me know if I can help in any way, especially in regard to looking after any Poles you may desire to send out of Russia.

Incidentally, I have several million Poles in the United States, very many of them in the Army and Navy. They are all bitter against the Nazis and knowledge of a complete diplomatic break between you and Sikorski would not help the situation.

Roosevelt

Stalin

· 91 ·

———

April 29, 1943
Private message of Premier Joseph V. Stalin to President Franklin D. Roosevelt.

I received your answer, unfortunately, only on April 27, whereas the Soviet Government was obliged to take a decision for the severance of relations with the Polish Government on April 25.

Since the Polish Government, throughout nearly two weeks, not only did not discontinue, but actually intensified, in its press and radio, a campaign which was hostile to the Soviet Union and advantageous only to Hitler, public opinion in the USSR grew extremely indignant over this conduct and postponement of the decision of the Soviet Government became impossible.

It is conceivable that Mr. Sikorski himself has no intention of cooperating with Hitler's gangsters. I should be only too glad if this supposition turned out to be correct. I do, however, consider that Mr. Sikorski allowed himself to be led by certain pro-Hitler elements, either within the Polish Government or in its entourage, and as a result the Polish Government, very possibly involuntarily, became a tool in Hitler's hands in the anti-soviet campaign of which you are aware.

I, too, believe that Premier Churchill will find a way to bring the Polish Government to reason and to help it in future to act according to the dictates of common sense. I may be mistaken, but it seems to me that one of our duties, as allies, consists in preventing any one ally from acting inimically, to the comfort and gratification of the common foe, against any other ally.

As regards Polish subjects in the Soviet Union and their further destinies, I can assure you that the Soviet authorities have always treated them as friends and comrades, and will continue to do so in the future. It is, therefore, clear that there is not, nor can be, any question of their being deported from the Soviet Union. Should they themselves wish to leave the USSR, the Soviet authorities which have never put obstacles in the way of this, do not intend to do so in future, and will render them all possible assistance.

Roosevelt

· 92 ·

Maj. Gen. Alexander Belyaev was chairman of the Soviet Purchasing Commission. The United States War Department awarded him the Legion of Merit a few weeks later for his part in arranging safe conduct of various flights of high government officials to and from Moscow.

May 5, 1943
Personal for Mr. Stalin

I want you to know that Mr. Churchill is coming to Washington next week to discuss our immediate next steps. We will of course keep General B[elyaev] currently informed.

Roosevelt

Roosevelt

· 93 ·

The following letter was carried by Joseph E. Davies, who agreed to make the trip to propose to Stalin that he and Roosevelt should meet in the near future without Churchill. ("Churchill will understand. I will take care of that," the president told Davies.)[73] While the meeting was a cherished wish of Roosevelt's, the letter was timed to precede Churchill's visit to Washington to mitigate Stalin's fear that Roosevelt and Churchill might plan something without him. Davies actually presented Roosevelt's message to Stalin on May 20.

Roosevelt later in June denied to Churchill that he had written asking Stalin—"Uncle Joe," in the private parlance of the president and the prime minister—for a private meeting: "I did not suggest to UJ that we meet alone but he told Davies that he assumed . . ."[74]

May 5, 1943

My dear Mr. Stalin;

I am sending this personal note to you by the hands of my old friend, Joseph E. Davies. It relates solely to one subject which I think it is easier for us to talk over through a mutual friend. Mr. Litvinov is the only other person with whom I have talked about it.

I want to get away from the difficulties of large Staff conferences or the red tape of diplomatic conversations. Therefore, the simplest and most practical method that I can think of would be an informal and completely simple visit for a few days between you and me.

I fully appreciate the desirability for you to stay in daily touch with your military operations; I also find it inadvisable to be away from Washington more than a short time. There are two sides to the problem. The first relates to timing. There is always the possibility that the historic Russian defense, followed by taking the offensive, may cause a crack-up in Germany next winter. In such a case we must be prepared for the many next steps. We are none of us prepared today. Therefore, it is my belief that you and I ought to meet this summer.

The second problem is where to meet, Africa is almost out of the question in summer and Khartoum is British territory, Iceland I do not like because for both you and me it involves rather difficult flights and, in addition would make it, quite frankly, difficult not to invite Prime Minister Churchill at the same time.

Therefore, I suggest that we could meet either on your side or my side of Bering Straits. Such a point would be about three days from Washington and I think about two days from Moscow if the weather is good. That means that you could always get back to Moscow in two days in an emergency.

It is my thought that neither of us would want to bring any staff. I would be accompanied by Harry Hopkins, an interpreter and a stenographer—and that you and I would talk very informally and get what we call "a meeting of the minds." I do not believe that any official agreements or declarations are in the least bit necessary.

You and I would, of course, talk over the military and naval situation, but I think we can do that without our Staffs being present.

Mr. Davies has no knowledge of our military affairs nor of the post-war plans of this Government, and I am sending him to you for the sole purpose of talking over our meeting.

I greatly hope that our forces will be in complete control of Tunisia by the end of May, and Churchill and I next week will be working on the second phase of the offensive.

Our estimates of the situation are that Germany will deliver an all-out attack on you this summer, and my Staff people think it will be directed against the middle of your line.

You are doing a grand job. Good luck!

Always sincerely
Franklin D. Roosevelt

Stalin

· 94 ·

Moscow, May 8, 1943
The President:

I congratulate you and the gallant American and British forces on the brilliant victory which has led to the liberation of Bizerte and Tunis from Hitlerite tyranny. I wish you continued successes.

Stalin

Roosevelt

· 95 ·

May 13, 1943
Personal and from the President to Mr. Stalin.

Thank you for your message of congratulation on the performance of our forces in liberating Tunisia. Now that we have the initiative it is reasonable to expect further successes on both the eastern and the western fronts, *and also further supplies including air.*

Roosevelt

Roosevelt

· 96 ·

May 18, 1943
Personal and From the President to Premier Stalin.

I know that you will be happy to learn that the following are the American estimates of Axis losses in North Africa from December 8, 1940, to May 12, 1943.

Total personnel losses, 625,000.

Total tank losses, not less than 2,100.

Total plane losses (in North Africa and in the Mediterranean): 7,596 destroyed, 1,748 probably destroyed, and 4,499 damaged.

Total merchant shipping losses: 625 ships totaling

2,200,000 tons sunk, and 371 ships totaling 1,600,000 tons damaged.

American estimate of Italian losses in East Africa,

Exclusive of natives, Italian losses in East Africa were, approximately, 150,000.

These figures agree substantially with British estimates except for personnel losses, in which their estimate is somewhat lower than ours.

Roosevelt

Stalin

· 97 ·

_____

In April 1941 Stalin had made the decision to dissolve the Comintern because he thought the agency constituted an "impediment" to the development of independent nationalistic Communist parties. Nothing was done at the time because of fear the dissolution might have appeared the result of German pressure, and then the war had preoccupied Stalin. However, on May 8, 1943, Georgi Dimitrov, the head of the Comintern, was informed by Molotov that the decision would immediately be implemented, and that the various operations and functions of the Comintern would forthwith be divided up among various Soviet agencies. On May 20 Stalin, undoubtedly thinking of his meeting with Davies scheduled for that evening, and conscious of how it would appear to Davies as well as Roosevelt, asked Dimitrov whether the dissolution could be announced immediately, saying, "We ought to rush with the publication." Dimitrov replied that the member parties had to see the announcement first; May 22 was set as the date for the announcement. On May 28, in answer to a question by a Reuters correspondent, keenly exploiting the propaganda value of the move, Stalin said, "The dissolution of the Communist International is both appropriate and timely, for it will ease the organization of pressure by all peace-loving nations against the common foe, Hitlerism, and expose the lie of the Hitlerites that Moscow allegedly intends to interfere in the life of other states and to 'bolshevize' them." Stalin was sure that world revolution would happen on its own, that it was, as he told Averell Harriman, "inevitable."[75]

Roosevelt, according to Hull, was "gratified" when he heard of the dissolution, but wondered what it portended, whether the Comintern's "activities would still be continued under some guise remained to be seen. It was at least a gesture of friendship."[76]

Davies's evening meeting with Stalin at which he presented Roosevelt's letter lasted two and a half hours. Again, as when Davies had been ambassador, he and Stalin got on very well. When Stalin asked Davies why Churchill was being excluded from the proposed meeting between himself and the president, Davies mentioned differences in regard to colonial and backward people, and volunteered that if Stalin would sit down with Roosevelt they would understand each other better. "I am not so sure," said Stalin. "Knowing what you both are trying to do I am absolutely sure," replied Davies. "Understanding alone is not enough," said Stalin. "There must be reciprocity and respect." To which Davies replied, "If you knew the President as I know him, you would know that this is exactly what you would get and in fact are getting now."[77]

On Sunday, May 23, Stalin entertained Davies at a formal dinner in the Kremlin, after which they watched *Mission to Moscow,* a Warner Brothers film starring Walter Huston and based on Davies's book extolling the Russians, which Davies had brought with him. After Stalin saw it he allowed it to be shown throughout the Soviet Union, where it became very popular. Ambassador Standley, who was included in the Kremlin dinner but was outraged at being excluded from the private meeting between Davies and Stalin, and further outraged that Davies refused to tell him what had transpired or show him the president's message, reported that the dinner "was the dullest Kremlin dinner I have ever attended" and that most of the Russians "including Stalin appeared bored."[78]

[Moscow] May 24, 1943
PERSONAL AND FOR THE PRESIDENT AND SECRETARY [From Davies]
    Last night Stalin handed me a memorandum which reads in close paraphrase as follows:

One. The expediting of shipment to the Soviet Union of equipment for the four oil refinery plants ordered in the United States.

Soviet orders placed with American firms for delivery to the Soviet Union of equipment for the four oil refinery plants complete with all the auxiliary equipment have been approved by the American Government.

The production of all the equipment in accordance with the Soviet specifications accepted by the American firms for the four plants mentioned above is to be completed before the end of June as it is provided for by the terms of delivery.

All the equipment to be transferred to ports and the loading on Soviet ships completed not later than July for plants numbers 1 and 2 and not later than August for plants numbers 3 and 4.

Two. The increasing of delivery of components for aviation gasoline.

It is necessary to increase the shipment to the Soviet Union [apparent omission] octane components for aviation gasolines—iso octane or alky benzine—in every way so that beginning from June to the end of 1943 the monthly shipment to the Union of Soviet Socialist Republics from the United States of America may amount to not less than 22 to 25,000 tons of components.

Three. Airplanes.

It is necessary that as many pursuit planes as possible be sent in an expeditious manner using to this effect every supply route.

He stated that this memorandum was given to me by reason of our previous conversation. At that time he had said that there were three vital military necessities which he most needed for his military defense now. Hitler's summer Russian offensive, he believed, might be most violent and desperate. When he first mentioned these necessities I told him that while it was out of my bailiwick I would be glad to take the matter up with you. Accordingly I conferred with Ambassador Standley and thereafter with General Burns, General Faymonville and through Admiral Standley with General Michela and they are all of the opinion that we should join in a recommendation to you to require immediate priority to secure as speedy compliance with these requests as physically possible.

The emphasis placed on the requests on both occasions indicates to me that great importance is attached to this matter. It would be helpful for me here if I could receive prompt acknowledgement setting forth your personal interest and disposition and anything that you could say consistent with your other commitments and your own judgment.

Will be leaving here shortly, immediately after receipt of formal reply to your letter. Proceeding direct home, respectfully and hastily.

DAVIES

Stalin

· 98 ·

_____

Davies believed that he had set up the basis for the meeting Roosevelt so desired, writing the president, "As to the particular mission I was engaged upon, I believe that the result thereof has been completely successful."[79] Stalin sent Davies home with two gifts, a Soviet Tommy gun and a German light hand machine gun, both of which Davies gave to the president.

May 26, 1943
Dear Mr. Roosevelt,

Mr. Davies has handed me your message.

I agree with you that this summer, possibly as early as June, the beginning a new large-scale offensive of Hitlerites is to be expected on the Soviet-German front. Hitler has already concentrated against us about 200 German divisions and as many as 30 divisions of his allies. We are preparing to meet the new German offensive and to launch counter attacks but we experience a shortage of airplanes and aircraft fuel. Now it is of course impossible to foresee all the military and other steps that we shall have to take. This will depend upon the developments at our front. Much will depend also on how speedy and active will be the anglo-american military operations in Europe.

I have mentioned these important circumstances in order to explain why my present answer to your proposal cannot be quite definite now.

I agree with you that such a meeting is necessary and that it should not be postponed. But I ask you to appreciate duly the importance of the circumstance set forth just because the summer months will be extremely serious for our Soviet armies. As I do not know how the events will develop at the Soviet-German front in June I shall not be able to leave Moscow during this month. Therefore I would suggest that our meeting should be arranged in July or in August. If you agree to this I undertake to I inform you two weeks before the date of the meeting when this meeting could take place in July or in August. In case you could upon receipt of my communication agree to the time of our meeting suggested by me I would arrive in the place of our meeting at the fixed time.

As to the place of the meeting this will be communicated to you by Mr. Davies personally.

I agree with you as to the limitation of the number of your and my advisers.

I thank you for sending Mr. Davies to Moscow who has a knowledge of the Soviet-Union and can unbiassedly judge of things.

With sincere respect,
[signed] J. Stalin

Roosevelt

· 99 ·

―――――

June 2, 1943
OPERATIONAL PRIORITY
Personal and from the President to Premier Stalin.

I am sending you through Ambassador Standley the recently approved decisions of our Combined Chiefs of Staff. These decisions have the joint approval of both Mr. Churchill and myself. In view of their extremely secret nature I am asking Ambassador Standley to deliver them to you personally.

Roosevelt
FDR

Roosevelt

· 100 ·

―――――

March 1943 had been a devastating month for convoys in the North Atlantic; German submarines sank twenty-seven merchant ships. To halt the carnage, Roosevelt ordered Admiral King to transfer sixty B-24 Liberator planes from the Pacific to the North Atlantic. Within weeks German submarines became the hunted instead of the hunters. Forty-three submarines were sunk in May alone. With the submarine casualty rate running at 75 percent and the average life of a submarine down to three months, Admiral Donitz on May 22 suspended U-boat operations. In the next four months 3,546 cargo ships crossed the Atlantic with not one casualty.[80]

The "recently approved decisions" message following was drafted by General Marshall, approved by Churchill, and edited by the president to make the message reflect Roosevelt's concern with keeping Stalin on an equal footing in the alliance. The president wrote to Marshall:

> For General Marshall from the President.
> 31 May 1943
> Despatch for Stalin approved with following amendment. Strike out under B following words, quote N. priority unquote, and include A and B as one priority stop in order to protect security suggest you wire Stalin telling him you are sending by courier by air to deliver message to him in Moscow or his agent at some convenient place. You may state that your message has my approval as well as Churchill's.
> Roosevelt

Standley wrote the president:

> Message delivered Moscow time 23 hours Friday June 4. Molotov and interpreter Pavlov present. Message translated in my presence. I advised Stalin of our plans to preserve secrecy and that he could use same channel for his reply. Stalin listened attentively to the message showing no evidence of surprise. He exhibited no reactions other than stating that he understood the general purport of the message and after careful study for two or three days would make a reply.
> Air raid warnings were sounded as I was leaving for the meeting. Found Stalin with staff in air raid shelter in Kremlin eighty feet underground much preoccupied over raid which consisted of fifty planes heading for Moscow. They veered eastward toward Gorki and all clear signal sounded during the meeting.[81]

June 2, 1943

1. In general, the overall strategy agreed upon is based upon the following decisions.

(a) To give first priority to the control of the submarine menace, ~~and~~ the security of our overseas lines of communication,

~~(b) next in priority~~ and employ every practicable means to support Russia.

(b) To prepare the ground for the active or passive participation of Turkey in the war on the side of the Allies.

(c) To maintain an unremitting pressure against Japan for the purpose of continually reducing her Military power.

(d) To undertake such measures as may be practicable to maintain China as an effective Ally and as a base of operations against Japan.

(e) To prepare the French forces in Africa for active participation in the assaults on Axis Europe.

2. With reference to (a) above regarding submarines, the immediate results of the recent deployment of longrange aircraft with new equipment and special attack groups of naval vessels give great encouragement, better than one enemy submarine a day having been destroyed since May 1. If such a rate of destruction can be maintained it will greatly conserve, therefore increase, available shipping and will exert a powerful influence on the morale of the German submarine armada.

With reference to the support of Russia, agreement was reached as follows:

(a) To intensify the present air offensive against the Axis powers in Europe. This for the purpose of smashing German industry, destroying German fighter aircraft and breaking the morale of the German people. The rapid development of this air offensive is indicated by the events of the past three weeks in France, Germany, and Italy, Sicily and Sardinia, and by the growth of the United States heavy bomber force in England from some 350 planes in March to approximately 700 today with a schedule calling for 900 June 30, 1,150 September 30 and 2,500 April 1. The British bomber force will be constantly increasing.

(b) In the Mediterranean the decision was taken to eliminate Italy from the war as quickly as possible. General Eisenhower has been directed to prepare to launch offensives immediately following the successful completion of HUSKY, (viz. the assault on Sicily,) for the purpose of precipitating the collapse of Italy and thus facilitating our air offensive against Eastern and Southern Germany as well as continuing the attrition of German fighter aircraft and developing a heavy threat against German control in the Balkans. General Eisenhower may use for the Mediterranean operations all those forces now available in that area except for three British and four American Divisions which are to participate in the concentration in England, next to be referred to.

(c) It was decided that the resumption of the concentration of ground forces in England could now be undertaken with Africa securely in our hands and that while plans are being continuously kept up to date by a joint U.S.-British Staff in England to take instant advantage of a sudden weakness in France or Norway, the concentration of forces and landing equipment in the British Isles should proceed at a rate to permit a full-scale invasion of the Continent to be launched. At the peak of the great air offensive in the Spring of 1944. Incidentally. the unavoidable absorption of large landing-craft in the Mediterranean, the South-West Pacific and the Aleutian Islands has been our most serious limiting factor regarding operations out of England.

3. We have found that undertakings listed utilize our full resources. We believe that these operations will heavily engage the enemy in the air and will force a dispersion of his troops on the ground to meet both actual attacks and heavy threats of attack which can readily be converted into successful operations whenever signs of Axis weakness become apparent.

Roosevelt

Roosevelt

· 101 ·

Mr. Brown was the code name given Molotov during his visit to Washington in May 1942.

June 4, 1943
Personal and from the President
Marshall Stalin—Moscow

I am very grateful to you for your courtesy extended to my government and me in your cordial reception of Ambassador Davies. He has returned safely, bearing your letter. I am very happy that you and I are in complete agreement in principle on all the matters contained in your letter and I will await your further communication in accordance with your letter and your understanding with Mr. Davies.

My warmest personal regards, with my kind remembrances also to Mr. Brown.

Roosevelt

Stalin

· 102 ·

June 11, 1943
PERSONAL MESSAGE OF PREMIER J. V. STALIN TO PRESIDENT ROOSEVELT

Your message in which you inform me about certain decisions on the questions of strategy made by you and Mr. Churchill I received on June 4. I thank you for the message.

As is apparent from your message these decisions are in contradiction with those made by you and Mr. Churchill at the beginning of this year, regarding the terms of the opening of the second front in Western Europe.

You of course remember that in the joint message of January 26 of this year you and Mr. Churchill informed me about the decision made at that time to divert considerable German land and air forces from the Russian front and to force Germany on her knees in 1943.

Later Mr. Churchill on his own behalf informed me on February 12 about the more precise terms of the British-American operation in Tunisia and in Mediterranean, as well as on the Western coast of Europe. It was said in this message, that preparations for the operation of forcing the Channel in August 1943 were energetically being carried out by Great Britain and the United States, and should weather or other reasons have prevented it, then this operation would be prepared for September 1943 with participation of larger forces in it.

Now, in May 1943 you and Mr. Churchill made the decision, postponing the British-American invasion of Western Europe until spring of 1944. That is the opening of the second front in Western Europe which was postponed already from 1942 to 1943, is being postponed again, this time until spring 1944.

This decision creates exceptional difficulties for the Soviet Union, which has already been fighting for two years, with utmost strain of its strength, against the main forces of Germany and her satellites, and leaves the Soviet Army, fighting not only for its own country, but also for its Allies, to its own strength, almost in single combat with yet very strong and dangerous enemy.

Is it necessary to say what painful and negative impressions will be made in the Soviet Union, upon its people and its Army, by the new postponement of the second front, and by leaving our Army, which has made so many sacrifices, without expected serious support from the British-American Armies?

As to the Soviet Government, it does not find it possible to agree with this decision, made, besides, without its participation and without attempt to discuss jointly this most important question, and which decision may result in grave consequences for the future progress of the war.

Roosevelt

· 103 ·

June 16, 1943
Memorandum for the President from Harry Hopkins
    This is the best I can get out of the WPB [War Production Board] but I think it means a substantial increase in aluminum to Russia.

June 16, 1943
Personal and from the President to Marshal Stalin.
    In response to your special request it has been decided to make available to your country from the production of the United States and Canada during July August and September five thousand long tons per month of primary aluminum and one thousand long tons of high grade secondary aluminum of the type we ourselves are using in aircraft manufacture. Because of the shortage of primary aluminum, it is not possible at this time to agree to increase the offer contained in the Third Protocol and it may therefore be necessary to curtail shipments during succeeding months to the extent that shipments of primary aluminum only exceed the four thousand long tons per month scheduled in the Protocol, although I hope this will not be necessary. The secondary aluminum is in addition to the Protocol offering. We will review the situation again within the next two months and let you know the shipping schedule during the last quarter of the calendar year and, if possible, for the balance of the Protocol year.
                                                        Roosevelt

Roosevelt

· 104 ·

    The president had asked General Arnold to increase the number of P-39 planes—maneuverable fighters—"over and above the protocol" so as to "do everything possible to strengthen Russia this summer," even if that meant postponement or replacement of the P-39s allotted to Britain. He asked as well that more B-25 bombers be sent to the USSR. General Arnold replied to the president that the P-39 was due for a model change, that the P-40N was the best plane to send to the USSR, and that more bombers would also be possible.[82]

June 16, 1943
Personal from the President to *Marshal* Stalin

In addition to our new protocol agreement I have directed that six hundred additional fighters be sent to you during the balance of 1943. They are P-40N type of fighter which we fought very successfully in Tunisia. This is the most maneuverable fighter we have. It provides our best protection against dive bombers and gives excellent protection to the ground strafing of the P-39s.

I have also directed the shipment of seventy eight additional B-25s during the same period. In November the airplane situation will again be reviewed and we will then inform you what the shipping schedule of the last half of the protocol year will be.

Roosevelt

Roosevelt

· 105 ·

The prime minister's cable to Stalin follows this message.

June 18, 1943
Personal and from the President to Marshal Stalin.

As I was away when your message came, I am a few days late in answering it. I am in full accord with what the Prime Minister telegraphed you. I assure you that we are really doing everything that is possible at this time.

I trust you will appreciate that our shipping situation is still tight, though we are cheered by the progress of our campaign against the submarines for the past two months, giving us a good net gain in shipping available.

Roosevelt

Prime Minister to Marshal Stalin personal and secret.

1. I have received a copy of your telegram of about 11th June to the President. I quite understand your disappointment but I am sure we are doing not only the right thing but the only thing that is physically possible in the circumstances. It would be no

help to Russia if we threw away 100,000 men in a disastrous cross-channel attack such as would, in my opinion, certainly occur if we tried under present conditions and with forces too weak to exploit any success that might be gained at very heavy cost. In my view and that of all my expert military advisers, we should, even if we got ashore, be driven into the sea, as the Germans have forces already in France superior to any we could put there this year, and can reinforce far more quickly across the main lateral railways of Europe than we could do over the beaches or through any of the destroyed channel ports we might seize. I cannot see how a great British defeat and slaughter would aid the Soviet Armies. It might, however, cause the utmost ill feeling here if it were thought it had been incurred against the advice of our military experts and under pressure from you. You will remember that I have always made it clear in my telegrams to you that I would never authorize any cross channel attack which I believed would lead only to useless massacre.

2. The best way for us to help you is by winning battles and not by losing them. This we have done in Tunisia where the long arm of Britain and United States sea power has reached across the Atlantic and 10,000 miles around the Cape and helped us to annihilate great Axis land and air forces. The threat immediately resulting to the whole Axis defensive system in the Mediterranean has already forced the Germans to reinforce Italy, the Mediterranean Islands, the Balkans and Southern France with land and air forces. It is my earnest and sober hope that we can knock Italy out of the war this year, and by doing so we shall draw far more Germans off your front than by any other means open. The great attack that is now not far off will absorb the capacities of every port under our control in the Mediterranean from Gibraltar to Port Said inclusive. After Italy has been forced out of the war the Germans will have to occupy the Riviera, make a new front either on the Alps or the Po, and above all provide for the replacement of the 32 Italian divisions now in the Balkans. The moment for inviting Turkish participation in the war, active or passive, will then arrive. The bombing of the Romanian oil fields can be carried through on a decisive scale. Already we are holding in the west and south or Europe the larger part of the German air forces and our superiority will increase continually. Out of a first line operational strength of between 4,800 and 4,900 aircraft, Germany, according to our information, has today on the Russian front some 2,000 compared with some 2,500 this time last year. We are also ruining a large part of the cities and munitions centers of Germany which

may well have a decisive effect by sapping German resistance on all fronts. By this coming autumn this great air offensive should have produced a massive return. If the favourable trend of the anti-U-boat warfare of the last few months continues, it will quicken and increase the movement of the United States forces to Europe which is being pressed to the full limit of the available shipping. No one has paid more tribute than I have to the immense contribution of the Soviet Government to the common victory, and I thank you also for the recognition which you have lately given to the exertions of your two western allies. It is my firm belief that we shall present you before the end of the year with results. which will give you substantial relief and satisfaction.

3. I have never asked you for detailed information about the strength and dispositions of the Russian armies because you have been, and are still, bearing the brunt on land. I should however be glad to have your appreciation of the situation and immediate prospects on the Russian front and whether you think a German attack is imminent. We are already again in the middle of June and no attack has been launched. We have some reason to believe that the unexpectedly rapid defeat of the Axis forces in North Africa has dislocated German strategy, and that the consequent threat to southern Europe has been an important factor in causing Hitler to hesitate and to delay his plans for a large scale offensive against Russia this summer. It is no doubt too soon to pronounce decidedly on all this, but we should be very glad to hear what you think about it.

4. At the end of your message you complain that Russia has not been consulted in our recent decisions. I fully understand the reasons which prevented you from meeting the President and me at Khartoum, whither we would have gone in January, and I am sure you were right not to relinquish even for a week the direction of your immense and victorious campaign. Nevertheless the need and advantages of a meeting are very great. I can only say that I will go at any risk to any place that you and the President may agree upon. I and my advisers believe that Scapa Flow, our main naval harbour in the north of Scotland would be the most convenient, the safest and if secrecy be desired probably the most secret. I have again suggested this to the President. If you could come there by air at any time in the summer you may be sure that every arrangement would be made to suit your wishes, and you would have a most hearty welcome from your British and American comrades.

PRIME

Roosevelt

· 106 ·

___

Marshal Joseph V. Stalin,
Commander in Chief of the Armed Forces of the USSR
The Kremlin, Moscow
June 22, 1943

Two years ago by an act of treachery in keeping with the long record of Nazi duplicity the Nazi leaders launched their brutal attack upon the Soviet Union. They thus added to their growing list of enemies the mighty forces of the Soviet Union. These Nazi leaders had underestimated the extent to which the Soviet Government and people had developed and strengthened their military power to defend their country and had utterly failed to realize the determination and valor of the Soviet people.

During the past two years the freedom loving peoples of the world have watched with increasing admiration the history-making exploits of the armed forces of the Soviet Union and the almost incredible sacrifices which the Russian people are so heroically making. The growing might of the combined forces of all the United Nations which is being brought increasingly to bear upon our common enemy testifies to the spirit of unity and sacrifice necessary for our ultimate victory.

This same spirit will, I am sure, animate us in approaching the challenging tasks of peace which victory will present to the world.

Franklin D. Roosevelt

Stalin

· 107 ·

___

Stalin refers to Roosevelt's message number 105, dated June 18 and delivered by Standley.

Personal message of Premier J. V. Stalin to President Roosevelt
June 24, 1943

I am sending you the text of my reply to the message of Mr. Churchill with which you are in full agreement as you informed me in your message handed over to me by Mr. Standley on June 20th.

PERSONAL MESSAGE OF PREMIER J. V. STALIN TO PRIME-MINISTER MR. W. CHURCHILL

June 24, 1943

Your message of June 19 was received by me.

I fully understand the complexity of the organization of Anglo-American invasion of Western Europe, particularly, the organization of transference of the troops across the Channel. This complexity was evident also from your message.

From your message of the last year and of this year I got confidence that you and the President fully realized the difficulties of the organization of such operation and that the appropriate preparation of this invasion is being carried out by you together with the President, with full consideration of these difficulties and with all necessary intensity of strength and means. As far back as last year you informed me that the large scale invasion of Europe by the British and American forces, will be carried out in 1943. In your memorandum, transmitted to V. M. Molotov on June 10, 1942, you wrote:

"Finally, and this is most important of all, we are concentrating our maximum efforts on organization and preparation of the large scale invasion of the continent of Europe by the British and American forces in 1943. We do not set any limits for the scale and aims of this campaign, which at the beginning, will be carried out by the British and American forces numbering more than one million men, with the appropriate support of aviation."

At the beginning of this year, you on your own behalf and on behalf of the President twice informed me about your decisions on the question of the invasion of Western Europe by the Anglo-American forces with the aim to "divert considerable German land and air forces from the Russian front."

In addition to that you set a task to force Germany to its knees in 1943 and defined the tine of the invasion not later than September.

In your message of January 26 of this year you wrote:

"We conferred with our military advisers and made the decisions on operations which must be undertaken by the American and British military forces within first nine months of the year 1943. We wish to inform you immediately about our intentions. We suppose that these operations together with your powerful offensive may, surely, force Germany to its knees in 1943."

In your subsequent message, received by me on February 12, of this year, defining more accurately the terms of the invasion of Western adopted by you and by the President you wrote: "We are also carrying out

preparations energetically and to the limits of our resources for the operation of forcing the Channel in August, in which operation the British and
the United States units will participate. The limiting factors here will be
also the tonnage and the offensive landing means. If the operation is postponed due to weather or other reasons, then it will be prepared for September with participation of larger forces in it.

In February when you wrote about these, adopted by you plans and
the terms of the invasion of Western Europe, the difficulties of this operation were far more considerable than at present. Since that time the Germans suffered more than one defeat: they were thrown back by our forces
in the south and suffered not a small loss; they were defeated and expelled
by the Anglo-American forces from the North Africa; in the submarine
warfare the Germans found themselves in more difficult position than at
any time before, and the superiority of Anglo-American forces has grown
considerably; it is known also that the Americans and the British have
achieved the superiority of their aviation in Europe, and the Navy and
Merchant fleet have grown in their might. Thus, the conditions for the
opening of the second front in Western Europe during the period of the
year 1943 did not become worse, but, on the contrary, became considerably better.

After all this the Soviet Government could not assume that the British
and the American Governments would change the decision adopted at the
beginning of this year in regard to the invasion of Western Europe this
year. On the contrary, the Soviet Government had all reasons to consider
that this Anglo-American decision would be realized, that the necessary
preparation was being carried out and that the second front in Western
Europe would be opened, finally, in 1943.

Therefore when you write now that "Russia would not have received
relief if we had thrown hundreds of thousand men across the Channel in
the disastrous offensive," there is no thing left for me but to remind you of
the following. Firstly, of your own memorandum of June of last year,
when you stated about the preparation for invasion not of one hundred
thousand men, but of more than one million men of Anglo-American
forces at the time of the beginning of the operation. Secondly, of your message of February, in which it was said about large scale preparatory measures for the invasion of Western Europe in August—September of this
year; this meant that, evidently, the operation was foreseen, by no means,
with the participation of one hundred thousand men, but with the sufficient number of forces. When you state now: "I cannot imagine how the
great British defeat and bloodshed would help the Soviet armies," then is
it not clear that the statement of such kind in regard to the Soviet Union

has no ground and is in direct contradiction with your other above-mentioned responsible decisions regarding the extensive and energetic Anglo-American measures on the organization of the invasion this year, which are being carried out, and on which the full success of the operation must depend.

I do not want to expatiate longer on your responsible decision of the annulment of your previous decisions regarding the invasion of Western Europe, adopted by you and by the President without participation of the Soviet Government and without any attempt to invite its representatives to the conference in Washington, although you cannot but know that in the war against Germany the role of the Soviet Union and its interest in the questions of the second front are great enough. It is not necessary to say that the Soviet Government cannot reconcile itself with such ignoring of the fundamental interests of the Soviet Union in the war against the common enemy.

You write to me that you fully understand my disappointment. I have to tell you that this is not simply matter of disappointment of the Soviet Government, but a matter of preservation of its confidence in the Allies which confidence is subjected to hard trials.

One must not forget, that it is the question of preservation of millions of lives in occupied regions of Western Europe and Russia, and reduction of the tremendous sacrifices of the Soviet armies in comparison with which the sacrifices of the Anglo-American forces constitute a small quantity.

June 24th, 1943

Stalin

· 108 ·

The following message was translated by Charles E. Bohlen, who subsequently was appointed Roosevelt's translator at Tehran and remained in that capacity through Yalta.

Moscow, June 26, 1943
The President:

I thank you for the high evaluation of the determination and courage of the Soviet people and of their armed forces in their struggle against the German brigands.

As a result of the two-year struggle of the Soviet Union against Hitlerite Germany and her vassals and as a result of the serious blows which have been delivered by the Allies to the Italian-German armies in North Africa the conditions for the final destruction of our common enemy have been created.

I am convinced that the sooner we deliver our joint united blows from the west and east against the enemy the sooner victory will come.

J. Stalin

Roosevelt

· 109 ·

A U.S. submarine in the vicinity of the Aleutian Islands, mistaking a Soviet trawler for an enemy ship, sank it. Two men were killed, the rest were rescued. An official apology had already been made.

On July 5 the Germans began their last offensive against Kursk, and when, in the greatest tank battle ever fought, involving more than two million men and six thousand tanks, the Soviet Army repulsed the might of the German Army, it was the death knell for German ambitions in Russia. After Kursk the Germans never again went on the offensive.

The "other matter" is almost certainly Roosevelt's desire for a meeting with Stalin.

July 15, 1943
Personal from the President to Marshal Stalin.

I am deeply sorry for unfortunate sinking of one of your ships in North Pacific and have directed every possible future precaution.

Although I have no detailed news, I think I can safely congratulate you on the splendid showing your armies are making against the German offensive at Kursk.

I hope to hear from you very soon about the other matter which I *still* feel to be of great importance *to you and me*.

~~Can you let me know answer to operations discussed in Moscow by Davies?~~

FDR

Roosevelt

· 110 ·

Retaking the city of Orel, captured by the Germans in October 1941, was a huge victory for the Russians. Of the original population of 114,000, however, only 30,000 remained; the rest had either been murdered, been deported to Germany, or joined the partisans in the hills.[83] In Moscow, to mark the day, twenty salvos from 120 guns were fired off, a ceremony that was repeated on the anniversary for years.

5 August 1943
Personal from the President to Marshal Stalin.

Sincere congratulations from the President to Marshall Stalin. Sincere congratulations to the Red Army, the People of the Soviet Union and to yourself upon the great victory of Orel.

During a month of tremendous fighting your forces by their skill, their courage, their sacrifices and their ceaseless effort have not only stopped the long planned German attack but have launched a successful counter offensive of far reaching import.

The Soviet Union can be justly proud of its heroic accomplishments.

Roosevelt

Stalin

· 111 ·

In spite of what he writes, Stalin had had plenty of time to answer Roosevelt: he didn't leave for the front until August 1 and stayed only two nights in the village of Khoroshevo. The remark "I have frequently to go to the different parts of the front," which he used as an excuse to put off the summit meeting with Roosevelt and Churchill, was certainly not true. This was, actually, only Stalin's second trip to the front; the first had been in 1941, when he went to watch antiaircraft fire. Although Stalin hated to travel, he gave the impression that he was constantly on the move with his troops. He wrote virtually the same thing a few days later to Churchill. In fact, he rarely left the Kremlin except to go to Kuntsevo, his nearby dacha.

On July 10, in the largest amphibian operation to date, one Canadian, four British, and three American divisions landed in Sicily. Gen. George S. Patton, head of the American forces, entered Palermo twelve days later to find crowds yelling "Down with Mussolini." On July 19 the United States Air Force bombed Rome for the first time, carefully targeting only the railway yards. On July 25th the Italian Fascist government fell; Mussolini was arrested on orders of Marshal Pietro Badoglio, who was appointed by King Victor Emmanuel to form a new cabinet; and surrender negotiations with the Allies began.

In a fireside chat on July 28 Roosevelt declared that "our terms to Italy are still the same as our terms to Germany and Japan—unconditional surrender."[84]

August 8, 1943
From Premier J. V. Stalin
To President Franklin D. Roosevelt

1. Only now, having come back from the front, I can answer your message of July 16th [Roosevelt's message number 109, sent on July 15]. I have no doubt that you take into account our military position and will understand the delay of the answer.

Contrary to our expectations, the Germans launched their offensive not in June, but in July, and now the battles are in full swing. As it is known, the Soviet Armies repelled the July offensive, recaptured Orel and Belgorod and now is putting the further pressure upon the enemy.

It is easy to understand that under the present acute situation at the Soviet-German front, a great strain and utmost vigilance against the enemy actions are required from the Command of the Soviet troops. In connection with the above, I have at the present time to put aside other questions and my other duties, but the primary duty—the direction of action at the front. I have frequently to go to the different parts of the front and to submit all the rest to the interests of the front.

I hope that under such circumstances you will fully understand that at the present time I cannot go on a long journey and shall not be able, unfortunately, during this summer and autumn to keep my promise given to you through Mr. Davi[e]s.

I regret it very much, but, as you know, circumstances are sometimes more powerful than people who are compelled to submit to them.

I consider that a meeting of the responsible representatives of the two countries would positively be expedient. Under the present military situation, it could be arranged either in Astrakhan or in Archangel. Should this proposal be inconvenient for you personally, in that case, you may send to one of the above-mentioned points your responsible and fully trusted person. If this proposal is accepted by you, then we shall have to determine a number of questions which are to be discussed and the drafts of proposals which are to be accepted at the meeting.

As I have already told Mr. Davi[e]s, I do not have any objections to the presence of Mr. Churchill at this meeting, in order that the meeting of the representatives of the two countries would become the meeting of the representatives of the three countries. I still follow this point of view on the condition that you will not have any objections to this.

2. I use this opportunity to congratulate you and the Anglo-American troops on the occasion of the outstanding successes in Sicily which are resulted in collapse of Mussolini and his gang.

3. Thank you for your congratulation sent to the Red Army and the Soviet people on the occasion of successes at Orel.

Roosevelt and Churchill

· 112 ·

The Quebec conference code-named QUADRANT, a meeting of Churchill, Roosevelt, and Canadian Prime Minister Mackenzie King in the relative coolness of Canada, was convened on August 17 primarily to work out the details of the surrender of Italy, but other matters were discussed as well. At the conference Roosevelt for the first time began to restrict British access to the Manhattan Project, and both leaders agreed to continue withholding all knowledge of it from Stalin. Roosevelt pushed Churchill forcefully for a commitment to the cross-Channel invasion. He also secured a draft of a four-power declaration, with T. V. Soong of China taking part in the deliberations.[85] Together Roosevelt and Churchill composed a message for Stalin.

18 August 1943
Personal to Marshal Stalin from Prime Minister Churchill and President Roosevelt.

We have both arrived here with our staffs and will probably remain in conference for about ten days. We fully understand the strong reasons which lead you to remain on the battlefronts, where your presence has been so fruitful of victory. Nevertheless, we wish to emphasize once more the importance of a meeting between all three of us. We do not repeat not feel that either Archangel or Astrakhan are suitable but we are prepared ourselves, accompanied by suitable officers, to proceed to Fairbanks in order to survey the whole scene in common with you. The present seems to be a unique opportunity for a rendezvous and also a crucial point in the war. We earnestly hope that you will give this matter once more your consideration. Prime Minister will remain on this side of the Atlantic for as long as may be necessary.

Should it prove impossible to arrange the much needed meeting of the three heads of governments, we agree with you that a meeting of the foreign office level should take place in the near future. This meeting would be exploratory in character as, of course, final decisions must be reserved to our respective governments.

Generals Eisenhower and [Sir Harold] Alexander have now completed the conquest of Sicily in thirty-eight days. It was defended by 315,000 Italians and 90,000 Germans, total 405,000 soldiers. These were attacked by thirteen British and United States Divisions and with a loss to us of about 18,000 killed and wounded, 23,000 German and 1,000 Italian dead and wounded were collected and 130,000 prisoners. Apart from those Italians who have dispersed in the countryside in plain clothes, it can be assumed that all Italian forces in the island have been destroyed. Masses of guns and munitions are lying scattered about all over the island. Over 1,000 enemy aircraft have been taken on the airfields. We are, as you know, about soon to attack the Italian mainland in heavy strength.

Churchill-Roosevelt

Roosevelt and Churchill

· 113 ·

This message, which included the terms of surrender for Italy prepared by the Combined Chiefs of Staff (not printed here), was sent in sections and the details of the terms reached Moscow incomplete and garbled. Sir Archibald Clark Kerr delivered the flawed and incomplete message to Stalin, promising delivery of an accurate one when he received it.

August 19, 1943
PRESIDENT AND PRIME MINISTER TO MARSHAL STALIN

1. On August 15th. the British Ambassador at Madrid reported that General [Giuseppe] Castellano had arrived from Badoglio with a letter of introduction from the British Minister at the Vatican. The General declared that he was authorized by Badoglio to say that Italy was willing to surrender unconditionally provided she could join the Allies. The British Representative at the Vatican has since been furnished by Marshal Badoglio with a written statement that he has duly authorized General Castellano. This therefore seems a firm offer. We are not prepared to enter into any bargain with the Badoglio Government to induce Italy to change sides. On the other hand, there are many advantages and the great speeding-up of the campaign which might follow there from. We shall begin our invasion of the mainland of Italy probably before the end of this month, and about a week later we shall make our full-scale thrust at AVALANCHE [the Salerno beachhead south of Naples] (see our immediately following telegram). It is very likely that the Badoglio Government will not last so long. The Germans have one or more armoured divisions outside Rome, and once they think that the Badoglio Government is playing them false they are quite capable of overthrowing it and setting up a Quisling Government of Fascist elements under for instance Farinacci. Alternatively, Badoglio may collapse and the whole of Italy pass into disorder.

2. Such being the situation, the Combined Chiefs of Staff have prepared and the President and Prime Minister have approved, as a measure of military diplomacy, the instructions which are given in our immediately following telegram. They have been sent to General Eisenhower for action.

3. To turn to another subject, following on the decisions taken at TRIDENT [a conference in Washington in late May] His Majesty's Government entered upon negotiations with the Portuguese in order to obtain naval and air facilities in LIFEBELT [the Azores]. Accordingly, His Majesty's Ambassador at Lisbon invoked the Anglo-Portuguese Alliance, which has lasted 600 years unbroken, and invited the Portuguese to grant the said facilities. [Portuguese dictator] Dr. [Antonio] Salazar was of course oppressed by fear of German bombing out of revenge, and of possible hostile movements by the Spaniards. We have accordingly furnished him with supplies of anti-aircraft artillery and fighter airplanes which are now in transit, and we have also informed Dr. Salazar that should Spain attack Portugal we shall immediately declare war on Spain and render such help as is in our power. We have not however made any precise military convention ear-marking particular troops, as we do not think either of these

contingencies probably. Dr. Salazar has now consented to the use of LIFEBELT by the British, with Portuguese collaboration, in the early part of October. As soon as we are established there and he is relieved from his anxieties, we shall press for the extension of these facilities to the United States ships and aircraft.

4. The possession of LIFEBELT is of great importance to the sea war. The U-boats have quitted the North Atlantic, where convoys have been running without loss since the middle of May, and have concentrated more on the southern route. The use of LIFEBELT will be of the utmost service in attacking them from the air. Besides this, there is the ferrying of United States heavy bombers to Europe and Africa, which is also most desirable.

5. All the above is of the most especially secret operational character.

Stalin

· 114 ·

As the Italian front collapsed, Marshal Pietro Badoglio, a slippery character as well as a patriot, assured Hitler that Italy would remain a loyal partner while secretly negotiating for terms with Allied representatives. Eisenhower had finally accepted a complicated surrender formula allowing the so-recently Fascist Badoglio to stay in power without consulting Stalin. Churchill, partial to constitutional monarchies, was hoping that Roosevelt would look favorably on a government headed by King Victor Emmanuel. But Roosevelt wrote to Churchill on November 9, diplomatically burying the idea of upholding the monarchy, "The old gentleman, I am told, only clicks before lunch."[86]

When Churchill read the following cable from Stalin he commented ominously, "Stalin is an unnatural man. There will be grave troubles." Harriman, however, reports no such reaction from Roosevelt.[87]

Not knowing the exact terms of surrender exacerbated all of Stalin's fears that his Allies might be selling him out. The complete accurate version of the terms of surrender reached the Kremlin later the same day.

August 22, 1943

PREMIER J. V. STALIN TO PRESIDENT FRANKLIN D. ROOSEVELT AND TO PRE-
MIER MINISTER WINSTON CHURCHILL.

1. I have received your message concerning the negotiations with the Italians and the new terms of armistice with Italy. Thank you for the information.

Mr. Eden told Mr. [Leonid] Sobolev that Moscow was fully informed about the negotiations. I have, however, to say, that Mr. Eden's statement does not correspond with reality, as I have received your message in which long passages are omitted and which has no concluding paragraphs. In view of this, it is necessary to state that the Soviet Government is not informed about the negotiations of the British and the Americans with the Italians. Mr. Kerr gives assurance that within a short time he will receive the complete text of your message; although the three days have passed, and Ambassador Kerr has not yet given me the complete text of the message. I cannot understand how such delay could have occurred during the transmission of the information on such important matter.

2. I believe that the time is ripe to organize the military-political commission of the representatives of the three countries: the United States, Great Britain and the USSR with the purpose of considering the questions concerning the negotiations with the different Governments dissociating themselves from Germany. Until now the matter stood as follows: The United States and Great Britain made agreements but the Soviet Union received information about the results of the agreements between the two countries just as a passive third observer. I have to tell you that it is impossible to tolerate such a situation any longer. I propose to establish this Commission and to assign Sicily at the beginning as the place of residence of the Commission.

3. I am waiting for the complete text of your message concerning the negotiations with Italy.

Stalin

· 115 ·

The Russian Army was making such great advances against the German Army that a new sense of optimism was very much in evidence. Kharkov was captured on August 23. In the far south five

thousand Germans were taken prisoner. A visible change was that
the whole diplomatic corps was allowed to return from Kuibyshev
to Moscow. The following message for the prime minister and the
president was handed to the foreign office by the Soviet chargé d'affaires on the night of August 26, 1943:

August 24, 1943
From Premier Stalin to Prime Minister Mr. W. Churchill and President Mr.
F. D. Roosevelt.

I have received your joint message of August 19th.

I entirely share your opinion and that of Roosevelt about the importance of a meeting between the three of us. In this connexion I request you
most earnestly to understand my position at this moment, when our
armies are carrying on the struggle against the main forces of Hitler with
the utmost strain and when Hitler not only does not withdraw a single division from our front but on the contrary has already succeeded in transporting, and continues to transport fresh divisions to Soviet-German
front. At such a moment, in the opinion of all my colleagues, I cannot
without detriment to our military operations leave the front for so distant
a point as Fairbanks although if the situation on our front were different
Fairbanks undoubtedly would be very convenient as a place for our meeting as I said before.

As regards a meeting of representatives of our states and in particular
of representatives in charge of Foreign Affairs, I share your opinion about
the expediency of such a meeting in the near future. This meeting however,
ought not to have a purely exploratory character but a practicable and
preparatory character in order that after that meeting has taken place our
Governments are able to take definite decisions and thus that delay in the
taking of decisions on urgent questions can be avoided. Therefore I consider it indispensable to revert to my proposal that it is necessary in advance to define the scope of questions for discussion by representatives of
the Three Powers and to draft the proposals which out to be discussed by
them and presented to our Governments for final decision.

Yesterday I received from Sir A. Clark-Kerr additions and corrections
to your and Mr. Roosevelt's message, in which you informed me about instructions sent to General Eisenhower in connexion with conditions of
surrender worked out for Italy in negotiations with General Castellano. I
and my colleagues think the instructions given General Eisenhower correspond entirely to the aim of unconditional surrender of Italy and therefore
cannot lead to any objections on our part.

But I think the information so far received is quite insufficient in order to be able to judge what measures are necessary on the part of the Allies during negotiations with Italy. This circumstance confirms the necessity of participation of a Soviet Representative in taking decisions in the course of negotiations. Therefore I think that the time has fully come for establishment of a military-political commission of representatives of the three countries which I mentioned to you in my message of August 22nd.

Roosevelt and Churchill

· 116 ·

August 25, 1943

To Marshal Stalin from President Roosevelt and Prime Minister Churchill

In our conference at Quebec, just concluded, we have arrived at the following decision as to military operations to be carried out during 1943 and 1944.

The bomber offensive against Germany will be continued on a rapidly increasing scale from bases in the United Kingdom and Italy.

The objectives of this air attack will be to destroy the German air combat strength, to dislocate the German military, industrial and economic system, and to prepare the way for a cross channel invasion.

A large scale buildup of American forces in the United Kingdom is now under way. It will provide an initial assault force of British and American divisions for cross channel operations. A bridgehead on the continent once secured will be reinforced steadily by additional American troops at the rate of from three to five divisions per month. This operation will be the primary British and American ground and air effort against the Axis.

The war in the Mediterranean is to be pressed vigorously. Our objectives in that area will be the elimination of Italy from the Axis alliance, and the occupation of that country as well as Sardinia and Corsica as bases for operations against Germany.

Our operations in the Balkans will be limited to the supply of Balkan guerrillas by air and sea transport, to minor raids by commandos, and to the bombing of strategic objectives.

We shall accelerate our operations against Japan in the Pacific and in Southeast Asia. Our purposes are to exhaust Japan's air, naval, and shipping resources, to cut the Japanese communications and to secure bases from which to bomb Japan proper.

Roosevelt and Churchill

· 117 ·

___

Stalin recalled Ivan Maisky and Maxim Litvinov, his ambassadors to London and Washington, respectively, at this time.

Litvinov, who had returned to Russia for consultations in May, was replaced by thirty-four-year-old Andrei Gromyko, who had been chargé d'affaires in Washington, and whom Hull had warmly praised to Molotov.

28 August 1943
From: The Prime Minister and the President
To: Marshal Stalin (Via Soviet Embassy, Washington).

We are considering your proposals and have little doubt that plans satisfactory all of us can be made both for the meeting on the Foreign Office level and for the Tripartite Commission. Prime Minister and I will be meeting again early next week and will telegraph you further.

Roosevelt and Churchill

· 118 ·

___

September 2, 1943
President and Prime Minister to Marshal Stalin, and personal.

1. We have received from General C. [Castellano] a statement that the Italians accept and that he is coming to sign, but we do not know for certain whether this refers to the short military terms which you have already seen, or to the more comprehensive and complete terms in regard to which your readiness to sign was specifically indicated.

2. The military situation there is at once critical and hopeful. Our invasion of the mainland begins almost immediately, and [a] the heavy blow called AVALANCHE will be struck in the next week or so. The difficulties of the Italian Government and people in extricating themselves from Hitler's clutches may make a still more daring enterprise necessary, for which General Eisenhower will need as much Italian help as he can get. The Italian acceptance of the terms is largely based on the fact that we shall send an airborne division to Rome to enable them to hold off the Germans, who have gathered Panzer strength in that vicinity and who may replace the Badoglio Government with a Quisling administration probably under

Farinacci. Matters are moving so fast there that we think General Eisenhower should have discretion not to delay settlement with the Italians for the sake of the differences between the short and the long terms. It is clear that the short terms are included in the long terms, that they proceed on the basis of unconditional surrender and Clause Ten in the short terms places the interpretation in the hands of the Allied Commander-in-Chief.

3. We are therefore assuming that you expect General Eisenhower to sign the short terms in your behalf if that be necessary to avoid the further journeying of General C. to Rome and consequent delay and uncertainty affecting the military operations. *We are of course anxious that the Italian unconditional surrender be to the Soviet Union as well as to Britain and the United States. The date of the surrender announcement must of course be fitted in with the military coup.*

> Roosevelt &
> Churchill

Roosevelt

· 119 ·

At Quebec, Roosevelt had finally compelled Churchill to agree that Britain would support a firm date of May 1, 1944, for the opening of the second front—the cross-Channel invasion; Churchill, in favor of invading Europe through the Balkans, "the soft underbelly of Europe," had long been sidestepping the issue.[88] U.S. troops and equipment were flowing to England in preparation.

On September 4, 1943, Stalin officially rescinded his antireligion policy. The new policy was announced the next day in *Pravda*. The appointment of a church council was announced, a patriarch was elected, licenses were issued for the opening and restoration of churches, a limited number of theological seminaries and academies were permitted to open, and the Russian Orthodox Church was allowed to resume publication of its journal. The timing was probably influenced by Stalin's upcoming meeting with Roosevelt, but the rationale behind it was the realization that the church was a powerful political instrument that could be used to advantage. It is a speculation, but a persuasive one, that it was Roosevelt who started him along the path.

4 September 1943
Personal from the President to Marshal Stalin;

1. The Prime Minister and I are both happy at the idea of the military, political meeting *on the State Department level.*

2. I think it should be held as soon as possible. What would you think of a date about September twenty-fifth?

3. In regard to location, the Prime Minister has suggested London or ~~Edinburgh~~ *somewhere in England* and I would be willing to have representatives go to either of these if you also think it best. However, I am inclined to the thought of a more remote spot where also the membership of the meeting would be less surrounded by reporters. I would be inclined to suggest Casablanca or Tunis. I do not object to Sicily but the communications from and to there are more difficult.

4. The political representatives would, of course, report to their respective Governments because I do not think we could give plenary powers to them. They could be advised on military developments by attaching one or two military advisers to them, though I do not want to have the meeting develop *at this stage* into a full-scale Combined Staffs' Conference.

5. If Mr. Molotov comes *and Mr. Eden* I would wish to send Mr. Hull, but I do not believe that the latter should make such a long journey and I would, therefore, send the Under Secretary of State, Mr. Welles. Mr. Harriman would go with Mr. Welles because he has such good knowledge of all shipping, lend-lease and commercial staff who is in complete touch with the work of the Combined Staffs.

6. The tenacity and drive of your Armies is magnificent and I congratulate you again.

7. While this coming Conference is a very good thing, I still hope that you and Mr. Churchill and I can meet as soon as possible. I personally could arrange to meet in a place as far as North Africa between November fifteenth and December fifteenth. I know you will understand that I cannot be away from Washington more than about twenty days because, under our Constitution, no one can sign for me when I am away.

8. *Turning now to a Commission to sit in Sicily, in connection with carrying out of further settlements with Italy, why not send an officer to Eisenhower's headquarters where he would join with the British and Americans who are now working on this very subject?*

9. I have no objection to adding a French member to *their* meetings because we are in the midst of equipping ten or eleven of their divisions in North Africa. However, I think it would be very unwise to have the French take part in discussions relating to the military occupation of Italy. If the Italians go through with *the* surrender terms *already signed* I hope they

will be able wholeheartedly to assist the occupation troops. On the whole, the Italians greatly dislike the French and if we bring the French into occupation discussions at this time the civil and military elements in Italy will greatly resent it.

10. We can discuss the problem of consulting the Greeks and Yugoslavs later on.

Roosevelt

Stalin

· 120 ·

September 7, 1943
Personal Message from Premier J. V. Stalin
to President Franklin D. Roosevelt
and Prime Minister Winston Churchill

I have received your message of September 4th. The question raised in your message as to whether the Soviet Government agrees to authorize General Eisenhower to sign the brief terms of the armistice with Italy in its behalf is answered by the letter of September 2nd of the People's Commissar for Foreign Affairs Mr. V. M. Molotov addressed to Mr. Kerr British Ambassador.

This letter said that the authority given by the Soviet Government to General Eisenhower covers also the signing of the brief terms of the Armistice.

Stalin

· 121 ·

Stalin had written Churchill on August 31 that he approved of having a French representative on the commission.[89]

September 8, 1943
Stalin to Roosevelt

Your message in which you touched upon several important questions I received on September 6 [Roosevelt's message number 119 of September 4].

First. I still consider, as I did before, that the question of the creation of the Military-Political Commission of the representatives of the three countries with its residence at the beginning in Sicily or in Algiers is the most urgent one. Sending of a Soviet officer to the Staff of General Eizenhower can by no means substitute the Military-Political Commission, which is necessary for directing on the spot the negotiations with Italy (as well as with other countries dissociating themselves from Germany). Much time has passed, but nothing is done.

As to the participation of the French representative in this Commission, I have already expressed my opinion on this subject. However, if you have any doubt, in this case this question can be discussed after the Commission is created.

Second. I consider that the beginning of October as the Prime Minister suggested would be a convenient time for the meeting of the three our representatives, and I propose as the place of the meeting—Moscow. By that time the three Governments could have reached an agreement regarding the questions which have to be discussed as well as the proposals on those questions, without which (agreement) the meeting will not give the necessary results in which our Governments are interested.

Third. As to our personal meeting with participation of Mr. Churchill I am also interested to have it arranged as soon as possible. Your proposal regarding the time of the meeting seems to me acceptable. I consider that it would be expedient to choose as the place of the meeting the country where there are the representations of all three countries, for instance, Iran. However, I have to say that the exact date of the meeting has to be defined later taking into consideration the situation on the Soviet-German front where more than 500 divisions are engaged in the fighting in all, and where the control on the part of the High Command of the USSR is needed almost daily.

Fourth. I thank you for congratulations on the occasion of the successes of the Soviet Armies. I take this opportunity to congratulate you and Anglo-American troops on the occasion of the new brilliant successes in Italy.

Roosevelt

· 122 ·

————

9 September 1943
From the President to Marshal Stalin personal.

Thank you for your message received today.

1. I agree on the immediate setting up of the Military-Political Com-

mission but I think Algiers better than Sicily on account of communications and, therefore, suggest that they meet in Algiers on Tuesday, September twenty-first. They will be given full information in regard to progress of current and future negotiations but, of course, should not have plenary powers. Such authority would, of course, have to be referred to their Governments before final action.

I am entirely willing to have a French representative on this Commission. It is important to all of us that the secrecy of all their deliberations be fully maintained.

2. In regard to the meeting of our three representatives, I will cheerfully agree that the place of meeting be Moscow and the date the beginning of October—say Monday, the fourth. I will send you in two or three days a suggested informal list of subjects to be discussed, but I think the three members should feel free, after becoming acquainted with each other, to discuss any other matters which may come up.

3. I am delighted with your willingness to go along with the third suggestion, and the time about the end of November is all right. I fully understand that military events might alter the situation for you or for Mr. Churchill or myself. Meanwhile, we can go ahead on that basis. Personally, my only hesitation is the place but only because it is a bit further away from Washington than I had counted on. My Congress will be in session at that time and, under our Constitution, I must act on legislation within ten days. In other words, I must receive documents and return them to the Congress within ten days and Tehran makes this rather a grave risk if the flying weather is bad. If the Azores route is not available, it means going by way of Brazil and across the South Atlantic Ocean. *For these reasons I hope that you will consider some part of Egypt, which is also a neutral state and where every arrangement can be made for our convenience.*

4. I really feel that the three of us are making real headway.

Roosevelt

Roosevelt and Churchill

· 123 ·

Eisenhower and the Badoglio government signed an armistice on September 8, as a result of which the German Army occupied Rome and the Badoglio government fled to safety in southern Italy.

On September 8 U.S. Gen. Mark Clark landed with four American and three British divisions just south of Naples.

September 9, 1943
From the President and the Prime Minister to Marshal Stalin.

We are pleased to tell you that General Eisenhower has accepted the unconditional surrender of Italy, the terms of which were approved by the United States, the Soviet Republics and the United Kingdom.

Allied troops have landed near Naples and are now in contact with German forces.

Allied troops are also making good progress in the Southern end of the Italian peninsula.

Stalin

· 124 ·

Novorossisk was one of the last two German strongholds in the Caucasus in the far south. The Russians recaptured the ruins of Novorossisk, which had been an important naval base on the Black Sea, on September 16.

September 11, 1943
Personal message from Premier J. V. Stalin to President Franklin D. Roosevelt and to Prime Minister Churchill.

I have received your message of September 10. I congratulate you with new successes and especially with landing at Naples. There is no doubt that the successful landing at Naples and break between Italy and Germany will deal one more blow upon Hitlerite Germany and will considerably facilitate the actions of the Soviet armies at the Soviet-German front.

For the time being the offensive of the Soviet troops is successfully developing. I think that we shall be in a position to achieve more successes within the next two-three weeks. It is possible that we shall have recaptured Novorossisk within the next few days.

Stalin

· 125 ·

September 12, 1943

Personal message from Premier J. V. Stalin to President Franklin D. Roosevelt

And Prime Minister Winston Churchill

I have received your message of September 10th.

1. The question of the creation of the Military-Political Commission we may consider in general to be solved. Vice-Chairman of the Council of the People's commissar for Foreign Affairs Mr. A. Y. Vishinsky, whom you know well, was appointed by the Soviet Government as its plenipotentiary. Mr. A. E. Bogamolov, Ambassador of the USSR to the Allied Governments in London[,] was appointed as Vice-Plenipotentiary. They will take with them the group of the responsible Military and Political experts and the small technical staff.

I think that the beginning of work of the Military-Political Commission can be set for September 25–30. I have no objections regarding Algiers as the place of work of the Commission at the beginning, having in view that the Commission itself will decide the question of expediency of its going to Sicily or to any other place in Italy.

I find that the consideration of the Prime Minister regarding the functions of the Commission are sound, but I consider that some time later, we shall able to determine more precisely the functions of the Commission regarding the first experience of the Commission's regarding Italy as well as other countries, taking into consideration the first experience of the Commission's work.

2. As to the question of the meeting of our representatives, I propose to consider, as agreed upon that Moscow be the place of the meeting, and October 4, as President suggested be the date of it.

I still consider, as I did before, and about what I had previously written to you, that in order to make this meeting successful it is necessary to know in advance text of the proposals, which the British and the American Governments have and which are to be considered at the meeting of the three representatives. I, however, do not propose any limitation regarding the agenda.

3. As to the meeting of the heads of the three Governments, I do not have any objections regarding Tegeran [Tehran] as the place of the meeting, which (Tegeran) is more appropriate than Egypt where the Soviet Union does not have its representation.

Roosevelt

· 126 ·

―――――

Cordell Hull had been trying to get Undersecretary of State Sumner Welles out of the State Department for years. Welles, like Roosevelt a Grotonian and graduate of Harvard, was such a good friend and confidant of the president that, much to Hull's discomfiture, the two often made policy behind Hull's back. In August, Hull had asked the president to replace Welles "if he desired the State Department to function properly."[90] Roosevelt agreed, but wanted Welles to attend the Moscow conference to give him a graceful exit. Hull at first went along with this plan, but as summer turned to fall, Welles, brooding in Bar Harbor, Maine, unhappy at losing his position, began giving stories to the press portraying Hull in an increasingly negative light. Hull, furious, dug in his heels and decided that although he was in poor health and had never been in an airplane, he would attend the conference "wherever the conference might be held—anywhere between here and Chungking."[91] Roosevelt, who was mindful of Wilson's failure to bring the United States into the League of Nations because of opposition in the Senate, and who had chosen Hull because of his prestige and great influence in the Senate, needed his secretary of state. He had no choice but to agree that Hull should go in place of Welles. But then, abruptly realizing that the trip might very well be too much for Hull, Roosevelt worriedly asked Stalin to change the venue.

Roosevelt announced the resignation September 25 and wrote the following message the same day.

25 September 1943
For Marshall Stalin
From the President.

[~~I am anxious to have Secretary Hull attend the preliminary conference with Mr. Molotov and Mr. Eden~~]*I regret that I feel it necessary to reopen the question of the meeting of the Foreign Ministers, but on further consideration I am most anxious that Secretary Hull attend in person in the meeting with Mr. Molotov and Mr. Eden.*

Mr. Hull ~~He~~ would find the long flight to Moscow *extremely difficult* ~~almost prohibitive~~ *for* physical reasons. Would it be possible therefore for the conference to be held in England? It would, I believe, be a great advantage to all of us if Mr. Hull could personally attend the conference.

I feel sure the British would be willing to make the change. Could the date be made October 15 for the opening session?

Roosevelt

Stalin

· 127 ·

This message is a reply to Roosevelt's message of September 25 (not September 27, which is the date that Stalin received it). The delay of his message evidently irritated Roosevelt beyond measure. As a result, Wilson Brown, naval aide to the president, cabled the following to the naval aide in Moscow who received all Roosevelt's messages:

> Will you go to the proper authorities and say quote the President is enquiring relative to his message concerning the place of the meeting of the heads of the foreign offices unquote.
>
> With all future messages to Marshal Stalin from the President, would appreciate it if you will continue to acknowledge receipt of message in Moscow immediately and in addition send later dispatch giving time of delivery to Stalin.

28 September 1943

PERSONAL message from Premier J. V. Stalin to President Franklin D. Roosevelt

Today I have received your message of September 27th.

I share your opinion regarding the desirability of the Secretary of State Mr. Hull's presence at the forthcoming conference of the representatives of the three governments.

At the same time I have to inform you about great difficulties which could have appeared in case of change of the decision, previously agreed upon, regarding Moscow as the place of the forthcoming conference.

The fact is that in case the conference would not be held in Moscow but in Britain, as you propose, Mr. V. M. Molotov could not have come to the conference at the appointed time, whose presence at the conference I consider to be necessary. Mr. V. M. Molotov's departure from the USSR, at least in near future, is absolutely impossible, because as you know Mr.

A. Y. Vishinsky, the Deputy Commissar for Foreign Affairs, will very soon go to Algiers.

Besides, as it is known the press in the United States and in Britain has already widely published the information that the forthcoming conference will take place not elsewhere but in Moscow, and, therefore, the choice of a new place for the conference could have caused undesirable perplexities.

I have no objections against October 15th as the date of the conference.

It is assumed that by that time the agenda of the three partite conference will be finally agreed upon among the three Governments.

Roosevelt

· 128 ·

---

28 September 1943
The President to Marshal Stalin.

The Prime Minister of Great Britain and I have agreed with a recommendation of General Eisenhower that the long term surrender document after it is signed by the Italian Government should be retained in a confidential status and not published at the present time.

Roosevelt

Roosevelt

· 129 ·

October 1, 1943

The Allied Supreme Commander in the Mediterranean Area, Eisenhower, has recommended the following changes in the "Instrument of Surrender of Italy":

1. Change the title to "Additional conditions of the armistice with Italy."

2. Change the last sentence of the preamble to read "and have been accepted unconditionally by Marshal Pietro Badoglio, Head of the Italian Government."

3. Omit the statement of unconditional surrender in paragraph one.

General Eisenhower and all of his senior commanders concur in this recommendation as highly advantageous to our progress in defeating the

German forces in Italy in that it will help to align the Italian Army, Navy, and civil populations on our side.

Eisenhower urgently requests that pending a decision on these recommendations secrecy in regard to the Terms of Surrender document is "absolutely vital to our success in Italy."

I hope that these recommendations of General Eisenhower will be approved by the Allied Powers because they are highly advantageous to our war effort and can be of no disadvantage to us.

Your concurrence is requested by telegraph at the earliest practicable date.

Roosevelt

Stalin

· 130 ·

President Roosevelt was at Shangri-La, as Camp David was then called, when this was delivered to General Watson by the Russian Embassy. Roosevelt saw it in the Map Room when he returned October 4. A paraphrase was sent to the prime minister.

October 2, 1943
Personal message from Premier J. V. Stalin to President Franklin D. Roosevelt

I have no objections to your consent and to that of the Prime Minister of Great Britain with the proposal of General Eisenhower, that the document with the extensive terms of capitulation, after it is signed by the Italian Government, is to be kept in secret and is not to be published at the present time.

Roosevelt

· 131 ·

-----

4 October, 1943
Personal to Premier Stalin from the President.

I have your wire and our delegation will be in Moscow on October fifteenth.

While I do not look upon this conference as one that will plan or rec-

ommend military strategy, I have no objection and, indeed, would welcome the fullest exchange on your proposal relative to an expedition directed against France.

General [John] Deane is a member of our mission and will be fully informed of our plans and intentions.

I agree that this is a three power conference and that the discussion on
our proposal should be limited to the future intentions and plans of these
powers exclusively.

This would, in a way, preclude a wider participation at a later date and
under circumstances which are mutually agreeable to our three governments.

I am sure that we are going to find a meeting of minds for the important
decisions which must finally be made by us. This preliminary conference
will clear the ground and if ~~points of difference~~ *difficulties* develop at the
meeting of our foreign ministers, I would still have every confidence that
they can be reconciled when ~~the three of us~~ *you and Churchill and I* meet.

It looks as if American and British armies ~~We~~ should be in Rome in another few weeks.

Roosevelt

Stalin

· 132 ·

———

October 5, 1943
Personal Message from Premier J. V. Stalin to President Franklin D. Roosevelt

I have received your message of October 1, only today, on October 5th.

On my part there are no objections against the proposed by you
changes in the "Document of the Capitulation of Italy."

Stalin

· 133 ·

———

October 6, 1943
Premier J. V. Stalin to Franklin D. Roosevelt

I received your message of October 4th.

As regards the military questions, i.e. British-American measures of shortening the war, you already know the point of view of the Soviet Government from my previous message. I hope, however, that in this respect a preliminary meeting of the three will bring useful results, having prepared our future important decisions.

If I understood you correctly, at the Moscow conference will be discussed questions concerning only our three countries, and, thus, it can be considered as agreed upon that the question of the declaration of four nations is not included in the agenda of the conference.

Our representatives have to do everything possible to prevent possible difficulties in their responsible work. It is understood that the decisions as such, can be made only by our governments and, I hope they will be made at my personal meeting with you and Mr. Churchill.

Best wishes to the American and British Armies to fulfill successfully their task and enter Rome, which will be a new blow inflicted on Mussolini and Hitler.

Roosevelt

· 134 ·

October 12, 1943
Personal to Marshal Stalin

Badoglio is going to declare war on Germany October 13th.

Based on old treaty relationship allied forces have secured air and naval facilities in Azores.

Roosevelt

Stalin

· 135 ·

October 14, 1943
Stalin to Roosevelt

I have received your message of October 13th. I thank you for the information. I wish the Armed Forces of the United States and Great Britain further successes.

Roosevelt

· 136 ·

———

October 14, 1943

Personal from President Roosevelt to Marshal Stalin.

The Secretary of State and his Staff are well on their way to Moscow, but it seems doubtful at this time that they will be able to get there before the seventeenth. I will let you know their progress.

I am much disturbed in regard to the location of the other meeting but I will send you this problem in another message.

Roosevelt

Roosevelt

· 137 ·

———

October 14, 1943

From President Roosevelt Personal to Marshal Stalin

The problem of my going to the place you suggested is becoming so acute that I feel I should tell you frankly that, for constitutional reasons, I cannot take the risk. The Congress will be in session. New laws and resolutions must be acted on by me after their receipt and must be returned to the Congress physically before ten days have elapsed. None of this can be done by radio or cable. The place you mentioned is too far to be sure that the requirements are fulfilled. The possibility of delay in getting over the mountain—first, east bound and then west bound—is insurmountable. We know from experience that planes in either direction are often held up for three or four days.

I do not think that anyone of us will need Legation facilities, as each of us can have adequate personal and technical staffs. I venture, therefore, to make some other suggestions and I hope you will consider them or suggest any other place where I can be assured of meeting my constitutional obligations.

In many ways Cairo is attractive, and I understand there is a hotel and some villas out near the pyramids which could be completely segregated.

Asmara, the former Italian Capital of Eritrea, is said to have excellent buildings and a landing field—good at all times.

Then there is the possibility of meeting at some port in the Eastern Mediterranean, each one of us to have a ship. If this idea attracts you we could easily place a fine ship entirely at your disposal for you and your party so that you would be completely independent of us and, at the same time, be in constant contact with your own war front.

Another suggestion is in the neighborhood of Bagdad where we could have three comfortable camps with adequate Russian, British and American guards. This last idea is worth considering.

In any event, I think the Press should be entirely banished, and the whole place surrounded by a cordon so that we would not be disturbed in any way.

What would you think of November twentieth or November twenty-fifth as the date of the meeting?

I am placing a very great importance on the personal and intimate conversations which you and Churchill and I will have, for on them the hope of the future world will greatly depend.

Your continuing initiative along your whole front heartens all of us.

Roosevelt

Roosevelt

· 138 ·

———

16 October 1943

From the President to Marshal Stalin and personal.

In view of Mr. Molotov's note to the American Chargé d'Affaires of October 14 and in order that there may be no misunderstanding with regard to representation on the Political Military Commission, I think I should make clear that, as indicated in my telegram to you of September 5, I feel that French representation should be restricted to matters other than the military occupation of Italy, in which the three Governments establishing the Commission decide that France has a direct interest. I feel that in this regard French representation should correspond to that which I suggested in my message of October 13 should be accorded to the Governments of China, Brazil, Greece and Yugoslavia, or to any other governments which may by mutual agreement be invited to participate. It was never my intention that the French Committee of National Liberation should function on the same plane as the Governments of the Soviet Union, Great Britain and the United States or enter into its deliberations on all subjects.

Roosevelt

Stalin

· 139 ·

October 17, 1943
Message from Premier J. V. Stalin to President Franklin D. Roosevelt

I have received both of your messages of October 14. I thank you for the information about the Secretary of State and his staff, who are on their way now. I hope they will soon arrive safely in Moscow.

I shall send my reply regarding the question raised in your second message, after I have counsel with my colleagues in the Government.

Stalin

· 140 ·

Stalin, as supreme commander in chief, was deeply involved in planning day to day tactics with his generals. Gen. Georgy Zhukov, Stalin's link to the field generals, commented on Stalin's "naturally analytical mind, great erudition and a rare memory."[92] He knew the name of every Russian army and front commander, who numbered over a hundred, could name any army formation at any time, and didn't hesitate to interfere with his generals' battle plans.

Harriman, in Moscow, was reporting to the president that Stalin's intransigence "was not based on stubbornness or considerations of prestige," but that, as Stalin said, the opportunity to defeat the Germans so decisively was "an opportunity which might only occur once in fifty years," and he had to be part of it. Hull agreed: "Military considerations come first." Roosevelt's extremely accommodating attitude must be seen in this light.[93]

19 October 1943
Paraphrase
From Premier Stalin to President Roosevelt.

Concerning the location for the forthcoming conference of the leaders of the three governments, I desire to convey the following information to you.

Unfortunately, not one of the places proposed instead of Tehran by you for the meeting is suitable for me.

It became clear, during the course of operations of the Soviet forces in the summer and fall of this year, that the summer campaign may overgrow into a winter one and that our troops can continue their offensive operations against the German Army.

It is considered by all my colleagues that these operations demand my personal contact with the Command and daily guidance on the part of the supreme Command. Conditions are better in Tehran, because wire telegraph and telephone communications with Moscow exist there. This cannot be said about the other locations. My colleagues insist on Tehran as the place of the meeting for this reason.

I accept your suggestion to designate November 20th or 25th as a possible date for the conference, and I also agree that representatives of the press should be excluded from the meeting.

I hope that a great deal of good will be accomplished by the direct participation in the Moscow meeting of Mr. Hull, who has arrived safely in Moscow.

Stalin

· 141 ·

October 21, 1943
Personal Message from Premier J. V. Stalin to President Franklin D. Roosevelt

I have received your message of October 17th. On my part I do not have any objections against your proposal regarding the extent of rights of the French presentation in the military-political commission of the allied countries.

Roosevelt

· 142 ·

Admiral Standley had submitted his resignation as ambassador to the Soviet Union in May, and Averell Harriman was named to succeed him. The admiral had compounded his unsuitability as ambassador by holding a press conference in March during which he complained that the Soviet government was hiding from its people the huge shipments of armaments, food, and raw materials that the

United States was sending to Russia. Harriman was, as Cordell Hull had told President Roosevelt, the "only" choice. Harriman and Hull, traveling with his doctor, met in Tehran and flew to Moscow together on October 18. Hull, traveling by plane and ship, took eleven days to reach Moscow.

Hull spent sixteen days in Moscow, meeting almost every afternoon with Eden and Molotov. In spite of Stalin's statement to Roosevelt that "the question of the declaration of four nations is not included in the agenda," Hull had with him the draft of a declaration on general security, which Roosevelt insisted be signed not just by the United States, Great Britain, and Russia but by China as well. Eden had already discussed this with Churchill: the inclusion of China was from their point of view inevitable, given Roosevelt's mindset. "To the President, China means four hundred million people who are going to count in the world of tomorrow, but Winston thinks only of the colour of their skin; it is when he talks of India or China that you remember he is a Victorian," Churchill's physician confided to his diary.[94] But Hull had had to make polite threats about diverting aid from Russia to China to bring Molotov around to the fact that China would be the fourth signatory. (Hull told Secretary of State Edward Stettinius when he returned that the "Chinese matter" had taken him ten days to work through.) The declaration bound the four countries to fight until Germany and Japan "laid down their arms on the basis of unconditional surrender" and provided for the creation of an international organization.[95] This was the first time the Soviet Union formally agreed with Roosevelt's policy of unconditional surrender. This first foreign ministers conference, a stopgap to the so-often-postponed meeting with Roosevelt, was the first of many.

Harriman wanted to know whether it was really a matter of communications that made Stalin insist the meeting of the heads of government be held in Tehran. Molotov maintained that it was, that the telephone and telegraph lines that linked Tehran to Moscow were guarded by Russian troops so that there was no possibility that communications could be disrupted.

General Faymonville, in charge of Lend-Lease, remained unpopular in Washington because of his zeal in carrying out Roosevelt's directives, with which most of the diplomatic corps and the army disagreed. Harriman solved this problem by reorganizing the Lend-Lease structure. He replaced Faymonville with Gen. John Deane, who had been secretary of the Combined Chiefs of Staff. Deane became head of the newly constituted Military Mission, which welded the political and military representation into a coordinated team. Deane reported to Harriman. More diplomatic than Faymonville, and much more powerful, by virtue of the new title and his background, Deane continued Roosevelt's Lend-Lease policy of dispensing unstinting aid without the quid pro quo of intelligence gathering, as Roosevelt had decreed. General Michela, the chargé d'affaires notorious for his anti-Soviet sentiments, was also sent home. Harriman also insisted that Charles Bohlen be brought back to Moscow as counsel of the embassy.

The following message was dictated by the president to Grace Tully:

October 21, 1943
Personal and from the President for the eyes of Secretary Hull only.

I have received a message from the Marshal stating that it is impossible for him to meet Churchill and me anywhere else but Tehran. A careful check-up on time risks and constitutional requirements here makes Tehran impossible for me.

In reply to my several messages the Marshal has shown no realization of my obligations.

Therefore, will you please deliver the following message from me to the Marshal and explain to him orally the definite and clear reasons which are not actuated by personal desires but are fixed in our Constitution. This is not a question of theory; it is a question of fact.

QUOTE — PERSONAL AND SECRET FOR MARSHAL STALIN

I am deeply disappointed in your message received today in regard to our meeting.

Please accept my assurance that I fully appreciate and understand your reason for requiring daily guidance on the part of the Supreme Command and your personal contact with the Command which is bringing such outstanding results. This is of high importance.

And I wish you would realize that there are other vital matters which, in this constitutional American Government, represent fixed obligations on my part which I cannot change. Our Constitution calls for action by the President on legislation within ten days of the passage of such legislation. That means that the President must receive and return to the Congress, with his written approval or his veto, physical documents in that period. I cannot act by cable or radio, as I have told you before.

The trouble with Tehran is the simple fact that the approaches to that city over the mountain often make flying an impossibility for several days at a time. This is a double risk; first for the plane delivering documents from Washington and, second, for the plane returning these documents to the Congress. I regret to say that as head of the Nation, it is impossible for me to go to a place where I cannot fulfill my constitutional obligations.

I can assume the flying risks for documents up to and including the Low Country as far as the Persian Gulf, through the relay system of planes, but I cannot assume the delays attending flights in both directions into the saucer over the mountains in which Tehran lies. Therefore, with much regret I must tell you that I cannot go to Tehran and in this my cabinet members and the Legislative leaders are in complete agreement.

Therefore, I can make on last practical suggestion. That is that all three of us should go to Basra where we shall be perfectly protected in three camps, to be established and guarded by our respective national troops. As you know, you can easily have a special telephone, under your own control, laid from Basra to Tehran where you will reach your own line into Russia. Such a wire service should meet all your needs, and by plane you will only be a little further off from Russia than in Tehran itself.

I am not in any way considering the fact that from the United States territory I would have to travel six thousand miles and you would only have to travel six hundred miles from Russian territory.

I would gladly go ten times the distance to meet you were it not for the fact that I must carry on a constitutional government more than one hundred and fifty years old.

You have a great obligation to your people to carry on the defeat of our common enemy, but I am begging you to remember that I also have a great obligation to the American Government and to maintaining the full American war effort.

As I have said to you before, I regard the meeting of the three of us as of the greatest possible importance, not only to our peoples as of today, but also to our peoples in relation to a peaceful world for generations to come.

It would be regarded as a tragedy by future generations if you and I and Mr. Churchill failed today because of a few hundred miles.

I repeat that I would gladly go to Tehran were I not prevented from doing so because of limitations over which I have no control.

I am suggesting Basra because of your communications problems.

If you do not like this I deeply hope you will reconsider Bagdad or Asmara or even Ankara in Turkey. The latter place is neutral territory, but I
think it is worth considering and that the Turks might welcome the idea of
being hosts though, of course, I have not mentioned this to them or anybody else.

Please do not fail me in this crisis.

Roosevelt

Stalin

· 143 ·

The conference went a long way toward satisfying the Russians
on the subject of Operation OVERLORD, the second front. In spite of
Ambassador Clark Kerr of Great Britain, who would have preferred not to discuss the second front, General Deane and the
British Gen. Hastings Ismay gave details of OVERLORD, including
the combined bomber offensive designed to soften German defenses and the plan for a second landing in the South of France, and
they went into the problems involved in supplying the invasion
forces on the Channel beaches. Harriman reported to Roosevelt
that "Mr. Hull has stood the trip well under the careful eye of his
capable physician." Furthermore, he reported, General Deane "appeared to satisfy and win the confidence of the Soviet delegates.[96]

Molotov queried Harriman about the closeness of Harriman's
relationship with the British, wondering whether it was based on a
treaty. "None whatsoever," Harriman answered. He said that Roosevelt and Churchill had a close personal relationship, which had
made it possible for British and American soldiers to fight as one,
with a single commander.

During the conference Stalin admitted that the victories Russia
had achieved in the summer had been made possible because the
threat of a second front had pinned down twenty-five German divisions in the west, as well as the ten to twelve divisions in Italy.[97]

At the dinner hosted by Stalin in Catherine Hall in the Kremlin
to mark the conclusion of the conference, Stalin, seated next to
Hull, gave his translator, Valentin Berezhkov on Hull's other side, a
message "in a barely audible whisper" for him to translate "word

for word" to Hull for the president. Stalin admonished Berezhkov to "speak in a low voice so that no one overhears you." Hull, according to Berezhkov, "became excited" when he heard the message. Hull himself said he was "astonished and delighted" by the "unsolicited" declaration.[98]

For President Roosevelt
October 30, 1943

The Soviet government has studied the situation in the Far East and has decided that immediately after the end of the war in Europe, when the Allies have defeated Hitler's Germany, it will come out against Japan. Let Hull transmit this to President Roosevelt as our official position. But for the time being, we want to keep this a secret.

Stalin

· 144 ·

Nov. 5, 1943
PERSONAL MESSAGE FROM PREMIER J. V. STALIN TO PRESIDENT FRANKLIN D. ROOSEVELT.

Mr. Hull has transmitted to me on October 25, your latest message and I had a chance to talk with him regarding it. My reply has been delayed because I was sure that Mr. Hull had transmitted to you the contents of the eventuated talk and my views regarding my meeting with you and Mr. Churchill.

I cannot but give consideration to the arguments you gave regarding the circumstances hindering you from traveling to Tehran. Of course, the decision of whether you are able to travel to Tehran remains entirely with yourself.

On my part, I have to say that I do not see any more suitable place for a meeting, than the aforementioned city.

I have been charged with the duties of Supreme Commander of the Soviet troops and this obliges me to carry out daily direction of military operations at our front. This is especially important at the present time, when the uninterrupted four-month summer campaign is overgrowing into a winter campaign and the military operations are continuing to develop on nearly all fronts, stretching 2,600 kilometers.

Under such conditions for myself as Supreme Commander the possibility of travelling farther than Tehran is excluded. My colleagues in the

Government consider, in general, that my travelling beyond the borders of the USSR at the present time is impossible due to great complexity of the situation at the front.

That is why an idea occurred to me about which I already talked to Mr. Hull. I could be successfully substituted at this meeting by Mr. V. M. Molotov, my first deputy in the Government, who at negotiations will enjoy, according to our Constitution, all powers of the head of the Soviet Government. In this case the difficulties regarding the choice of the place of meeting would drop off. I hope that this suggestion could be acceptable to us at the present time.

Roosevelt

· 145 ·

Roosevelt's hand against isolationist opposition to U.S. membership in a world peacekeeping organization was immeasurably strengthened, and his partnership with Hull justified, when the Senate on November 5 overwhelmingly approved a resolution "providing for postwar collaboration to secure and maintain peace for the world and for the establishment of a general international organization."[99]

Strikethroughs and italics additions are Hopkins's.

November 8, 1943
PERSONAL FROM THE PRESIDENT TO MARSHAL STALIN
Thank you for your message of November fifth which Mr. Gromyko was good enough to deliver.

I hope to leave here in a few days and to arrive in Cairo by the twenty-second of November.

You will be glad to know that I have worked out a method so that if I get word that a bill requiring my veto has been passed by the Congress and forwarded to me, I will fly to Tunis to meet it and then return to the Conference.

Therefore, I have decided to go to Tehran and this makes me especially happy.

As I have told you, I regard it as of vital importance that you and Mr. Churchill and I should meet. The psychology of the present excellent feeling really demands it even if our meeting lasts only two days. Therefore, it is my thought that the Staffs begin their work in Cairo on November twenty-second, and I hope Mr. Molotov and your military representative, who I hope can speak English, will come there at that time.

Then we can all go to Tehran on the twenty-sixth and meet with you there on the twenty-seventh, twenty-eighth, twenty-ninth or thirtieth, for as long as you feel you can be away. Then Churchill and I and the top Staff people can return to Cairo to complete the details.

I ~~have asked Generalissimo Chiang Kai-Shek to come to Cairo for a few days.~~ The whole world is watching for this meeting of the three of us. And even if we make no announcements as vital as those announced at the recent highly successful meeting in Moscow, the fact that you and Churchill and I have got to know each other personally will have far reaching effect on the good opinion *within* ~~of~~ our three nations and *will assist in* the further disturbance of Nazi morale.

I am greatly looking forward to a good talk with you.

Roosevelt

Stalin

· 146 ·

November 10, 1943
Personal Message from Premier J. V. Stalin to President Franklin D. Roosevelt

I have received Your message of November 8th. I thank You for Your answer.

Your plan concerning the organization of our meeting in Iran, I accept. I hope, and Mr. Churchill will agree with this proposal.

By November 22nd, Mr. V. M. Molotov and our military representative will arrive in Cairo, where together with you they will agree upon everything necessary in connection with our meeting in Iran.

Roosevelt

· 147 ·

This message was written by the president aboard the battleship USS *Iowa* while at Norfolk, Virginia, then flown back to Washington for transmission by the Map Room.

The brand new USS *Iowa,* commissioned in April, sailed from Hampton Roads, Virginia, on November 13. With the president were Harry Hopkins, Generals Marshall, Arnold, Watson, Brehon Somervell, and T. T. Handy, and Admirals King, Brown, McIntire, Cooke, and William Leahy, Roosevelt's chief of staff. A major point of discussion among the military leaders was how to prevent Churchill from again postponing the second front in the upcoming conference. It was accepted among them that although Churchill kept saying he was in favor of OVERLORD, in fact he kept putting roadblocks in its way.

Roosevelt kept a diary of the trip. In it he wrote, "This will be another Odyssey—much further afield & afloat than the hardy Trojan whose name I used to take at Groton when I was competing for school prizes."[100]

November 12, 1943
Personal for Marshal Stalin from the President

I am of course made very happy by your telegram of ten November and the definite prospect of our meeting, and I shall be very glad to see Mr. Molotov in Cairo on the twenty second. I am just leaving for French North Africa. Warm regards, Roosevelt.

Stalin

· 148 ·

Stalin canceled Molotov's trip to Cairo upon learning that Chiang Kai-shek would be there, for fear that Japan might construe a Russian-Chinese conference as an unfriendly act and close the port of Vladivostok.

Churchill was delighted that Molotov would not be in Cairo. He had been counting on having "many meetings" of the British and the American staff before Molotov's arrival, and had even been worried enough to ask of Roosevelt "that the date of the arrival of Molotov and his Military representative shall be postponed till the 25th of November at the earliest."[101] He insisted that "a Soviet observer cannot possibly be admitted to the intimate conversations which our own Chiefs of Staff must have."[102]

November 12, 1943

Personal Message From Premier J. V. Stalin to President Franklin D. Roosevelt

As it appeared, Mr. V. M. Molotov, due to some circumstances, which are of a serious character, cannot come to Cairo by November 22. He will come together with me to Iran at the end of November. On the above I inform at the same time Mr. Churchill, and on this matter you will receive the information.

P.S. Sending the present message, unfortunately, was delayed, because of the fault of some office clerks, but I hope, it will arrive, nevertheless, in time.

Stalin

· 149 ·

———

November 12, 1943

Personal message from Premier J. V. Stalin to President Franklin D. Roosevelt.

I consider necessary to inform You that I have sent today a message to Mr. Churchill of the following content:

"Today I have received two messages of Yours.

Although I had already written to the President, that Mr. V. M. Molotov would be in Cairo by November 22, I have, however, to say that due to some reasons, which are of a serious character, Mr. Molotov, unfortunately, cannot come to Cairo. He will be able to be in Tehran at the end of November and will come there together with me. And some military men will come with me.

It goes without saying that in Tehran a meeting of only three heads of the Governments is to take place, as it was agreed upon. And the participation of the representatives of any other countries must be absolutely excluded.

I wish success to Your conference with the Chinese on Far Eastern Affairs."

Roosevelt

· 150 ·

20 November 1943

For Marshal Stalin personal from the President.

I have just landed. I am sorry about Mr. Molotov and hope he is all well again. I will be glad to see him with you in Tehran. Let me know when you expect to get there. I will be in Cairo tomorrow on and Mr. Churchill will be nearby.

I am sincerely happy about the fine continuance of your gains.

Roosevelt

Roosevelt

· 151 ·

Roosevelt's last-minute question to Stalin, "Where do you think we should live?" was artful. For safety's sake he knew he had to lodge either at the British or the Russian embassy, which backed onto each other; otherwise, Stalin and Churchill would be exposed to snipers and assassination attempts as they rode back and forth from meetings at the American embassy, half a mile distant, as he himself would be when visiting with them. What is notable is that Roosevelt refused to lodge with Churchill. He wanted to stay in the Russian quarters. So a certain element of trust and intimacy immediately existed between Roosevelt and Stalin, which Churchill tried to penetrate but could not. Roosevelt and his personal entourage, consisting of Hopkins, Leahy, his son-in-law Maj. John Boettiger, and his naval aide Adm. Wilson Brown, stayed at the American compound the first night. Some time after midnight Molotov summoned Harriman and the British ambassador Clark Kerr to a meeting. He told them that he had just learned that German agents had found out that Roosevelt was in Tehran and were planning a demonstration, and that it would be wise if Roosevelt moved into the Russian embassy. Harriman tried to press him for details, "but nothing of importance was forthcoming." (Later, in Moscow, Harriman realized that there had been no specific threat, just a general concern about safety on the part of Stalin.) The next morning, after a brief discussion, all present—Hopkins, Pa Watson, and McIntire—agreed that the president should move to the Russian compound; Roosevelt, who after all had engineered the move, pronounced himself "delighted at the prospect." According to Elliot Roosevelt, Stalin gave the president the main building in the Russian complex, with rooms adjacent to the board room, where all the plenary meetings were held, and lodged himself in one of the smaller houses.[103]

Once installed in the Soviet embassy, which dated from the tsarist years, the American delegation observed the bulges at the hips under the white coats of all the servants who made their beds, cleaned their rooms, and waited on them, and realized that their Russian servants were in fact members of the NKVD.

22 November 1943
Personal and Secret for Marshal Stalin from President Roosevelt

I have arrived in Cairo this morning and begin discussions with the Prime Minister. Conferences will follow with the Generalissimo by the end of the week. He will thereupon return to China. The Prime Minister and I with our senior staff officers can then proceed to Tehran to meet you, Mr. Molotov and your staff officers. If it suits your convenience I could arrive the afternoon of November 29. I am prepared to remain for two to four days depending upon how long you can find it possible to be away from your compelling responsibilities. I would be grateful if you would telegraph me what day you wish to set for our meeting and how long you can stay. I realize that bad weather sometimes causes delays in travel from Moscow to Tehran at this tine of the year and therefore would appreciate your keeping me advised of your plans.

I am informed that your Embassy and the British Embassy in Tehran are situated close to each other whereas my Legation is some distance away. I am advised that all three of us would be taking unnecessary risks by driving to and from our meetings if we were staying so far apart from each other.

Where do you think we should live?

I look forward to our talks with keen anticipation.

ROOSEVELT

Stalin

· 152 ·

---

26 November 1943

Personal and strictly————from Premier Stalin to President Roosevelt.

Your message from Cairo received. I will be at your service in Tehran the evening of November twenty-eighth.

Roosevelt

· 153 ·

November 26, 1943

Thank you very much for your message of November 23rd informing me of your intention to reach Tehran on the 28th or 29th. I expect to reach there on the 27th. It will be good to see you.

Roosevelt.

Roosevelt flew to Tehran from Cairo aboard his special new four-engine army air corps Douglas C-54, which the press named the Sacred Cow. He was accompanied by about seventy people altogether. Churchill also brought a large contingent. Stalin did not; with him were Marshal Kliment Yefremovich Voroshilov, a member of the Politburo and his trusted aide ("a good fellow but he is no military man," Stalin characterized him), and Molotov.[104] Voroshilov flew with Stalin to Tehran from Baku. Stalin's plane hit several air pockets above the mountains and, reportedly, Stalin clung to his armrests with an expression of utter terror on his face. He had never been in a plane before and he would never fly again.

That first morning Churchill, wanting to settle military matters before meeting with Stalin at the plenary session at 4 P.M., requested a meeting with Roosevelt either immediately or at lunch. Roosevelt, realizing that Stalin would learn of it, refused.

Stalin called on Roosevelt at 3 P.M. Alone except for their interpreters, Charles Bohlen and V. N. Pavlov, the two leaders talked for forty-five minutes. Roosevelt presented as topics to be discussed at the conference actions that would remove thirty to forty German divisions from the eastern front and offered Russia surplus merchant ships after the war was over. Stalin replied that a merchant fleet was not only of great value but would lead to closer relations between the two countries, and that Russia could reciprocate by supplying raw materials. Roosevelt also drew Stalin to him by cautioning him not to bring up problems of India with Churchill. They further had similar views on French Gen. Charles de Gaulle. Neither believed the French would rally behind him. Stalin expressed the opinion that Pétain rather than de Gaulle represented "the real physical France."[105] Roosevelt refused to recognize de Gaulle's French Committee of National Liberation as the government-in-exile. Stalin brought up Indochina, saying that the Allies should not shed blood to restore it to French colonial rule. Roosevelt, agreeing, proposed a United Nations trusteeship, and remarked that after a hundred years of French occupation, Indochina was in worse condition than it had been before.

Stalin had never been to an international conference outside his own country. When it came to the first elaborate dinner—Churchill's birthday dinner, held at the British embassy (ironically, guarded by turbaned Indian soldiers)—according to A. H. Birse, the British interpreter seated at Stalin's left, "Stalin, who sat uncomfortably on the edge of his chair, looked with anxiety at the display of different-sized knives and forks before him, turned to me and said, 'This is a fine collection of cutlery. It is a problem which to use. You will have to tell me, and also when I can begin to eat. I am unused to your customs.'"[106]

Churchill later told the *New York Times* writer Harrison Salisbury that there had been "absolute agreement . . . a melding of minds, a union of spirit. We were," he remembered, "on the crest of a wave."[107]

Harriman, as well as Hopkins and Bohlen, carried away the clear impression that Stalin respected Roosevelt. As Harriman observed,

> When the President spoke Stalin listened closely with deference, whereas he did not hesitate to interrupt or stick a knife into Churchill whenever he got the chance. I felt at the time that Stalin's attitude was motivated not only by the greater power of the

United States but also by his understanding that Roosevelt represented something new; his New Deal was reforming capitalism to meet the needs and desires of the "working class." There was nothing about that in Communist doctrine.[108]

At their second private meeting Roosevelt and Stalin had a free-ranging discussion about the postwar world. Roosevelt outlined his concept of the world peacekeeping organization which he envisioned at that time as consisting of an assembly of all the members, an executive committee which would deal with nonmilitary matters, and the Four Policemen, which would be the enforcing agency. But Stalin, according to Hopkins, "expressed the opinion that this proposal for the Four Policemen would not be favorably received by the small nations of Europe."[109] Addressing Stalin's overriding concern, Roosevelt spoke of the importance of a strong world organization—an organization that would be sufficiently strong and motivated to prevent repetition of Germany's secret rearmament.

Roosevelt accomplished his two main objectives: to bring Stalin to an understanding and acceptance of a postwar organization to maintain world peace; and, because his military advisers were telling him that the United States faced a long, bloody war with Japan, to nail down the commitment from Stalin that the Soviet Union would enter the war against Japan. Stalin finally achieved his one objective, a definite date for the invasion of France. OVERLORD would take place, Roosevelt told him, May 1.

Roosevelt

· 154 ·

General John Deane, head of the U.S. Military Mission, had asked Molotov in October for bases in the Soviet Union so that American planes could more efficiently bomb industrial sites in Germany. But although Germany was his "talking point," the "major objective," according to Deane, "was ultimate Soviet-American collaboration in the war against Japan. Bombing bases in western Russia would be a proving ground for the vast American air operations which we visualized would later take place in Siberia."[110] The

Russians, always suspicious of foreign incursions into their society, had agreed "in principle" to the granting of bases for American bombers but had done nothing to implement the bases.

Tehran
President Roosevelt to Marshal Stalin
November 29, 1943

During the recent Moscow Conference the United States Delegation proposed that air bases be made available in the USSR on which United States aircraft could be refueled, emergency repaired and rearmed in connection with shuttle bombing from the United Kingdom. It was also proposed that a more effective mutual interchange of weather information be implemented and that both signal and air communication between our two countries be improved.

It was my understanding that the USSR agreed to these proposals in principle and that appropriate Soviet authorities would be given instructions to meet with my Military Mission for the purpose of considering concrete measures which would be necessary to carry out the proposals.

I hope that it will be possible to work out these arrangements promptly.

Roosevelt

· 155 ·

———

Tehran
November 29, 1943
Advance Planning for Air Operations in Northwestern Pacific

With a view of shortening the war, it is our opinion that the bombing of Japan from your Maritime Provinces, immediately following the beginning of hostilities between the USSR and Japan, will be of the utmost importance, as it will enable us to destroy Japanese military and industrial centers.

If agreeable, would you arrange for my Military Mission in Moscow to be given the necessary information covering airports, housing, supplies, communications, and weather in the Maritime Provinces and the route thereto from Alaska. Our objective is to base the maximum bomber force possible, anywhere from 100 to 1,000 four engined bombers, with their maintenance and operating crews in that area; the number to depend upon facilities available.

It is of the utmost importance that planning to this end should be started at once. I realize that the physical surveys by our people should be limited at this time to a very few individuals and accomplished with the utmost secrecy. We would of course meet any conditions you might prescribe in this regard.

If the above arrangements are worked out now, I am convinced that the time of employment of our bombers against Japan will be materially advanced.

Roosevelt

· 156 ·

Tehran
November 29, 1943
Advance Planning for Naval Operations in Northwestern Pacific

I would like to arrange with you at this time for the exchange of information and for such preliminary planning as may be appropriate under the present conditions for eventual operations against Japan when Germany has been eliminated from the war. The more of this preliminary planning that can be done, without undue jeopardy to the situation, the sooner the war as a whole can be brought to a conclusion.

Specifically, I have in mind the following items:

a. We would be glad to receive combat intelligence information concerning Japan.

b. Considering that the ports of your Far Eastern submarine and destroyer force might be threatened seriously by land or air attack, do you feel it desirable that the United States should expand base facilities sufficiently to provide for these forces in U.S. bases?

c. What direct or indirect assistance would you be able to give in the event of a U.S. attack against the northern Kuriles?

d. Could you indicate what ports, if any, our forces could use, and could you furnish date on these ports in regard to their naval use as well as port capacities for dispatch of cargo?

These questions can be discussed as you may find appropriate with our Military Mission in Moscow, similar to the procedure suggested for plans regarding air operations.

Roosevelt

· 157 ·

_____

December 3, 1943
Dear Marshal Stalin,

The weather conditions were ideal for crossing the mountains the day of our departure from Tehran so that we had an easy and comfortable flight to Cairo. I hasten to send you my personal thanks for your thoughtfulness and hospitality in providing living quarters for me in your Embassy at Tehran. I was not only extremely comfortable there but I am very conscious of how much more we were able to accomplish in a brief period of time because we were such close neighbors throughout our stay.

I view those momentous days of our meeting with the greatest satisfaction as being an important milestone in the progress of human affairs. I thank you and the members of your staff and household for the many kindnesses to me and to the members of my staff.

I am just starting home and will visit my troops in Italy on the way.

Roosevelt

· 158 ·

_____

3 December 1943
FOR MARSHAL STALIN PERSONAL FROM THE PRESIDENT

Our party has arrived safely at our destination and we earnestly hope that by this time you have also arrived safely. The conference, I consider, was a great success and I feel sure that it was an historic event in the assurance not only of our ability to wage war together but too work for the peace to come in the utmost harmony. I enjoyed very much our personal talks together and particularly the opportunity of meeting you face to face. I look forward to meeting you sometime again. Until that time, I wish the greatest success to you and your Armies.

Roosevelt

· 159 ·

***

6 December 1943
From the President to Marshal Stalin Personal

The decision has been made to appoint General Eisenhower immediately to command of cross-Channel operations.

Roosevelt

Roosevelt

· 160 ·

***

6 December 1943
OPERATIONAL PRIORITY

FOR MARSHAL STALIN FROM THE PRESIDENT AND THE PRIME MINISTER, AND PERSONAL

In addition to the agreements arrived at by the three of us at Tehran, we have reached the following decisions in the conference just concluded in Cairo regarding the conduct of the war against Germany in 1944:

The highest strategic priority will be given to the bomber offensive against Germany, with the purpose of dislocating the German military, economic and industrial system, destroying the German air combat strength, and paving the way for an operation across the Channel.

In order to permit the reinforcement of amphibious craft for the operation against southern France, the operation scheduled for March in the Bay of Bengal has been reduced in scale.

To provide the reinforcement of cross-Channel operations, we have directed the greatest effort be made to increase the production of landing craft in the United States and the United Kingdom, and for the same purpose, the diversion of certain landing craft from the Pacific has also been ordered.

ROOSEVELT–CHURCHILL

Stalin

· 161 ·

———

PERSONAL TO PRESIDENT FRANKLIN D. ROOSEVELT FROM PREMIER J. V.
STALIN
December 6, 1943

Thank you for your telegram.

I agree with you that the Tehran Conference was a great success and
that our personal meetings were, in many respects, extremely important. I
hope that the common foe of our peoples—Hitlerite Germany will soon
feel it. Now there is confidence that our peoples will harmoniously act together during the present time as well as after this war is over.

I wish the best successes to you and your armed forces in the coming
important military operations.

I also hope that our meeting in Tehran should not be regarded as the
last one, and we shall meet again.

Stalin

· 162 ·

———

The following message was transmitted to the President aboard
the USS *Iowa*.

December 10, 1943

PERSONAL TO PRESIDENT ROOSEVELT FROM PREMIER STALIN

I have received your message regarding the appointment of General
Eisenhower. I welcome the appointment of General Eisenhower. I wish
him success in the task of preparation and carrying out the coming decisive operations.

Stalin

· 163 ·

PERSONAL TO PRESIDENT ROOSEVELT AND PRIME-MINISTER CHURCHILL
FROM PREMIER STALIN
December 10, 1943

I thank you for your joint message in which you inform me of the additional decisions regarding the prosecution of the war against Germany in 1944.

Greetings.

Stalin

· 164 ·

The Tehran conference marked a turning point in Soviet-American relations. Roosevelt arrived back in Washington on December 17. His speechwriter Sam Rosenman, waiting to greet him at the south entrance to the White House, recalled, "I do not remember ever seeing the President look more satisfied and pleased than he did that morning. He believed intensely that he had accomplished what he had set out to do—to bring Russia into co-operation with the Western powers in a formidable organization for the maintenance of peace—and he was glad. . . . He was indeed the champ who had come back with the prize."[111]

The Declaration of Tehran, issued after the meeting, emphasized plans for "a world family of democratic nations."

"We are sure that our concord will win an enduring peace. We recognize fully the supreme responsibility resting upon us and all the United Nations to make a peace which will command the good will of the overwhelming mass of the peoples of the world and banish the scourge and terror of war for many generations."[112]

According to Harriman, Roosevelt's bread-and-butter thank-you letter of December 3 didn't reach Stalin for two weeks. Through some mysterious mistake, never explained, Harriman gave it to Stalin, unopened, on December 18. This was Stalin's reply:

20 December 1943
PERSONAL AND SECRET MESSAGE TO PRESIDENT ROOSEVELT FROM PRE-
MIER STALIN

I thank you for your letter which Your Ambassador has extended to
me on December 18TH.

I am glad that fate has given me an opportunity to render you a service
in Tehran. I also attach important significance to our meeting and to the
conversations taken place there which concerned such substantial questions of accelerating of our common victory and establishment of future
lasting peace between the peoples.

Stalin

· 165 ·

Stalin was also very pleased with the meeting at Tehran. In the
aftermath the American embassy in Moscow reported that the Soviet press "was citing the 'historic decisions' taken at Teheran almost daily," that the change in Soviet attitude toward the United
States and Great Britain was almost "revolutionary." Nevertheless,
the pressure of the conference showed in the fact that when they returned home all three leaders took sick: Churchill came down with
pneumonia, Stalin complained of an ear attack lasting two weeks as
a result of the flight, and President Roosevelt returned with a hack-
ing cough that turned into a bronchial infection he couldn't shake
off. He wrote to his cousin Polly on January 14, "This 'flu' is Hell,
as you know. I am not over mine yet."[113]

January 4, 1944
Message from Premier J. V. Stalin to President Roosevelt

I am glad to learn from the information published in the press that you
feel better. I convey to you the best wishes, and mainly—the wishes for a
quick and complete recovery.

Roosevelt and Churchill

· 166 ·

Suddenly, seemingly without provocation, *Pravda* published two attacks, one on England, one on the United States. According to the first article, on January 17, the Soviet Union had just learned that "two leading British personalities" had recently met in a coastal town on the Iberian Peninsula with the German diplomat Joachim von Ribbentrop to probe the possibilities of striking a separate peace with Germany excluding the Soviet Union. Harriman thought it "a patently false dispatch" and suspected that "party zealots had warned Stalin against letting the post-Tehran euphoria go too far, lest some Russians relax their revolutionary vigilance against Western influence." but as Admiral Leahy noted in a memo to Roosevelt, there was probably truth to the allegation, because Magic intercepts showed a history of meetings in Lisbon between British and German anti-Hitler representatives.[114] The second article, which appeared in *Pravda* soon after the first, was an attack on Wendell Willkie as a meddler in Soviet affairs. When told that Willkie thought the attack unwarranted because he had always upheld Soviet aid, Stalin suggested sending him a cable to read, "I like you but I don't want you to be President."[115]

Roosevelt drafted the following message. When Churchill saw it, he asked Roosevelt to omit the crossed-out paragraph, which Roosevelt agreed to do. OVERLORD-ANVIL was the code name for the invasion of southern France.

January 23, 1944
FROM: THE PRESIDENT AND THE PRIME MINISTER
TO: MARSHAL STALIN
LONDON

With regard to the handing over to the Soviets of Italian shipping asked for by the Soviet Government at the Moscow Conference and agreed to with you by us both at Tehran, we have received a memorandum by the Combined Chiefs of Staff contained in our immediately following telegram. For these reasons set out in this memorandum we think it would be dangerous to our triple interests actually to carry out any transfer or to say anything about it to the Italians until their cooperation is no longer of operational importance.

Nevertheless, if after full consideration you desire us to proceed, we will make a secret approach to Badoglio with a view to concluding the necessary arrangements without their becoming generally known to Italian naval Forces. If in this way agreement could be reached, such arrangements with Italian naval authorities as were necessary could be left to him. These arrangements would have to be on the lines that Italian ships selected should be sailed to suitable Allied port where they would be collected by Russian crews who would sail into Russian northern ports which are the only ones now open where any refitting necessary would be undertaken.

We are, however, very conscious of dangers of above course for the reasons we have laid before you and we have, therefore, decided to propose the following alternative, which, from the military point of view, has many advantages.

The British battleship, ROYAL SOVEREIGN, has recently completed refitting in the U.S.A. she is fitted with radar for all types of armament. The United States will make one light cruiser available at approximately the same time.

His Majesty's government and the United States are willing for their part that these vessels should be taken over at British ports by Soviet crews and sailed to North Russian ports. You could then make such alterations as you find necessary for Arctic conditions.

These vessels would be temporarily transferred on loan to the Soviet and would fly the Soviet flag until without prejudice to military operations the Italian vessels can be made available.

His Majesty's Government and the United States will each arrange to provide 20,000 tons of merchant shipping to be available as soon as practicable and until the Italian merchant ships can be obtained without prejudice to projected essential operations OVERLORD-ANVIL.

~~An effort will be made at once to make available from the surrendered Italian war ships 8 destroyers and 4 submarines to be taken over by the Soviet as soon as they can be made available under conditions stated above for the British and U.S. ships.~~

This alternative has the advantage that the Soviet Government would obtain the use of vessels at a very much earlier date than if they all had to be refitted and rendered suitable for northern waters. Thus if our efforts should take a favorable turn with Turks and the Straits become open these vessels would be ready to operate in the Black Sea. We hope you will very carefully consider this alternative which we think is in every way superior to first proposal.

ROOSEVELT. CHURCHILL.

Roosevelt and Churchill

· 167 ·

This telegram was drafted by Roosevelt and sent to Churchill, who made no changes.

January 23, 1944
FROM: THE PRESIDENT AND THE PRIME MINISTER
TO: MARSHAL STALIN
LONDON

Our Combined Chiefs of Staff have made the following positive recommendation with supporting date:

(a) The present time is inopportune for effecting the transfer of captured Italian ships because of pending Allied operations.

(b) To enforce the transfer at this time would remove needed Italian resources now employed in current operations, would interfere with assistance now being given by Italian repair facilities, might cause the scuttling of Italian war ships, and result in loss of Italian cooperation thus jeopardizing OVERLORD and ANVIL.

(c) At the earliest moment permitted by operations the implementation of the delivery of Italian vessels may proceed.

ROOSEVELT. CHURCHILL.

Stalin

· 168 ·

At the Moscow conference Hull had offered as a major inducement for the Russians to agree to the inclusion of China as one of the four powers a promise to Molotov to be generous to the Soviet Union when it came time to distribute the captured Italian naval and merchant ships.

Churchill's comment on the following letter was "What can you expect from a bear but a growl."[116]

FROM PREMIER J. V. STALIN

TO: FRANKLIN D. ROOSEVELT AND WINSTON CHURCHILL

29 January 1944

On January 23 I have received your two joint messages, signed by you, Mr. President, and you, Mr. Prime-Minister, on the question of transference for the use of the Soviet Union of Italian vessels.

I have to say, that after your joint affirmative reply in Tehran to my question regarding the transference to the Soviet Union of Italian vessels before the end of January 1944, I considered this question as settled and it did not occur to me that there was possibility of revision of this accepted and agreed upon, among the three of us, decision. So much the more, as we came to an agreement that in the course of December and January this question should have been settled with the Italians as well. Now I see that this is not so, and that the Italians have not been approached on that question at all.

In order not to delay, however, this matter, which is of vital importance for our common struggle against Germany, the Soviet Government is ready to accept your proposal regarding the transference from British ports to the USSR of the battleship "Royal Sovereign" and one cruiser for temporary use by the naval Command of the USSR until adequate Italian vessels are put at the disposal of the Soviet Union. Likewise we are ready to accept from the United States and England merchant vessels 20,000 tons each, which will also be used by us until Italian vessels of the same tonnage are transferred to us. It is important to avoid any delay in this matter now, so that all vessels in question be transferred to us still in the course of February.

In your reply, however, is no mention made of the transference to the Soviet Union of eight Italian squadron destroyers and four submarines, regarding the transference of which to the Soviet Union still at the end of January, you Mr. President, and you Mr. Prime-Minister, gave your consent in Tehran. Undoubtedly for the Soviet Union primarily is this question, the question regarding destroys and submarines, without which the transference of a battleship and a cruiser is of no value. You will understand yourself that cruisers and battleships are powerless without destroyers escorting them. Since you have at your disposal the whole Italian naval fleet, fulfillment of the decision agreed upon in Tehran pertaining to the transference for the use of the Soviet Union of eight destroyers and four submarines from this fleet should not be difficult. I agree, that instead of Italian destroyers and submarines the Soviet Union be given to use the same number of American or English destroyers and submarines. Besides, the question of transference of destroyers and submarines cannot be postponed, but must be solved simultaneously with the transference of the battleship and cruiser, as it was agreed upon, among the three of us, in Tehran.

Roosevelt

· 169 ·

Harriman was directed to present this message directly to Stalin, which he did on February 11.

"Views of your Government as outlined by Mr. Molotov" included the refusal of the Polish government in London to accept the Curzon Line, recommended by the Allies after World War I as the frontier, instead insisting on the frontier established by the Riga Treaty of 1921, which gave Poland the western Ukraine and western Byelorussia, as well as to the Poles' calls for further investigation of the Katyn massacre.[117]

THE WHITE HOUSE
7 February 1944
Marshal Joseph Stalin
The Kremlin,
Moscow

I have followed with the closest attention the recent developments in your relations with Poland. I feel that I am fully aware of your views on the subject and am therefore taking this opportunity of communicating with you on the basis of our conversations at Tehran. First of all, let me make it plain that I neither desire nor intend to attempt to suggest much less to advise you in any way as to where the interests of Russia lie in this matter since I realize to the full that the future security of your country is rightly your primary concern. The observations which I am about to make are prompted solely by the larger issues which affect the common goal towards which we are both working.

The overwhelming majority of our people and Congress, as you know, welcomed with enthusiasm the broad principles subscribed to at the Moscow and Tehran Conferences, and I know that you agree with me that it is of the utmost importance that faith in these understandings should not be left in any doubt. I am sure that a solution can be found which would fully protect the interests of Russia and satisfy your desire to see a friendly, independent Poland, and at the same time not adversely affect the cooperation so splendidly established at Moscow and Tehran. I feel that it is of the utmost importance that we should bear in mind that the various differences which inevitably arise in the conduct of international relations should not be permitted to jeopardize the major all important question of cooperation and collaboration among nations which is the only sound basis for a just and lasting peace.

I have given careful consideration to the views of your Government as outlined by Mr. Molotov to Mr. Harriman on January 18 regarding the impossibility from the Soviet point of view of having any dealings with the Polish Government-in-exile and Mr. Molotov's suggestion that the Polish Government should be reconstituted by the inclusion of Polish elements at present in the United States, Great Britain and the Soviet Union. I fully appreciate your desire to deal only with a Polish Government in which you can repose confidence and which can be counted upon to establish permanent friendly relations with the Soviet Union, but it is my earnest hope that while this problem remains unsolved neither party shall by hasty word or unilateral act transform this special question into one adversely affecting the larger issues of future international collaboration. While public opinion is forming in support of the principle of international collaboration, it is especially incumbent upon us to avoid any action which might appear to counteract the achievement of our long-range objectives. I feel I should ill serve our common interest if I failed to bring these facts to your attention.

Prime Minister Churchill tells me that he is endeavoring to persuade the Polish Prime Minister to make a clean-cut acceptance as a basis for negotiation of the territorial changes which have been proposed by your Government. Is it not possible on that basis to arrive at some answer to the question of the composition of the Polish Government which would leave it to the Polish Prime Minister himself to make such changes in his Government as may be necessary without any evidence of pressure or dictation from a foreign country?

As a matter of timing it seems to me that the first consideration at this time should be that Polish guerillas should work with and not against your advancing troops. That is of current importance and some assurance on the part of all Poles would be of great advantage as a first step.

Roosevelt

Roosevelt and Churchill

· 170 ·

Roosevelt composed this message and sent it to Churchill with the admonition, "Please let me have your reaction to these suggestions and your draft of a reply to U.J.'s growl." Churchill had already told Roosevelt that he would give Stalin old destroyers, "those that we got from you in 1941," but the submarines were a problem. Churchill worried that the Italian Navy might mutiny at having their submarines given to the Soviet Union, and knowing how strongly Roosevelt felt about honoring the commitment to Stalin, he reluctantly decided to offer four of Britain's own subs and therefore changed the message as indicated, adding the italicized words.

The message was delayed and reached the Kremlin on February 24.

FROM: THE PRESIDENT AND THE PRIME MINISTER
TO: MARSHAL STALIN
London
7 February 1944

The receipt is acknowledged of your message in regard to handing over Italian shipping to the Soviet.

It is our intention to carry out the transfer agreed to at Tehran at the earliest date practicable without hazarding the success of ANVIL or OVERLORD which operations we all agree should be given first priority in our common effort to defeat Germany at the earliest possible date.

There is no thought of not carrying through the transfers agreed at Tehran. The British battleship and the American cruiser can be made available without any delay, and an effort will be made at once to make available from the British Navy eight destroyers. Four submarines will ~~be taken from Italy~~ *also be provided temporarily by Great Britain.*

I am convinced that disaffecting the Italian Navy at this time would be what you have so aptly termed an unnecessary diversion and that it would adversely affect the prospects of our success in France.

Roosevelt. Churchill.

Roosevelt

· 171 ·

On February 2 Stalin invited Harriman to the Kremlin to discuss the plan that Roosevelt had asked him to implement on November 29 for shuttle bombers to land and refuel at Russian bases. Harriman made the case that the bombers could penetrate more deeply into Germany if they were permitted to land in the Soviet Union and didn't have to fight their way back to the United Kingdom and Italy, and Stalin readily agreed. Within four months three airfields expressly built for this purpose in the Ukraine—at Poltava, Mirgorod, and Pyryatin—were ready.[118] Harriman reported to the president that he also discussed with Stalin the use by American bombers of Soviet air bases in the east after the Soviet Union entered the war against Japan, and that the premier wanted the discussions kept between "the narrowest limits."[119]

8 February 1944
FOR AMBASSADOR HARRIMAN PERSONAL FROM THE PRESIDENT
    Please convey to Stalin my appreciation of the information contained in your message and my congratulations on the daily successes of his valiant Army. Please also tell him that our operations in the Pacific are increasing their tempo and that the success of our amphibious attacks have met expectations.

Roosevelt

Stalin

· 172 ·

----

16 FEBRUARY 1944
PERSONAL
FROM
PREMIER J. V. STALIN
TO
PRESIDENT FRANKLIN D. ROOSEVELT
    I have received your message on the Polish question. It goes without saying that a correct solution of this question of great importance for us as well as for our common cause.

There are two principle points: first—the Soviet-Polish border, second—the composition of the Polish Government. The point of view of the Soviet Government is known to you from the recently issued statements and from Mr. Molotov's letter sent in reply to Mr. Hull's note received in Moscow on January 22 through Soviet Ambassador Gromyko.

First of all about the Soviet-Polish border. As it is known the Soviet Government officially stated that it did not consider the border line of 1939 unalterable and has agreed to the Curzon line, thus having made considerable concessions to the Poles in the border question. We had the right to expect an appropriate statement from the Polish Government. The Polish Government should have made an official statement that the border line established by the Riga Treaty, was subject to change and that the Curzon line was being accepted by it as the new border line between the USSR and Poland. Such a statement of recognition of the Curzon line should have been made by the Polish Government in the same official manner as it was done by the Soviet Government. None the less the Polish Government in London did not make any move stating, as before, in its official declarations that the border line, which was forced upon us at a difficult moment by the Riga Treaty, should remain unalterable. Hence there is no ground for an agreement, as the point of view of the present Polish Government, as it appears, is excluding the possibility of an agreement.

In connection with the above-mentioned circumstances the questions regarding the composition of the Polish Government became more acute. Besides, it is clear that the Polish Government, in which the principal role is played by hostile to the Soviet Union pro-fascist imperialist elements, such as [Kazimierz] Sosnkovsky, and in which there are almost no democratic elements, can find no ground in Poland itself, and cannot, as experience has shown, establish friendly relations with Soviet democratic states. Naturally, that such a Polish Government is unable to establish friendly relations with the Soviet Union and it cannot but bring discord amidst the democratic countries which, on the contrary, are interested in strengthening of unity among them. From the above follows that the basic improvement of the composition of the Polish Government proves to be a ripe task.

I delayed with the reply because of pressing duties at the front.

Roosevelt

· 173 ·

After nine hundred days of incredible hardship, during which they never gave up hope or thought of surrendering, the Russian Army finally broke through the ring of concrete and armored pill-boxes and the mine fields and the German soldiers and rescued the people still alive in Leningrad. It had been a city of three million; almost a third of the population died.

February 17, 1944
HIS EXCELLENCY JOSEPH V. STALIN
SUPREME COMMANDER OF THE ARMED FORCES
OF THE UNION OF SOVIET SOCIALIST REPUBLICS

On this twenty-sixth anniversary of the Red Army I wish to convey to you as supreme commander my sincere congratulations on the great and significant victories of the armed forces of the Soviet Union during the past year. The magnificent achievements of the Red Army under your leadership have been an inspiration to all. The heroic defense of Leningrad has been crowned and rewarded by the recent crushing defeat of the enemy before its gates. Millions of Soviet citizens have been freed from enslavement and oppression by the victorious advance of the Red Army. These achievements together with the collaboration and cooperation which was agreed upon at Moscow and Tehran assure our final victory over the Nazi aggressors.

Franklin D. Roosevelt

Roosevelt

· 174 ·

PRESIDENT TO PREMIER STALIN
February 17, 1944
PERSONAL FROM THE PRESIDENT FOR MARSHAL STALIN

Replying to your message of January 29, I am pleased to inform you that the following United States ships are available for temporary use by the Naval Command of the USSR until adequate Italian tonnage to replace them can be placed at the disposal of the Soviet Union.

The merchant ship (10,000 tons) "HARRY PERCY," now at Glasgow.

The merchant ship "JOHN GORRIE" (10,000 tons), now at Liverpool.

The cruiser "MILWAUKEE" will arrive in some port in the United Kingdom March 8.

Roosevelt

Roosevelt

· 175 ·

In a recent operation in the Ukraine the Soviet army had eliminated thirty-five thousand German troops and broken through into Romania.

19 February 1944

FROM THE PRESIDENT FOR MARSHAL STALIN

We have been following with keen interest and deep satisfaction the recent successes of your troops, especially in the Ukraine *and in the Northwest*. My congratulations and best wishes.

Roosevelt

Stalin

· 176 ·

The joint message which Roosevelt and Churchill sent Stalin on February 7 on the subject of Italian ships reached the Kremlin only on February 24, leading Stalin to write the following.

PERSONAL FROM PREMIER J. V. STALIN

TO PRESIDENT ROOSEVELT

February 21, 1944

I have received your message of February 18. Thank you for the information.

It, however, does not exhaust the question, since there is nothing mentioned in it about the Anglo-American destroyers and submarines instead of Italian ones (8 destroyers, 4 submarines), as it was agreed upon at Tehran. I hope to receive a speedy reply regarding these questions, touched in my communication of January 29th.

Roosevelt

· 177 ·

21 February 1944
FROM THE PRESIDENT FOR MARSHAL STALIN

I am informed as to the text of the message sent to you on February 20 by Mr. Churchill on the subject of a tentative settlement of the Polish post-war boundary by agreement between the Soviet and the Polish Governments.

This suggestion by the Prime Minister, if accepted, goes far toward advancing our prospects of an early defeat of Germany and I am pleased to recommend that you give to it favorable and sympathetic consideration. ~~In view of the large number of citizens of the United States who are of Polish descent, it is of much importance to me that the Polish dispute be adjudicated without any avoidable delay.~~

As I intimated before, I think the most realistic problem of the moment is to be assured that your armies will be assisted by the Poles when you get to Poland.

Roosevelt

Stalin

· 178 ·

February 23, 1944
PERSONAL TO PRESIDENT FRANKLIN D. ROOSEVELT
FROM PREMIER J. V. STALIN

I have received your message with greetings on the occasion of the latest successes of the Soviet troops. Please accept my thanks for your friendly wishes.

Roosevelt

· 179 ·

February 23, 1944
PERSONAL FROM THE PRESIDENT FOR MARSHAL STALIN.

In recent months a number of important steps have been taken by the Governments of the United Nations toward laying the foundations for post-war cooperative action in the various fields of international economic relations. You will recall that the United Nations Conference on Food and Agriculture, held in May 1943, gave rise to an Interim Commission which is now drafting recommendations to lay before the various governments for a permanent organization in this field. More recently, there has been established—and is now in operation—the United Nations Relief and Rehabilitation Administration. For nearly a year, there have been informal technical discussions at the expert level among many of the United Nations on mechanisms for international monetary stabilization; these discussions are preparatory to a possible convocation of an United Nations Monetary Conference. Similar discussions have been taking place, though on a more restricted scale, with regard to the possibility of establishing mechanisms for facilitating international developmental investment. To some extent, informal discussions have taken place among some of the United Nations with regard to such questions as commercial policy commodity policy, and cartels. Discussions are in contemplation on such questions as commercial aviation, oil, and others. In April a conference of the International Labor Organization will take place, in part for the purpose of considering the future activities of that organization

In a document presented by the Secretary of State at the Moscow meeting of Foreign Ministers, entitled "Bases of our Program for International Economic Cooperation," the need was emphasized for both informal discussions and formal conferences on various economic problems. It was suggested that "the time has come for the establishment of a Commission comprising representatives of the principal United Nations and possibly certain others of the United Nations for the joint planning of the procedure to be followed in these matters."

It is clear to me that there is a manifest need for United Nations machinery for joint planning of the procedures by which consideration should be given to the various fields of international economic cooperation, the subjects which should be discussed, the order of discussion, and the means of coordinating existing and prospective arrangements and activities. I do not mean to raise at this time and in this connection the broader issues of international organization for the maintenance of peace and security. Preliminary discussions on this subject are currently in contemplation between our three governments under the terms of the Moscow Protocol. What I am raising here is the question of further steps toward the establishment of United Nations machinery for post-war economic collaboration, which was raised by the Secretary of State at the Moscow meeting and was discussed by you, Prime Minister Churchill, and myself at Tehran.

I should appreciate it very much if you would give me your views on the suggestion made by the Secretary of State at Moscow, together with any other thoughts as to the best procedures to be followed in this extremely important matter.

Roosevelt

· 180 ·

February 23, 1944
PRESIDENT TO STALIN.

I have received your message of February 21 regarding the loan of Anglo-American ships to the Soviet Navy.

It was my understanding that Great Britain would provide the one battleship, the eight destroyers and the four submarines. I have telegraphed to Prime Minister Churchill in regard to this and will let you know when I hear from him.

Roosevelt

Roosevelt

· 181 ·

February 24, 1944
FOR MARSHAL STALIN FROM THE PRESIDENT

Referring to my message of 23 February 1944, I have had a reply from the Prime Minister, and our understanding as expressed to you is now confirmed.

ROOSEVELT

Stalin

· 182 ·

PERSONAL FROM PREMIER J. V. STALIN
TO PRESIDENT F. D. ROOSEVELT AND
PRIME-MINISTER W. CHURCHILL
February 26, 1944

I have received through Ambassador Harriman your two messages of February 24 [23] and 25 [24] regarding the Italian vessels. I have also received your joint with Mr. Prime-Minister message of February 7, transmitted to me by the British Ambassador Kerr on February 24. Thank you and Mr. Prime-Minister for the communication about your decision to accomplish the transference for temporary use to the Soviet Union by Great Britain of 8 destroyers and 4 submarines, and also a battleship and 20,000 tons of merchant vessels, and by the United States of a cruiser and 20,000 tons of merchant vessels. Since Mr. Kerr specially warned that all the destroyers are old, I have a certain fear regarding the fighting qualities of these destroyers. Meanwhile it seems to me, that for the British and American fleets it will not present much difficulty to allot in the number of eight destroyers at least half of them modern and not old ones. I still hope that you and Mr. Prime-Minister will find it possible that among the destroyers being transferred there be at least four modern ones. In the issue of military operations on the part of Germany and Italy we lost a considerable part of our destroyers. Therefore it is quite important for us to have at least a partial replacement of these losses.

Stalin

· 183 ·

This message was published in U.S. newspapers before the president, at Hyde Park, received it. The president was amazed to read a headline like "Stalin Reaffirms Teheran Ties, Cables Roosevelt Allies Will Soon Strike Final Blow Decided On at Conference," and he "directed a thorough investigation" into how the message could have been leaked.[120] It turned out that three events had occurred simultaneously. First, the message had come in unciphered, by commercial cable, and had gone straight to the White House instead of to the Map Room, so press secretary Steve Early released it. Second, as the message was being sent to Hyde Park, Western Union engineers who were rewiring the circuits there accidentally cut them, so the message was not received. Finally, the sending operator in Washington did not notice that the receiving operator in Hyde Park had not acknowledged receipt as he should have.

Feb. 28, 1944

MARSHAL STALIN TO PRESIDENT ROOSEVELT

I ask you to accept my sincere thanks for your friendly congratulations on the occasion of the twenty-sixth anniversary of the Red Army and on the successes of the armed forces of the Soviet Union in the struggle against the Hitlerite invaders. I am strongly convinced that the time is near when the successful struggle of the armed forces of the Soviet Union, together with the armies of the United States and Great Britain, on the basis of the agreements reached at Moscow and Tehran, will lead to the final defeat of our common enemy, Hitlerite Germany.

Roosevelt

· 184 ·

In the course of various questions by reporters on the progress of the war, Roosevelt was asked about a matter "that the [Russian] Ambassador brought in." Roosevelt answered, "It isn't settled yet, and that is as to what particular ships would go to the Russian navy from the Italian navy."[121]

March 3, 1944

In reply to insistent questioning at a press conference today I stated that Italian merchant ships and war ships are now being used in our war effort by the Allied Mediterranean command and that some of the Italian ships or substitutes therefore from the British and American tonnage will be allocated to the Soviet Navy to assist in their requirements for their war effort.

Roosevelt

Stalin

· 185 ·

This message didn't reach the Map Room until March 14. The president said, on March 15, "No reply necessary."

PERSONAL FROM PREMIER J. V. STALIN TO PRESIDENT F. D. ROOSEVELT
March 3, 1944

Despite the strongest desire on my part to consider favorably the familiar to you message regarding the Poles, addressed to me by Mr. Churchill, I have to state, that the emigrant Polish Government does not want the establishment of normal relations with the USSR. It is sufficient to say, that the Polish emigrants in London not only reject the Curzon line, but lay claim to Lwow and Vilno (capital of Lithuania).

It is necessary therefore to state, that the solution of the question regarding Polish-Soviet relations has not ripened yet. For your orientation I am enclosing a copy of my reply to Mr. Churchill regarding the said matter.

March 3, 1944
Personal from Premier J. V. Stalin to Prime Minister, Mr. W. Churchill

On February 27 I have received though Mr. Kerr both your messages of February 20 regarding the Polish question.

Having acquainted myself with the detailed account of your conversations with the members of the emigrant Polish government, I have time and again come to the conclusion, that such people are not able to establish normal relations with the USSR. It is desirable to point out that they not only reject the Curzon line but lay claim to Lwow as well as Vilno. Soviet territories, we cannot accept such wishes as subject for discussion, because even the raising of such a question we consider as insulting to the Soviet Union.

I have already written to the President, that the solution of the question regarding Soviet-Polish elations has not ripened yet. It becomes necessary to state once more the correctness of this conclusion.

Stalin

· 186 ·

PERSONAL FROM PREMIER J. V. STALIN TO PRESIDENT F. D. ROOSEVELT
March 6, 1944

I have received your message about your statement at the press conference in Washington regarding the transference of a part of Italian fleet or its equivalent from among the American and British tonnage to the Soviet Union. Thank you.

Roosevelt

· 187 ·

Oskar Lange, a professor of economics at Chicago University who had left Poland in 1937 and become an American citizen, thought that if Poland were given parts of eastern Prussia in place of eastern Poland, which Russia claimed, the Polish nation would have a more homogeneous population. He favored the establishment of a more democratic Polish government than the Polish government-in-exile.

Father Stanislaus Orlemanski, born in America of Polish parents, pastor of Our Lady of the Holy Rosary Catholic Church in Springfield, Massachusetts, also considered the Polish government-in-exile insufficiently democratic. He had written to Stalin asking to meet with him to discuss the future of Poland. Stalin extended him an invitation to come to Moscow.

Although Roosevelt worried that granting passports to the two men might be interpreted as the first step in abandoning the legal government-in-exile, there were no grounds for refusing permission to American citizens invited by the Soviet government.

March 8, 1944
Personal from the President to Marshal Stalin

In accordance with your suggestion Dr. Lange and Father Orlemanski will be given passports in order to accept your invitation to proceed to the Soviet Union. Due, however, to military movements our transportation facilities are greatly overcrowded at the present time, and transportation, therefore, from the United States to the Soviet Union will have to be furnished by Soviet facilities. I know you will realize that Dr. Lange and Father Orlemanski are proceeding in their individual capacity as private citizens and this Government can assume no responsibility whatsoever for their activities or views and should their trip become the subject of public comment it might be necessary for this Government to make this point clear.

Roosevelt and Churchill

· 188 ·

Churchill wrote the following message, which Roosevelt approved without change.

From: The President and The Prime Minister
To: Marshal Stalin
March 8, 1944

Although the Prime Minister instructed Ambassador Clark Kerr to tell you that the destroyers we are lending you were old, this was only for the sake of absolute frankness. In fact they are good, serviceable ships, quite efficient for escort duty. There are only 7 fleet destroyers in the whole Italian Navy, the rest being older destroyers and torpedo boats. Moreover these Italian destroyers, when we do get them, are absolutely unfitted for work in the North without very lengthy refit. Therefore we thought the 8 which the British Government have found would be an earlier and more convenient form of help to you.

The Prime Minister regrets that he cannot spare any new destroyers at the present time. He lost 2 last week, one in the Russian convoy, and for the landing at OVERLORD alone he has to deploy, for close inshore work against the batteries, no fewer than 42 destroyers, a large proportion of which may be sunk. Every single vessel that he has of this class is being used to the utmost pressure in the common cause. The movement of the Japanese fleet to Singapore creates a new situation for us both in the Indian Ocean. The fighting in the Anzio bridgehead and generally throughout the Mediterranean is at its height. The vast troop convoys are crossing the Atlantic with the United States Army of Liberation. The Russian convoys are being run up to the last minute before OVERLORD with very heavy destroyer escorts. Finally there is OVERLORD itself. The President's position is similarly strained, but in this case mainly because of the great scale and activity of the operations in the Pacific.

Our joint intentions to deliver to you the Italian ships agreed upon at Moscow and Tehran remain unaltered, and we shall put the position formally to the Italian Government at the time when it is broadened and the new ministers take over their responsibilities. There is no question of our right to dispose of the Italian Navy, but only of exercising that right with the least harm to our common interests. Meanwhile, all our specified ships are being prepared for delivery to you on loan as already agreed.

Roosevelt. Churchill.

Stalin

· 189 ·

___

This message is in response to Roosevelt's message of February 23, reiterating that "the time has come" to establish a United Nations economic planning group.

The Bretton Woods Conference, attended by 730 delegates from forty-four Allied nations, convened that summer in Bretton Woods, New Hampshire. Chaired by Secretary of the Treasury Henry Morgenthau, Jr., it resulted in the establishment of the International Monetary Fund (IMF) and the International Bank for Reconstruction and Development (later the World Bank and the Bank for International Settlements). The USSR was a signatory.

March 10, 1944
Personal from Premier J. V. Stalin to President F. D. Roosevelt
I have received your message on the question of post-war economic collaboration. Undoubtedly the questions touched upon in Mr. Hull's note regarding international collaboration in the sphere of economics are of great importance and demand attention. I consider as quite expedient the establishment at the present time of a United Nations apparatus for the working out of these questions and also for the establishment of conditions and order of consideration of various problems of the international economic collaboration in accordance with the decisions of the Moscow and Tehran Conferences.

Roosevelt

· 190 ·

___

The Joint Chiefs of Staff had requested and Roosevelt had authorized Brig. Gen. William J. Donovan, director of the Office of Strategic Services, to set up an OSS intelligence liaison mission with the NKVD and to offer to exchange information with them. The Joint Chiefs' rationale was that the Russians "had long since planted innumerable agents in their large purchasing mission." Donovan visited Moscow and discussed the project with Lt. Gen.

P. N. Fitin, chief of the External Intelligence Service, and Maj. Gen. A. P. Ossipov, head of the section that conducted subversive activities in enemy countries. The spymasters got along well and reached an agreement as to which Russian would be stationed in Washington and which American in Moscow, and they proceeded to set up a communications channel. Then suddenly Roosevelt scuttled the plan. Harriman thought that the cancellation was "the height of stupidity since we were dealing with a small group of marked men who would have had to be particularly circumspect in their behavior. I later learned," he wrote, "that J. Edgar Hoover and Admiral Leahy had been responsible for changing the President's mind."[122]

President to Harriman
March 15, 1944
   Referring to General Donovan's proposal that arrangements for an exchange of representatives of O.S.S. personnel in Russia for N.K.V.D. personnel in the United States, which Donovan says has your and Deane's approval, the question presented has been carefully examined here and has been found to be impracticable *at this time.*
   Please inform ~~Stalin~~ *the Marshal* when you have an opportunity that for purely domestic political reasons *which he will understand* it is not appropriate *just now* to exchange these missions ~~at the present time and that I am sure he will understand.~~ *The timing is not good.*

Roosevelt

Stalin

· 191 ·

PERSONAL FROM PREMIER J. V. STALIN TO PRESIDENT F. D. ROOSEVELT AND PRIME MINISTER W. CHURCHILL
March 17, 1944
   I have received your message regarding the transference by the British Government of eight destroyers to the Soviet Union, I am ready to agree that these destroyers are quite good for escort duty but you, of course, understand that the Soviet Union needs destroyers good also for other military operations. The right of the Allies to control the Italian fleet is, of course, quite indisputable, and it is necessary to make this point clear to

the Italian Government, and in particular regarding the Italian vessels which are subject to transference to the Soviet Union.

Roosevelt

· 192 ·

———

Germany supplied Turkey with certain necessary commodities in return for the delivery of chrome, which Germany desperately needed. For months the deliveries of Turkish chrome to Germany had been materially increasing, accompanied by a "considerable" decrease in the movement of chrome to Great Britain. Roosevelt sent exactly the same message and the same paraphrase of the letter to Churchill.

Churchill thought that the letter to Inonu was a bad idea and might have the opposite result of increasing the delivery of chrome ore to Germany because the Turks might regard it as a sign of weakening.

But as a result of continuing U.S. and British diplomatic pressure, the course of the war (the United States launched its first air attack on Berlin on March 4), and various other considerations, such as the possibility of Allied bombing of the Turkish rail lines and bridges that made the delivery of chrome possible, Turkey reversed its policy and agreed to reduce dramatically deliveries to Germany. By the end of April they suspended all further shipments.

Stalin thought that the letter was merely pointless. The letter was not sent.

March 16, 1944
F. Roosevelt to J. V. Stalin

As I am impressed by the importance to Germany of Turkish chrome, I have today forwarded by air a personal letter to President Inonu on the subject of chrome for delivery in Ankara by Ambassador Steinhardt. I feel sure that you will concur, but if this action runs counter to any steps you are now taking or contemplating, please let me know so that I can stop delivery of the letter. The following is a paraphrase of the text of my letter.

There are many matters about which I would like to talk to you almost every day in the week, and I wish that you and I were not several thousand miles apart.

I want to write you about the subject of chrome at this time.

By the capture of Nikopol the Russians, as you are aware, have succeeded in denying to the Germans an important source of manganese, and the denial to the Germans of manganese from Nikopol therefore multiplies the importance to the German war key.

It is obvious that it has now become a matter of grave concern to the United Nations that large supplies of chrome ore continues to move from Turkey to Germany.

How the Germans can be denied further access to Turkish chrome ore can best be decided by you. I know of your inventive genius and I hope you will find some method of accomplishing this.

It is my firm belief that you will recognize this opportunity for a unique contribution to what really is the welfare of the world to be made by Turkey.

There is no need to tell you how happy I was in our talks in Cairo, and I feel that now you and I can talk to each other as old friends.

Please accept all my good wishes. I am counting on our meeting again in the near future.

A similar telegram is being sent by me to Mr. Churchill

Stalin and Churchill were sent paraphrases of the letter for security reasons; following is the letter to President Inonu as written.

March 10, 1944
My dear Mr. President:

I wish much that you and I were not four thousand miles apart, for I find that there are many matters I would like to talk with you about almost every day of the week.

At the present moment I want to write you about the subject of chrome.

As you know, the Russians by the capture of Nikopol have succeeded in denying an important source of manganese to the Germans. This, therefore, multiplies the importance to the German war machine of Turkish chrome ore, which for many purposes can be substituted for manganese.

You will readily see that the continuation of large supplies of chrome ore from turkey to Germany has now become a matter of grave concern to the United Nations.

You will know best how the Germans can be denied further access to Turkish chrome ore. You have inventive genius and I hope you will find some method!

I am confident that you will recognize this opportunity for Turkey to make a unique contribution to what really is the welfare of the world.

I do not have to tell you how very happy I was in our talks in Cairo. Now you and I can talk to each other as old friends.

I send you all good wishes, and I am counting on our meeting again very soon.

Very sincerely yours,
Franklin D. Roosevelt

Stalin

· 193 ·

March 20, 1944
PERSONAL FROM PREMIER J. V. STALIN TO PRESIDENT F. D. ROOSEVELT
I have received your message which contains the draft of your letter to the Turkish President regarding chromium which Turkey delivers to Germany.

I consider your representation to the Turks quite timely, although I have to say that I have little hope to count on positive results.

Roosevelt

· 194 ·

Roosevelt thought it "would be a great pity" not to have a Russian observer at the upcoming International Labor Organization conference.

March 20, 1944
from the president for marshal stalin
I have just been informed by *Harriman* ~~the United States Ambassador in Moscow~~ that the *Soviet* Union is not planning to participate in the conference of the International Labor Organization to be held in Philadelphia starting April 20.

I have given considerable thought to the role that the International Labor Organization should play in constantly improving the labor and social standards throughout the world. I am anxious that you should know my thoughts on this matter.

It is my opinion that the International Labor Organization should be the instrument for the formulation of international policy on matters directly affecting the welfare of labor and for international collaboration in this field. I should like to see it become a body which will also serve as *an important* ~~the principal~~ organ of the United Nations for discussing economic and social matters relating to labor and an important agency for the consideration of international economic policies which look *directly* toward improvement in standard of living. It would be unfortunate if both our Governments did not take advantage of the conference in Philadelphia to *help* ~~cooperate in~~ developing ~~an instrument to implement these~~ *our common* objectives ~~of the United Nations~~. We could thereby adapt the existing International Labor Organization to the tasks facing the world without loss of valuable time.

I am instructing the United States Government delegates to the Philadelphia Conference to propose measures to broaden the activities and functions of the International Labor Organization and raise the question of its future relationship to other international organizations. In view of your interest in these matters and since there is a great range of social and economic problems that are of common interest to both our governments, I *greatly hope* ~~am convinced that it is extremely important~~ that your government *will* participate ~~in the Conference and in the future activities which I envisage for the International Labor Organization.~~

~~I sincerely hope that your Government will participate in this Conference.~~

ROOSEVELT

Stalin

· 195 ·

On March 21, 1944, Churchill sent a message to Stalin setting forth his position on Poland. Upon receipt of the message Stalin was furious, viewing Churchill's declaration that "all questions of territorial change must await the armistice" as a betrayal of the agreement reached at Tehran, which in fact it was; at Tehran it had been agreed that the Curzon Line would be the Polish border. Both Churchill and Stalin sent Roosevelt copies of the correspondence. Churchill's complete statement follows:

> I shall have very soon to make a statement to the House of Commons about the Polish position. This will involve my saying that

the attempts to make an arrangement between the Soviet and Polish Governments have broken down; that we continue to recognize the Polish Government, with whom we have been in continuous relations since the invasion of Poland in 1939; that we now consider all questions of territorial change must await the armistice or peace conferences of the victorious powers; and that in the meantime we can recognize no forcible transferences of territory.

From: Premier J. V. Stalin
To: President F. D. Roosevelt
March 23, 1944

Since Mr. Churchill, as he informed me, has sent to you a copy of his message of March 21, addressed to me on the Polish question I do not consider it superfluous to send you for your information a copy of my reply to this message.

Copy is enclosed.

From: Premier J. V. Stalin
To: Prime Minister Churchill
March 23, 1944

Recently I received from you two messages on the Polish question and have acquainted myself with Mr. Kerr's statement to Mr. Molotov, made on your instructions on the same question.

I give answers to questions inherent.

It stands out that your message as well as, and particularly, Kerr's statement are interspersed with threats in regard the Soviet Union. I should like to draw your attention to this fact as the method of threats is not only incorrect in the relationship of the Allies but is harmful, as it can bring about reverse results.

The efforts of the Soviet Union in the matter of defending and realization of the Curzon line you qualified, in one of your messages, as a policy of force. This means that now you try to qualify the Curzon line as not rightful and the fight for it as injust. I cannot at all agree with that position. I cannot but remind you that in Tehran you, the President and I came to an agreement regarding the rightfulness of the Curzon line.

You considered then the position of the Soviet Government on this question entirely correct, and you called the representatives of the emigrant Polish Government insane if they reject the Curzon line. But now you are defending something entirely opposite. Does not that mean that you do not recognize any more the matters we agreed upon in Tehran and that by doing this you are breaking the Tehran Agreement? I do not doubt that if you had continued to stand firmly on your Tehran position the conflict with the Polish emigrant Government would have already been solved. As to me and the Soviet Government, we shall continue to stand on the Tehran position and do not think to depart from it, as we consider that the realization of the Curzon line is not a manifestation of a policy of force but is a manifestation of reestablishment of lawful rights of the Soviet Union to those lands which even Curzon and the Supreme Council of the Allied powers still in 1919 recognized as non-Polish.

You state in your message of March 7 that the question of the Soviet-Polish border should be postponed until the peace conference. I think that we have here a certain misunderstanding. The Soviet Union is not at war and does not intend to fight against Poland. The Soviet Union has no conflict with the Polish people and considers itself an Ally of Poland and the Polish people. That is why the Soviet Union is shedding blood for the liberation of Poland from German oppression. Therefore it would be strange to talk about armistice between the USSR and Poland. But the Soviet Government has a conflict with the emigrant Polish Government which is not expressing the interests of the Polish people and does not express its hopes. It would be the stranger to identify with Poland the separated from Poland emigrant Polish Government in London. It is difficult for me even to point out a difference between the emigrant Government of Poland and the like emigrant Government of Yugoslavia, as well as between certain generals of the Polish emigrant Government and the Serbian General [Drazha] Mikhailovich.

In your message of March 21 you inform me that you intend to speak before the House of Commons and make a statement that all questions regarding territorial changes should be postponed until armistice or peace conference of the victorious powers and that until you cannot recognize any transference of territory *effected by force.* As I understand it, you are showing the Soviet Union as a hostile to Poland power and are practically renouncing the liberative character of war of the Soviet Union against German aggression. This is equal to the effort to ascribe the Soviet Union things that do not exist in reality and thus discredit it. I do not doubt that the people of the Soviet Union and the world public opinion will regard such a speech of yours as an undeserved insult to the Soviet Union.

Of course, you are free to make any speech in the House of Commons—this is your affair. But if you make such a speech I shall consider that you have committed an act of injustice and unfriendliness toward the Soviet Union.

In your message you express the hope that the failure of the Polish question will not influence our cooperation in other spheres. As to me, I stood and continue to stand for cooperation. But I am afraid that the method of threats and discreditation, if it will be used in the future as well, will not favor this cooperation.

Roosevelt

· 196 ·

Admiral Leahy and Cordell Hull advised the president that he shouldn't reply to Stalin "until you know what the Prime says in his speech to the House of Commons"; Roosevelt agreed. Churchill did not include the offending phrase in his speech; the following message was not sent.

March 26, 1944

Referring to your message dated March 23, thank you for giving me a copy of your reply to Mr. Churchill. Without reference to the merits, I am sure we are all in agreement that we must constantly keep our eyes on the main objectives and do our utmost to reconcile any divergence of views.

Stalin

· 197 ·

Because the League of Nations had expelled the Soviet Union after it invaded Finland, the International Labor Organization had to sever relations with the League before the Kremlin could allow the USSR to participate.

The trade-unionist organizations were simply following Kremlin orders, in spite of what Stalin wrote.

March 25, 1944

Personal from Premier J. V. Stalin to President F. D. Roosevelt

I share your endeavor toward cooperation of our two governments in working out economic and social matters connected with the tasks of improving working conditions on a world scale. The Soviet Union is unable, however, to send its representatives to the International Labor Bureau

Conference in Philadelphia due to the motives, stated in the letter to Mr. Harriman, as the Soviet trades-unionist organizations expressed themselves against such a participation and the Soviet Government cannot but take into account the opinion of the Soviet trades-unionist organizations.

It goes without saying that, if the International Labor Organization in reality becomes an organ of the United Nations and not of the League of Nations, with which the Soviet Union cannot have connections, the participation in its work also of representatives of the Soviet Union will be possible. I hope that this will become possible and that appropriate measures will be carried out already in the near future.

Stalin

· 198 ·

March 28, 1944

Personal from Premier J. V. Stalin to President F. D. Roosevelt

I have received your message containing information regarding the issuance of passports to Dr. Lange and priest Orlemanski. Although the Soviet transport is considerably overloaded we shall provide Lange and Orlemanski with necessary transport facilities. The Soviet Government is considering the trip of Lange and Orlemanski to the Soviet Union as that of private citizens.

Roosevelt

· 199 ·

March 31, 1944

Personal from the President for Marshal Stalin.

Thank you much for your message of March twenty-fifth. I hope that at the coming meeting the International Labor Organization will make it clear that it is no longer an organ of the League of Nations, and that it will become affiliated with the United Nations. Therefore, I trust that the Soviet Union will have representatives at the following conference.

I will keep you informed of what happens at the Philadelphia meeting.

Roosevelt

Stalin

· 200 ·

From: Marshal Stalin
To: The President
April 6, 1944

I have received your message of April 4 regarding the International Labor Bureau. Thank you for your reply. I believe that the realization of measures on reorganization of the International Labor Bureau will create the necessary conditions for the participation in its work in the future of the Soviet representatives.

Roosevelt

· 201 ·

The racking cough that Roosevelt brought home with him from Tehran never left him. By March it had turned into what Roosevelt called "grippe," accompanied as it was with intermittent temperature and malaise. He was also bothered by headaches. His worried personal physician, Dr. Ross McIntire, called in Lt. Comm. Howard Bruenn of the U.S. Naval Reserve to examine the president. Dr. Bruenn, a cardiologist at the Bethesda Naval Hospital, examined Roosevelt at the hospital on March 27 and found that the president had the early stages of congestive heart failure, as well as acute bronchitis. He prescribed digitalis. He insisted that the president from then on sleep in a hospital bed, which would elevate his head and make breathing easier. He also ordered Roosevelt to cut down on his smoking, lose weight, and drastically reduce his workday—in fact, that he take a complete rest immediately. With some reluctance, Roosevelt agreed to follow the doctor's orders.

On April 8, accompanied by Dr. Bruenn, Roosevelt left for Hobcaw Barony, the legendary Washington insider Bernard Baruch's sprawling twenty-three-thousand-acre plantation in South Carolina at the confluence of the Pee Dee and Waccamaw Rivers, which Baruch put at his disposal.

Churchill suggested to Roosevelt that they jointly write a letter informing Stalin of the particulars of OVERLORD and presented the following, which he suggested Roosevelt might amend. Instead, Roosevelt rejected the draft and wrote his own, which went out over both their signatures. Churchill's rejected draft:

> 1. Pursuant to our talks at Tehran, the general crossing of the sea will take place around the date mentioned in my immediately following, with 3 days margin on either side for weather. We shall be acting at our fullest strength.
>
> 2. Our action in the Mediterranean Theatre will be designed to hold the maximum number of German divisions away from the Russian front and from OVERLORD. The exact method by which this will be achieved will depend on the outcome of the heavy offensive which we shall launch in Italy with all our strength about mid-May.
>
> 3. Since Tehran your armies have gained and are gaining a magnificent series of unforeseen victories for the common cause. Even in months when you thought they would not be active they have gained these great victories. We ask you to let us know, in order to make our own calculations, what scale your effort will take in the 3 months following the date mentioned, when we shall certainly strike. We send you our very best wishes and hope we may all fall on the common foe together.

Roosevelt's cable, which went out over both their signatures, is more to the point, and doesn't ask for military information.

From: The Prime Minister and The President
To: Marshal Stalin
April 18, 1944

1. Pursuant to our talks at Tehran, the general crossing of the sea will take place around a date which Generals Deane and [M. B.] Burrows have recently been directed to give the Soviet General Staff. We shall be acting at our fullest strength.

2. We are launching an offensive on the Italian mainland at maximum strength about mid May.

3. Since Tehran your Armies have been gaining a magnificent series of victories for the common cause. Even in the months when you thought they would not be active, they have gained these great victories. We send you our very best wishes and trust that your Armies and ours, operating in unison in accordance with our Tehran agreement, will crush the Hitlerites.

Roosevelt. Churchill.

Stalin

· 202 ·

———

Personal from Premier J. V. Stalin to President F. D. Roosevelt
and Prime Minister W. Churchill
April 22, 1944

I have received your message of April 18. The Soviet Government is satisfied with your information, that, in accordance with the Tehran Agreement, the crossing of the sea will take place on the date planned, regarding which the Generals Dean[e] and Barrows [Burrows] have already informed our general staff, and that you will act with the maximum forces. I express my confidence in the success of the planned operation.

I have also confidence in the successfulness of the operation being undertaken by you in Italy.

As we agreed upon in Tehran, the Red Army will undertake by that date its new offensive in order to render the maximum support to the Anglo-American operations.

I beg you to accept my gratitude for the expressed by you wishes on the successes of the Red Army. I join your statement that your and our armies, supporting each other, will rout the Hitlerites and will fulfill their historic task.

Stalin

· 203 ·

———

Knox had been the vice presidential nominee in 1936. As part of Roosevelt's effort to enlist bipartisan support for aid to Britain and the draft, he had appointed Knox secretary of the navy in 1940. He died April 28 after a brief series of heart attacks.

From: Marshal Stalin
To: The President
April 30, 1944

I beg you to accept the sincere sympathy of the Soviet Government in connection with the tragic burden brought upon the United States of America in connection with the death of the Navy Minister of the USA, Frank Knox.

Roosevelt

· 204 ·

_____

May 5, 1944
Personal from the President for Marshal Stalin.

   Please accept my *real* ~~sincere~~ appreciation and that of the Government and people of the United States of your kind message in connection with the tragic death of the Secretary of the Navy, Mr. Frank Knox.

Franklin D. Roosevelt

Stalin

· 205 ·

_____

   Stalin sent this unusually friendly and personal message to the president the day he left Hobcaw Barony for Washington. It is possible that Stalin knew that Roosevelt was taking an extended vacation outside Washington for health reasons.

To Franklin Delano Roosevelt,
President of the United States
May 6, 1944
   My dear friend:
   I am extremely grateful for your assistance in permitting Reverend Stanislaus Orlemanski to come to Moscow.
   I wish you health and success.

Sincerely yours,
(Stalin)

Roosevelt and Churchill

· 206 ·

_____

   Roosevelt wanted Stalin to be informed about the delay of ANVIL, the assault on southern France, and suggested that Churchill write a joint message to Stalin informing him. The revisions are Roosevelt's, except for one final change, insertion of the word "planning," made by British chiefs of staff:

May 12, 1944
From: The President and the Prime Minister
To: Marshal Stalin

In order to give maximum strength to the attack across the sea against Northern France, we have transferred part of our landing craft from the Mediterranean to England. This, together with the need for using our Mediterranean land forces in the present Italian battle[,] makes it impracticable to attack the Mediterranean coast of France ~~in conjunction~~ *simultaneously* with the OVERLORD assault. We are ~~considering~~ ~~*expecting*~~ *planning to make* such an attack later, *for which purpose additional landing craft are being sent to the Mediterranean from the United States.* In order to keep the greatest number of German forces away from Northern France and the eastern front, we are attacking the Germans in Italy at once on a maximum scale and, at the same time, are maintaining a threat against the Mediterranean coast of France.

Roosevelt. Churchill.

Stalin

· 207 ·

———

Personal from Premier J. V. Stalin to President F. D. Roosevelt and Prime Minister Winston W. Churchill
May 15, 1944

I have received your joint message. It is clearer for you how and in what sequence to distribute your forces. The principal thing is, of course, to secure complete success of OVERLORD. At the same time I express confidence in the success of the offensive against the Germans that has started in Italy.

Roosevelt

· 208 ·

———

Roosevelt returned to Washington ten pounds lighter, as the doctors had ordered, and finally free of the bronchial infection that had dogged him since December. He sent the following message to Churchill five days earlier than he sent it to Stalin.

May 23, 1944
Personal from the President for Marshal Stalin.

Instead of a tripartite statement to be issued by the Soviet, U.K. and U.S. Governments, what would you think of a statement by me along these lines, to be issued after D DAY?

QUOTE. It has been suggested that the Allied Governments join in a general statement to the German people and their sympathizers emphasizing the landings recently made on the Continent of Europe. I have not been in agreement with this because it might over-emphasize the importance of these landings. What I want to impress on the people of Germany and their sympathizers is the inevitability of their defeat. What I want to emphasize to them is their continuation of the war from now on is unintelligent on their part. They must know in their hearts that under their present leadership and under their present objectives it is inevitable that they will be totally defeated.

Every German life that is lost from now on is an unnecessary loss. From a cold-blooded point of view it is true that the Allies will suffer losses as well, but the Allies so greatly outnumber the Germans in population and in resources that on a relative basis the Germans will be far harder hit—down to every family—than the Allies. And in the long run mere stubbornness will never help Germany. The Allies have made it abundantly clear that they do not seek the total destruction of the German people. They do seek total destruction of the philosophy of those Germans who have announced they could subjugate the world.

The Allies are seeking the long range goal of human freedom—a greater true liberty—political, religious and intellectual; and a greater justice, social and economic.

Our times are teaching us that no group of men can ever be strong enough to dominate the whole world.

The Government and people of the United States—with nearly twice the population of Germany—send word to the people of Germany that this is the time to abandon the teachings of evil.

By far the greater part of the world's population of nearly two billion people feel the same way. Only Germany and Japan stand out against all the rest of humanity.

Every German knows this in his heart. Germany and Japan have made a terrible and disastrous mistake. Germany and Japan must atone reasonably for the wanton destruction of lives and property which they have committed; and they must give up an imposed philosophy of falsity of which by now must be very clear to them.

The more quickly the end of the fighting and the slaughter the more quickly shall we come to a more decent civilization in the whole world.

The attacks which are now being made in the European theater by the Americans, by the British, by the Russian armies and their associates will, we hope, continue with success, but the German people can well realize that they are only a part of a series of attacks which will increase in number and volume until the inevitable victory is completed. UNQUOTE

Churchill has agreed to follow up with a similar message along the same lines.

Roosevelt

· 209 ·

Harriman delivered this message, with the scrolls mentioned in it, to Marshal Stalin.

May 25, 1944
To: His Excellency Joseph V. Stalin
Supreme Commander of the Armed Forces
The Union of Soviet Socialist Republics
Moscow

I am sending to you two scrolls for Stalingrad and Leningrad, which cities have won the wholehearted admiration of the American people. The heroism of the citizens of these two cities and the soldiers who so able defended them has not only been an inspiration to the people of the United States, but has served to bind even more closely the friendship of our two nations. Stalingrad and Leningrad have become synonyms for the fortitude and endurance which has enabled us to resist and will finally enable us to overcome the aggression of our enemies. I hope that in presenting these scrolls to the two cities you will see fit to convey to the citizens my own personal expressions of friendship and admiration and my hope that our people will continue to develop that close understanding which has marked our common effort.

Stalin

· 210 ·

———

Churchill had no objection to Roosevelt's idea of a post-D-day speech to the German people but thought the statement ill timed. He brought Roosevelt's letter before his cabinet, which also worried that the message might be taken by the German people as a peace feeler if sent before the battle was won. Stalin summarily rejected it.

Personal from Premier J. V. Stalin to President F. D. Roosevelt
May 26, 1944

I have received your message regarding the appeal to the German people.

Taking into consideration the whole experience of war with the Germans and the character of the Germans, I think, that the proposed by you appeal cannot bring positive effect, since it is timed to the moment of the beginning of the landing but not to the moment of sign of serious successes as a result of the landing of Anglo-American troops and as a result of the coming offensive of the Soviet Armies.

We could return to the question of character of the appeal itself when favorable circumstances for such an appeal arrive.

Roosevelt

· 211 ·

———

May 27, 1944
Personal from the President for Marshal Stalin.

Referring to my message of May 23 proposing for consideration a message to be issued by me with the purpose of influencing the German people, I am informed now that the Prime Minister of Great Britain and his Cabinet do not approve of the suggestion.

In view of a positive and definite objection by the British Government, and because the proposed statement is not of essential importance, I propose to do nothing at the present time in the way of a statement of that nature.

Roosevelt

Roosevelt

· 212 ·

_____

May 30, 1944
Personal from the President for Marshal Stalin.

The receipt is acknowledged of your message of May 26 regarding my proposal to make a statement designed to influence the German people.

My message to you dated May 27 which evidently crossed yours in transit is in agreement with your opinion that such a statement should not be made at the present time.

Roosevelt

Stalin

· 213 ·

_____

Personal from Premier J. V. Stalin to President F. D. Roosevelt
May 30, 1944

I have received your message informing me that you have decided not to undertake anything at the present time on the matter of appealing to the German people.

Thank you for your information.

Stalin

· 214 ·

_____

June 5, 1944
From Premier J. V. Stalin to President F. D. Roosevelt

The news of the capture of Rome was received in the Soviet Union with great satisfaction. I congratulate you upon this great victory of Allied Anglo-American troops.

Stalin

· 215 ·

The Normandy invasion, Operation OVERLORD, involving more than 5,000 ships and more than 600,000 American, British, and Canadian soldiers, began at dawn on June 6. The Germans, with sixty divisions in France and the Low countries, expected the invasion at the Pas de Calais to the north of where the troops landed and did not put up the devastating defense that Eisenhower feared; within twenty-four hours all beachheads had been secured. The most difficult landing and the worst fighting took place at Omaha Beach.

Stalin was elated. He later described the crossing of the channel and the Normandy landing, Harriman reported, as "an unheard of achievement, the magnitude of which had never been undertaken in the history of warfare."[123] On June 12 Molotov gave Harriman a silver-framed photo of Stalin in uniform with all decorations to send to Roosevelt, inscribed as follows:

To President Franklin D. Roosevelt in memory of the day of the invasion of Northern France by the Allied American and British liberating armies. From his friend Joseph V. Stalin. June 6, 1944

Stalin

· 216 ·

June 7, 1944
Personal to President F. D. Roosevelt from Premier J. V. Stalin

I consider it necessary to bring to your attention that on June 6 in reply to Mr. Churchill's message I have sent him the stated below personal message regarding the plan of the summer offensive of the Soviet troops:

"I have received your communication on the success of the beginning of the OVERLORD's operations. It rejoices all of us and makes us confident of future successes.

The summer offensive of the Soviet troops organized in accordance with the agreement at the Tehran Conference will begin in the middle of

June at one of the important sectors of the front. The general offensive of
the Soviet troops will develop in phases by successive throwing in of
armies into the offensive operations. By the end of June and during July
the offensive operations will become a general offensive of the Soviet
Union.

I pledge to give you timely information about the progress of the offensive operations."

Roosevelt

· 217 ·

Personal from the President for Marshal Stalin.
June 7, 1944

Thank you very much for your message of congratulation on the fall of
Rome, and also for sending me a copy of your message to Mr. Churchill.

All of this makes me very happy.

The news from Northern France is that everything is progressing according to schedule.

I send you my warm regards.

Roosevelt

Roosevelt

· 218 ·

Premier Sikorski had died in a plane accident at Gibraltar in
1943 and been replaced by Stanislaw Mikolajczyk, head of the Polish Peasant Party, who did not share the prevailing antagonism of
the Polish government-in-exile toward the Soviet Union. Mikolajczyk had written the president a long letter in early April emphasizing how much he desired to meet with him. Roosevelt, concerned
that Stalin might misinterpret such a meeting and needing the marshal's undivided attention to be fixed on positioning the Russian
Army to draw off German forces during and after the Normandy
invasion, put off meeting with Mikolajczyk until the day after the
invasion took place. The president gave a dinner in honor of the
Polish premier and met with him four times. He told him that he fa-

vored the return of Lwow to Poland and urged Mikolajczyk to replace some of the people in his cabinet. As a result on June 20 it was
announced that the reputedly anti-Soviet Gen. Kazimierz Sosnkovsky, whom Stalin had objected to in his message of February 16 to
Roosevelt, was to be removed as successor designate to the Polish
presidency, although he continued to serve as commander in chief
of the Polish forces.[124] After this message and another from Churchill, Stalin agreed to meet with Mikolajczyk.

June 17, 1944
For the Ambassador
   Please transmit the following message to Marshal Stalin from the Pres-
ident.

Personal
   As you know, the Polish Prime Minister Mr. Mikolajczyk has just completed a brief visit to Washington. For reasons which Ambassador Harriman has already explained to you I considered his visit at this time to be
necessary and desirable.
   You are aware, therefore, that his visit was not connected with any attempt on my part to inject myself into the merits of the differences which
exist between the Polish Government-in-exile and the Soviet Government.
Although we had a frank and beneficial exchange of views on a wide variety of subjects affecting Poland, I can assure you that no specific plan or
proposal in any way affecting Soviet-Polish relations was drawn up. I believe, however, that you would be interested in my personal impression of
Mr. Mikolajczyk and of his attitude toward the problems confronting his
country.
   Premier Mikolajczyk impressed me as a very sincere and reasonable
man whose sole desire is to do what is best for his country. He is fully cog-
nizant that the whole future of Poland depends upon the establishment of
genuinely good relations with the Soviet Union and, in my opinion, will
make every effort to achieve that end.
   His primary concern is the vital necessity for the establishment of the
fullest kind of collaboration between the Red Army and the forces of the
Polish Underground in the common struggle against our enemy. He believes that coordination between your Armies and the organized Polish
Underground is a military factor of the highest importance not only to
your Armies in the East but also to the main task of finishing off by our
combined efforts the Nazi beast in lair.

My impression is that the Prime Minister is thinking only of Poland and the Polish people and will not allow any petty considerations to stand in the way of his efforts to reach a solution with you. In fact it is my belief that he would not hesitate to go to Moscow, if he felt that you would welcome such a step on his part, in order to discuss with you personally and frankly the problems affecting your two countries particularly the urgency of immediate military collaboration. I know you will understand that in making this observation I am in no way attempting to press upon you my personal views in a matter which is of special concern to you and your country. I felt, however, that you were entitled to have a frank account of the impressions I received in talking with the Polish Prime Minister.

Stalin

· 219 ·

———

Admiral Leahy was so pleased with the following message that he directed the Map Room to start a new "Stalin" file as "the first of its kind to give us official information of their battles."

Stalin had agreed at Tehran to launch a major Red Army offensive immediately after the Normandy invasion to pin down the German divisions on the eastern front. The offensive began the day following this message.

Personal to President F. D. Roosevelt from Premier J. V. Stalin
June 21, 1944

I have the opportunity to inform you that not later than in a weeks time will begin the second turn of the summer offensive of the Soviet troops. In this offensive will participate 130 divisions, including armored-tank divisions. I and my colleagues count on serious success. I hope that our offensive will render substantial support to the operations of the Allied troops in France and Italy.

Roosevelt

· 220 ·

___

June 22, 1944

Personal from The President for Marshal Stalin.

Thank you for your message of June 21st. Your *good* action together with out efforts on the Western Front should quickly put the Nazis in a very difficult position.

Roosevelt

Stalin

· 221 ·

___

Stalin had no personal objection to Mikolajczyk, but his plans for a Polish government called for the posts of minister of war, foreign affairs, and internal affairs to go to the USSR-controlled Polish Committee of National Liberation, the so-called Lublin government: he wanted control.[125]

June 24, 1944

From: Premier J. V. Stalin

To: President F. D. Roosevelt

Thank you for the information regarding your meeting with Mr. Mikolajczyk.

If to bear in mind the establishment of military cooperation between the Red Army and the fighting against Hitlerite invaders forces of the Polish underground movement, then this, undoubtedly, is now an essential matter for the final rout of our common foe.

Great significance, of course, has in this respect the correction solution of the question of Soviet-Polish relations. You are familiar with the point of view of the Soviet Government and its endeavor to see Poland strong, independent and democratic, and the Soviet-Polish relations—good neighborly and based upon durable friendship. The Soviet Government sees the most important premises of this in the reorganization of the émigré Polish Government, which would provide the participation in it of Polish statesmen in England, as well as Polish statesmen in the United States and the USSR, and especially Polish democratic statesmen in Poland itself, and also in the recognition by the Polish Government of the Curzon Line as the new border between the USSR and Poland.

It is necessary to say however, that from the statement of Mr. Mikolajczyk in Washington is not seen that he makes in this matter any steps forward. That is why it is difficult for me at the present moment to express any opinion in respect to Mr. Mikolajczyk's trip to Moscow.

Your opinion on the question of Soviet-Polish relations and your efforts in this matter are highly valued by all of us.

Roosevelt

· 222 ·

It was reported that tens of thousands of Germans were killed and captured at Vitebsk.

June 27, 1944
Personal from the President for Marshal Stalin.

I have been made very happy by the news of your major victory at Vitebsk and send herewith my congratulations to you personally and to your gallant Army.

Roosevelt

Stalin

· 223 ·

Premier Stalin for the President
June 27, 1944

I have received your message concerning the scrolls of honor for Stalingrad and Leningrad. The scrolls will be sent to the addressees. I made the following statement in receiving the scrolls.

I accept the Scrolls of Honor from the President as a symbol of the fruitful collaboration between our Governments which is being effected in the name of the freedom of our peoples and the progress of humanity. The Scrolls of Honor will be presented to representatives of Leningrad and Stalingrad.

Please accept my sincere appreciation of your high estimation of the efforts of Stalingrad and Leningrad in the struggle with the German invaders.

Stalin

· 224 ·

_____

British forces, under General Montgomery, had failed in their efforts to take Caen and were stopped in their tracks. General Bradley, although hampered by lack of supplies due to Channel storms, finally managed to take Cherbourg. Stalin sent this message immediately, the day of Bradley's victory.

June 27, 1944
Personal to President F. D. Roosevelt from Premier J. V. Stalin
My warm congratulations go to you on the liberation of Cherbourg from the German usurpers. The valiant American and British troops are greeted by me on the occasion of their brilliant success.

Roosevelt

· 225 ·

_____

June 27, 1944
Personal from the President for Marshal Stalin,
I have been made very happy by the news of your major victory at Vitebsk and send herewith my congratulations to you personally and to your gallant Army.
Roosevelt

Stalin

· 226 ·

_____

Personal to President F. D. Roosevelt from Premier J. V. Stalin
June 30, 1944
I, personally, thank you and thank you in the name of the Red Army for the greetings on the occasion of liberation of Vitebsk by the Soviet troops.

Roosevelt

· 227 ·

On July 11, the eve of the Democratic national convention, Roosevelt finally announced, as the media had been predicting for months, that he would indeed run for an unprecedented fourth term: "If the people elect me, I will serve."[126] On July 14 he left on a trip to Hawaii and the Aleutian Islands, proceeding west in a private Pullman car accompanied by a huge delegation that included his wife and daughter, his two doctors, Vice Admiral McIntire and Lieutenant Commander Bruenn, as well as Admiral Leahy, reporters, speech writers, secretaries, Secret Service agents, navy cooks and waiters, his valet, and even Fala, his dog. There were several reasons for the trip: one was so that the president could be in Chicago, where the Democratic convention was taking place, in case there were problems with the selection of Harry Truman as the vice presidential candidate (in which case he could make an appearance), but an equally compelling reason for the journey was to meet with Admiral Nimitz and General MacArthur in Honolulu to settle the dispute between them about strategy in the war against Japan. And, of course, the president loved sea voyages.

After the train left Chicago and was rolling along somewhere in the Southwest, Roosevelt dictated the following message. When Harriman received it he recommended that one sentence be deleted because it implied that it was dangerous for Stalin to fly over enemy-occupied territory. Roosevelt approved Harriman's suggestion and crossed out the words himself. Harriman delivered the revised message to Stalin on July 19.

July 17, 1944
Personal from the President for Marshal Stalin.

Things are moving so fast and so successfully that I feel there should be a meeting between you and Mr. Churchill and me in the reasonably near future. The Prime Minister is in hearty accord with this thought. I am now on a trip in the far West and must be in Washington for several weeks on my return. It would, therefore, be best for me to have a meeting between the tenth and fifteenth of September. The most central point for you and me would be the north of Scotland. I could go by ship and you could come either by ship or by plane. ~~Your Army is doing so magnificently that the hop would be much shorter to Scotland than the one taken by Molotov two years ago.~~ I hope you can let me have your thoughts. Secrecy and security can be maintained either aboard ship or on shore.

Roosevelt

Roosevelt

· 228 ·

———

The mail pouch from Washington caught up with Roosevelt in San Diego. While there and viewing a practice amphibious landing exercise at Camp Pendleton he got what he called "the collywobbles," probably an attack of dysentery, but he felt better the next day.

On July 20, as Hitler was leaning over a conference table at headquarters, a group of German officers managed to explode a bomb very close to him. Thirteen members of the German staff were injured, four died, but Hitler was unharmed. The leader of the assassination attempt, Col. Claus von Stauffenberg, the former ambassador to the Soviet Union, was executed.

On June 15 armored amphibian boats landed nearly 100,000 U.S. troops—soldiers, marines, and Seabees—onto the beaches of Saipan in the Mariana Islands. In the ensuing battle virtually the entire Japanese garrison died, but the cost was high: 3,426 Americans were killed and 14,000 wounded before the island was secured in mid-July. Saipan was key because it put Tokyo within range of American B-29 bombers.

Meanwhile, the Soviet army was storming through Byelorussia, liberating its capital, Minsk, and capturing huge numbers of Germans. On July 17, 57,000 captured German soldiers, led by their generals and officers, were marched through Moscow.

Roosevelt dictated this message before he boarded the USS *Baltimore,* bound for Honolulu.

July 21, 1944

My dear Marshal:

Just as I was leaving on this trip to the Pacific I received the very de-lightful framed photograph of you which I consider excellent. I am partic-ularly happy to have it and very grateful to you.

The speed of the advance of your armies is amazing and I wish much that I could visit you to see how you are able to maintain your communi-cations and supplies to the advancing troops.

We have taken the key island of Saipan after rather heavy losses and are at this moment engaged in the occupation of Guam. At the same time, we have just received news of the difficulties in Germany and especially at Hitler's headquarters. It is all to the good.

With my very warm regards, I am

Very sincerely yours,
Franklin D. Roosevelt

Stalin

· 229 ·

July 22, 1944

Personal from Premier Stalin to President F. D. Roosevelt

I share your thought about the desirability of a meeting between you, Mr. Churchill, and myself.

However, I must say, that now, when the Soviet Armies are involved in battles on such a wide front, it would be impossible for me to leave the country and depart for a certain period of time from the conducting of front matters. All my colleagues consider it absolutely impossible.

Stalin

· 230 ·

Even Harriman looked on the Polish government-in-exile with a wary eye, characterizing it as dominated by a group of aristocrats intent on getting back their landed properties. Not surprisingly, Stalin viewed the return of Poland to this government as unaccept-able. But Stalin was aware that the government-in-exile, the legitimate government of Poland, was backed by Roosevelt and Churchill and that as a consequence he had to make some sort of rapprochement between it and the Lublin government. As Stalin had been genuinely surprised to learn, Stanislaw Mikolajczyk, the new premier of the government-in-exile, who was in Moscow waiting to meet with him, was peasant born.

The Russian Army was advancing at a stupendous rate; on July 18 it swept across the Curzon Line. On July 23, the day of the following message, the Russian army entered Lublin, Poland, and viewed, on its outskirts, Maidenak, the camp built by the Third Reich for the efficient mass extinction of human life by gassing of those it considered unsuitable. Russians and Poles toured the crematorium encircled by a mix of white ash and small human bones, the warehouse containing such things as gold fillings extracted from corpses, prisoners' toys, boots and shoes waiting to be shipped to Germany, and, some distance away, the cabbages being grown under the mantle of human ash. "The effect of Maidenak was to be enormous, not least in the Red Army," wrote Werth.[127]

Personal from Premier J. V. Stalin to President F. D. Roosevelt
July 23, 1944
    I am sending you for your information the text of my message to Prime Minister W. Churchill on the Polish question.

Personal from Premier J. V. Stalin to Prime Minister W. Churchill
    I have received your message of July 20. I am writing now only on the Polish question.

    The events at our front are proceeding at an extremely rapid rate. Lublin, one of the big cities of Poland[,] was occupied today by our troops which continue to advance.

    Under these circumstances we are confronted in practice with the question of administration on Polish territory. We do not want and we will not establish our administration of the territory of Poland as we do not want to interfere with the internal matters of Poland. This should be done by the Poles themselves. Therefore, we deemed it necessary to establish contact with the Polish Committee of National Liberation, recently created by the National Council of Poland, which has been formed in Warsaw at the end of last year from among representatives of democratic parties and groups, about which you must already have been informed by your Ambassador from Moscow. The Polish Committee of National Liberation intends to take up the creation of an administration on Polish territory, and this will, I hope, be realized. In Poland we did not find any other forces which could create the Polish administration. The so-called underground organizations guided by the Polish Government in London, proved themselves ephemeral, deprived of influence. I cannot consider the Polish Committee as Government of Poland, but it is possible that in the future it will serve as kernel for the formation of a provisionary Polish government from democratic forces.

As regards Mikolajczyk, I, of course, shall not refuse to accept him. It would, however, be better if he would get in touch with the Polish National Committee which regards Mikolajczyk favorably.

Roosevelt

· 231 ·

_____

July 27, 1944
Personal from the President to Marshal Stalin

I have received your telegram about the Polish question and I hear from the Prime Minister that Mikolajczyk is leaving to call on you. It goes without saying that I greatly hope you can work this whole matter out with him to the best advantage of our common effort.

Roosevelt

Roosevelt

· 232 ·

_____

July 27, 1944
For Marshal Stalin from the President

I can fully understand the difficulty of your coming to a conference with the Prime Minister and me in view of the rapid military progress now being made but I hope you can keep such a conference very much in mind and that we can meet as early as possible. Such a meeting would help me domestically and we are approaching the time for further strategical decisions.

Roosevelt

Stalin

· 233 ·

On July 29 the Russian Army, having advanced almost three hundred miles in a month, reached the east bank of the Vistula River; on the other side lay Warsaw. Exhausted, the army stopped.

At five P.M. on August 1, intercepting a coded German radio message stating that the Fourth German Panzer Army was retreating across the Vistula, Gen. Tadeusz Bor-Komorowski and an army of some 35,000 Poles, armed only with handguns and short of ammunition, rose up and began fighting the Nazis for their city. They were met by SS units, convicts, and Russian renegades, according to Simon Sebag Montefiore in *Stalin: The Court of the Red Tsar,* in addition to three new army divisions that Hitler had ordered to raze the city. Instead of asking the Red Army for help, however, according to Harriman, General Bor-Komorowski"directed his appeals to London." Although it was not clear to the world, the Russian Army in its pell-mell advance had outrun its supplies and had no boats or bridges with which to cross the Vistula, five to six hundred yards wide at Warsaw. Montifiore recounts that "Stalin pressured the generals—could their armies advance? Zhukov and [Marshal Konstantin] Rokossovsky said they must rest. Stalin seemed angry." The situation was complicated by Stalin's refusal to admit that his army was insufficiently prepared, and by the satisfaction he took at the outcome of the uprising. As Harriman observed, Stalin "thought of them [the Polish Army] as enemies of the Soviet Union, as indeed many of their leaders were." The result was that the German Army killed or wounded nearly 250,000 Poles and torched the city, while the world watched in horror.[128]

From: Marshal Stalin
To: The President
August 2, 1944

I have received your messages of July 28.

I share you opinion regarding the significance which our meeting could have, but circumstances, connected with military operations on our front about which I wrote previously, do not allow me, to my regret[,] to count on an opportunity of such a meeting in the nearest future.

As regards the Polish question, the matter depends, first of all, on the Poles themselves and on the capability of these or other persons from the Polish émigré government to cooperate with the already functioning in Poland Polish Committee of National Liberation around which more and more are rallying the democratic forces of Poland. On my part, I am ready to render to all Poles any possible assistance in this matter.

Stalin

· 234 ·

Mikolajczyk was offered the post of premier of the new Communist-dominated Polish government, but the London government-in-exile was offered in total only four of the eighteen cabinet seats.

Stalin met with Mikolajczyk on August 3, two days after the doomed Warsaw uprising, at which time Stalin told him that he had to come to an understanding with the Lublin Poles. "We cannot tolerate two governments," he said.[129] At his final meeting with Stalin, Mikolajczyk was assured by the marshal that a Soviet communications officer would be parachuted into Warsaw to coordinate efforts to air-drop supplies.

Stanislaw Grabski was head of the Soviet-backed Polish National Council, Tadeusz Romer foreign minister of the Polish government-in-exile, Boleslaw Bierut and Edward B. Morawski the heads of the Lublin government.

Stalin sent the identical cable, minus the last paragraph about Lange, to Churchill.

From: Marshal Stalin
To: The President
August 9, 1944
I wish to inform you about my meeting with Mikolajczyk, Grabski and Romer. My talk with Mikolajczyk convinced me that he has unsatisfactory information about affairs in Poland. At the same time, I was left with the impression that Mikolajczyk is not opposed to the finding of ways to unite the Poles.

As I did not consider it possible to press any decision on the Poles, I suggested to Mikolajczyk that he and colleagues should meet and themselves discuss their questions with representatives of the Polish Committee of National Liberation and, above all, the question of the speediest possible union of all the democratic forces of Poland on liberated Polish territory. These meetings have taken place. I have been informed about them by both sides. The delegation of the National Committee proposed that the 1921 Constitution should be taken as the basis of the activity of the Polish Government, and, in the event of agreement, offered Mikolajczyk's group four portfolios, among them the post of Prime Minister for Mikolajczyk. Mikolajczyk, however, could not bring himself (literally—could not decide) to give his agreement to this. Unfortunately, these meetings have not yet led to the desired results, but they have all the same had a positive significance, inasmuch as they have permitted both Mikolajczyk and also Morawski and Bierut, who had only just arrived from Warsaw, to inform each other in a broad way about their points of view and especially of the fact that both the Polish National Committee and Mikolajczyk expressed the wish to work together and to seek the practical possibilities to that end. One may consider this as the first stage in relations between the Polish Committee and Mikolajczyk and his colleagues. We shall hope that the business will go better in the future.

I have information that the Polish Committee of National Liberation in Lublin has decided to invite Professor Lange to join its body as a Director on Foreign Affairs. If Lange, well-known Polish democratic leader, could get the opportunity to come to Poland to take this post, this would be, undoubtedly, in the interests of consolidation of the Poles and in the interest of struggle against our common foe. I hope that you share this opinion and, on your part, will not refuse the necessary support in this matter, which is of such great significance to the cause of the Allies.

Roosevelt

· 235 ·

On August 12 Ambassador Harriman told Undersecretary of State Edward R. Stettinius what he had learned in a talk with Molotov, which Stettinius summarized as follows to Roosevelt:

Molotov stated Stalin viewed the situation as a definite step forward. He said the Soviets very anxious to see consolidation of the two groups. Molotov said he considered Mikolajczyk "A wise man," that latter had made a good impression, and both groups desired him to be Prime Minister.

Molotov confirmed impression Harriman had received from Mikolajczyk that 1935 constitution, which neither group apparently likes, stumbling block to Mikolajczyk. Molotov seemed to feel London group could work out better representation in a new government than the four places in Committee's proposal.

Molotov referred to Lange matter and Harriman expressed personal feeling this government would not want to become involved.

Molotov confirmed Stalin's promise to help in Warsaw. He stated resistance had started prematurely without Soviet knowledge.

Only discordant note in conversation was Molotov's comment Poles have always been too late and will be too late this time unless they make up their minds promptly.

Harriman feels unquestionably Soviets want to see agreement between Polish groups but will work with Committee regardless and delay by Mikolajczyk group will injure their interests.

Stettinius followed those comments up with the following:

From Stettinius to the President:
August 11, 1944

In regard to the question of Professor Lange there is much more involved in the present suggestion than there was in his previous visit as a private citizen to the Soviet Union, and I do not see how this Government can lend its support or offer any facilities to an American citizen even should he renounce such citizenship, accepting an official post in a Committee which is frankly and openly a rival to the government which we officially recognize. Any such action on our part, apart from its obvious impropriety would be particularly unfortunate at this moment when, as Stalin indicates, the conversations between Mikolajczyk and the Polish Committee offer some prospect of compromise solution.

The desire to have Professor Lange is obviously a tactical move designed to strengthen the claims of the Polish Committee to be recognized as the legal government of Poland, since until Poland is liberated and such government set up, questions of foreign affairs do not arise.

Any disinclination to have Dr. Lange go over now to take a post on this Polish Committee would be without prejudice to any question of his being invited later to accept a portfolio of a Polish government legally constituted as a result of a reconstruction of that government following the present conversations between Mikolajczyk and the Polish Committee.

From: The President
To: Marshal Stalin
August 12, 1944

I am most grateful for your telegram of August 9 in which you were good enough to give me a resumé of Prime Minister Mikolajczyk's conversations in Moscow both with you and with the Polish Committee.

As you know it is my earnest hope that some solution satisfactory to all concerned will emerge out of these conversations, which will permit the formation of an interim legal and truly representative Polish Government.

In regard to Lange, *I am sure you will recognize the difficulty of this Government of taking official action at this stage.* Oof course he as a private citizen has every right under our law to do what he sees fit, including the renunciation of his American citizenship. You will, I am sure, understand why, under the circumstances and particularly pending the outcome of the conversations between Premier Mikolajczyk, whose government we *still* recognize *officially*[,] and the Polish Committee, the Government of the United States ~~cannot in any way~~ *does not want to* become involved in or express any opinion concerning the request of the Polish Committee that Professor Lange join it as head of the Section on Foreign Affairs.

Roosevelt

· 236 ·

President Roosevelt sent the following message to Ambassador Harriman, with a note leaving it up to Harriman to deliver it to Stalin if he thought it would be helpful. Harriman delivered it to Stalin.

August 19, 1944
From: The President
To: Marshal Stalin

I have just seen our commanders in the Pacific Theater. I am highly pleased with the progress that is being made but greatly impressed with the magnitude of the task. Harriman has reported to me your agreement to inaugurate promptly planning for future joint cooperation between our respective forces.

General Deane has told me of the proposals which he submitted to the Red Army General Staff concerning Soviet American collaboration. I hope that you will instruct your staff to pursue expeditiously the joint preparation of plans with the United States Military Mission in Moscow which has been authorized to represent the United States Joint Chiefs of Staff in this planning in preparation for the time when you are ready to act. I feel that there is nothing we could do now that would be of more assistance in preparing to bring the Pacific war to a speedy conclusion.

Roosevelt

Roosevelt and Churchill

· 237 ·

The following message was written by Roosevelt and approved by the prime minister. The American request for approval for a shuttle mission of American bombers from England to drop arms to the Warsaw defenders, bomb nearby German targets, and land in the Ukraine had been turned down. It was "a purely adventuristic affair to which the Soviet Government could not lend its hand," Vishinsky informed Harriman on August 15.[130]

This was Roosevelt's last message to Stalin on the subject of Warsaw. Roosevelt refused Churchill's request to send a second joint message requesting permission to send American planes to help Warsaw defenders. Harriman thought that the United States should persevere, but the State Department and Roosevelt did not.

August 20, 1944
From: The President and the Prime Minister
To: Marshal Stalin

We are thinking of world opinion if the anti-Nazis in Warsaw are in effect abandoned. We believe that all three of us should do the utmost to save as many of the patriots as possible. We hope that you will drop immediate supplies and munitions to the patriot Poles in Warsaw, or you will agree to help our planes in doing it very quickly. We hope you will approve. The time element is of extreme importance.

Stalin

· 238 ·

___

From Premier J. V. Stalin
To: President F. D. Roosevelt
August 22, 1944

I have received your message on the Pacific Ocean matters.

I understand the significance you attach to these matters.

We also attach great importance to your successes there. I am confident at the same time that you are well aware to what an extent our forces are strained in order to secure success for the unfolding struggle in Europe. All this allows to hope that the time is not far off when we shall attain a solution of our urgent task and will be able to take up other questions. I hope that General Dean[e] will already now successfully cooperate with our staff.

Stalin

· 239 ·

___

Personal from Premier J. V. Stalin to President F. D. Roosevelt
and Prime Minister W. Churchill.
August 22, 1944

I have received your and Mr. Churchill's messages regarding Warsaw. I would like to express my considerations.

Sooner or later but the truth about a handful of criminals, who for the sake of seizure of power undertook the Warsaw adventure, will be universally known. These people have used the trustfulness of the Warsawites, having thrown many almost unarmed people under German guns, tanks and aviation. A situation has been created when every coming day is used not by the Poles for the task of liberation of Warsaw but by the Hitlerites, who are inhumanly annihilating the citizens of Warsaw.

From a military point of view the created situation which is attracting increased attention of the Germans to Warsaw is extremely unprofitable for the Red Army as well as for the Poles. Meanwhile the Soviet troops having met lately with new significant attempts of the Germans to develop counterattacks, are making everything possible to crush those counterattacks of the Hitlerites and develop a new broad offensive at Warsaw. There can be no doubt that the Red Army will not spare any efforts in order to crush the Germans at Warsaw and liberate Warsaw for the Poles. This will be the best and real help to Poles—Anti-Naziists.

Roosevelt

· 240 ·

At Dumbarton Oaks in Washington, D.C., on August 21, the United States formally presented the blueprint for the postwar peacekeeping organization to representatives of the governments of England, the Soviet Union, and China. This was the ultimate fruition of Roosevelt's Four Policemen concept and the only time representatives of the four nations convened, although because of Russia's neutrality toward Japan, the conference occurred in two separate stages: the United States, Great Britain, and the USSR met in the first stage, with China replacing the Soviet Union in the second. Directed by Roosevelt, the blueprint was the end result of three years' work in the State Department and was to form the basis for the United Nations Charter. The purpose of this first conversation, as it was called, between the nations, was to secure general agreement on the major principles set forth. It would be further refined at Yalta and the following spring at San Francisco. Undersecretary of State Stettinius, elected permanent chairman of the conversations, headed the American delegation, Sir Alexander Cadogan the British, and Andrei Gromyko the Russian.

The State Department had submitted its "tentative proposals" to the three powers in July. The Security Council, which had primary responsibility for peacekeeping, consisted of the five permanent members—the Four Policemen plus France—and generally held the reins of power.

The Soviet Union had serious qualifications. The Soviets proposed an international air force which the Security Council could authorize to swiftly respond to threats, a request that was eventually dropped. A major stumbling block for the Russians was the British and U.S. proposal that a member of the Security Council could not vote in matters to which it was a party. Gromyko objected to the lack of veto power. According to Stettinius, "He said his government wished to reaffirm that it considers the principle of unanimity of the four Great Powers must be carried out unconditionally."[131]

On Monday, August 28, the Russians revived an earlier proposal: they demanded that all sixteen Soviet republics be members of the world organization. When Stettinius told Roosevelt of this, the president responded, "My God," and instructed Stettinius to tell Gromyko privately that the United States would never agree to it. The last paragraph, in Roosevelt's handwriting, effectively took the proposal off the table as a matter of discussion.[132]

August 31, 1944
Personal from the President for Marshal Stalin.

I am much concerned at the reference made by your delegation at Dumbarton Oaks that the Soviet Government might desire to have the sixteen constituent republics considered for individual membership in the new international organization. Although it was made clear by your delegation that this subject would not be raised again during this present stage of the conversations, I feel I must tell you that to raise this question at any stage before the final establishment and entry into its functions of the international organization would very definitely imperil the whole project, certainly as far as the United States is concerned and undoubtedly other important countries as well. I hope you will find it possible to reassure me on this point.

This would not prejudice later discussion of the question after the organization came into being. The Assembly would then have full authority to act.

> Roosevelt

Stalin

· 241 ·

From: Marshal Stalin
To: The President
September 7, 1944

I have received your message on the question of participation of the Union Soviet Republics in the International Security Organization.

I attach exceptional importance to the statement of the Soviet delegation on this question. After the known constitutional reforms in our country in the beginning of this year, the governments of the Union Republics are extremely alert as to what attitude the friendly states will take toward the adopted in the Soviet Constitution broadening of their rights in the sphere of international relations. You, of course, know that for instance the Ukraine, Byelorussia which area constituent parts of the Soviet Union, by the number of their population and by their political importance are surpassing certain countries in respect to which all of us agree that they should belong to the number of initiators of the establishment of the International Organization. Therefore, I hope to have an opportunity to explain to you the political importance of the question brought up by the Soviet delegation at Dumbarton Oaks.

Roosevelt

· 242 ·

On September 7 Gromyko told Stettinius, "I am 99 percent sure I could clean up everything except the voting procedure and this is a serious matter to us." It was decided that the President should talk to Gromyko. Early the morning of September 8 Gromyko and Stettinius met with Roosevelt in the president's bedroom. Gromyko told Roosevelt that "he would be able to yield on everything else except the voting question, specifically mentioning that he could approve our economic and social council proposal. He also seemed perfectly open minded on the question of the international air force." Gromyko, according to Stettinius, "asked a number of questions . . . and discussed the way in which he could explain our position clearly to his people at home." The meeting ended after a half hour. Roosevelt and Stettinius decided to send a cable to Stalin explaining the matters under discussion.[133]

September 8, 1944
Personal for Marshal Stalin from the President.
    I have just had a pleasant and interesting talk with your Ambassador in regard to the progress of the Dumbarton Oaks talks. There is apparently only one issue of importance on which we have not yet reached agreement and that is the question of voting in the Council. The British and ourselves both feel strongly that parties to a dispute should not vote in

the decisions of the Council even if one of the parties is a permanent member of the Council, whereas I gather from your Ambassador that your Government hold the opposite view. Traditionally since the founding of the United States parties to a dispute have never voted in their own case and I know that public opinion in the United States would neither understand nor support a plan of international organization in which this principle was violated. Furthermore I know that this same view is held by many nations of the world and I am entirely convinced that the smaller nations would find it difficult to accept an international organization in which the great powers insisted upon the right to vote in the Council in disputes in which they themselves were involved. They would most certainly see in that an attempt on the part of the great powers to set themselves up above the law. *Finally, I would have real trouble with the Senate.* For these reasons I hope you will find it possible to instruct your delegation to agree with our suggestion on voting. If this can be done the talks at Dumbarton Oaks can be speedily concluded with complete and outstanding success.

Roosevelt

Stalin

· 243 ·

Personal from Premier J. V. Stalin to President F. D. Roosevelt
September 14, 1944

I have received your message regarding the discussions at Dumbarton Oaks.

I also hope that these important discussions may end successfully. This may be of serious significance for the further strengthening of cooperation of our countries and for the whole cause of future peace and security.

I must say that for the success of the activities of the international security organization of great significance will be the order of voting in the council, having in mind the importance that the council work on the basis of the principle of coordination and unanimity of the four leading powers on all questions, including and those which directly relate to one of these nations. The initial American proposal that there should be established a special procedure of voting in case of a dispute in which one or several members of the council, who have the statute of permanent members, are directly involved, seems to me correct. Otherwise will be brought to naught the agreement achieved among us at the Tehran Conference which is proceeding from the principle of provision, first of all, *the unanimity of agreement of four powers* necessary for the struggle against aggression in the future.

Such a unanimity proposes, of course, that among these powers there is no room for mutual suspicions. As to the Soviet Union, it cannot also ignore the presence of certain absurd prejudices which *often* hinder an actually objective attitude toward the USSR. And the other nations also should weigh the consequences which the lack of unanimity among the leading powers may bring about.

I hope that you will understand the seriousness of the considerations expressed here and that we shall find a harmonious solution of this question as well.

Roosevelt and Churchill

· 244 ·

———

The following was written by the chiefs of staff at OCTAGON, the code name for the second conference at Quebec, just concluded, and presented to Stalin by Ambassador Harriman and the British ambassador, Archibald Clark Kerr.

From: The United States Government and His Majesty's Government
To: Marshal Stalin
September 18, 1944

1. In our conference at Quebec just concluded we have arrived at the following decisions as to military operations.
Operations in North West Europe:

2. It is our intention to press on with all speed to destroy the German armed forces and penetrate into the heart of Germany. The best opportunity to defeat the enemy in the west lies in striking at the Ruhr and Saar since it is there that the enemy will concentrate the remainder of available forces in the defense of these essential areas. The northern line of approach clearly has advantages of the southern and it is essential that we should upon up the northwest ports, particularly Antwerp and Rotterdam, before bad weather sets in. Our main effort will therefore be on the left.
Operations in Italy.

3. As a result of our present operations in Italy

(a) Either [Gen. Albert] Kesselring's forces will be routed, in which case it should be possible to undertake a rapid regrouping and a pursuit towards the Ljubljana gap; or

(b) Kesselring's army will succeed in effecting an orderly withdrawal, in which event we may have to be content with clearing the Lombardy Plains this year.

Our future action depends on the progress of the battle. Plans are being prepared for an amphibious operation on the Istrian peninsula to be carried out if the situation so demands.

Operations in the Balkans

4. Operations of our air forces and Commando type operations will continue.

Operations against Japan

5. We have agreed on further operations to intensify the offensive against the Japanese in all theaters, with the ultimate objective of invading the Japanese homeland.

6. Plans for the prompt transfer of power to the Pacific theater after the collapse of Germany were agreed upon.

Roosevelt. Churchill.

Stalin

· 245 ·

From: Marshal Stalin
To: The President
September 29, 1944

I have received your and Mr. Churchill's message on the Conference in Quebec with information regarding your future military plans. It is clear from your message what important tasks are to be solved by the American and British armed forces. Allow me to wish you and your troops all success.

At the present time the Soviet forces are busy with the annihilation of the Baltic group of German troops hanging over our right flank. Without the liquidation of this group it is impossible for us to advance into Eastern Germany. Besides, our troops have two immediate tasks: to knock Hungary out of war and feel through the German defenses on the Eastern front by an onslaught of our troops, and, under favorable circumstances—to smash them.

Roosevelt

· 246 ·

Roosevelt was loath to have Churchill meet with Stalin without him at this juncture, fearing that they would lock him into decisions regarding the fate of southeastern Europe. But unable to leave the country until after the election, he could do little to stop Churchill, alarmed by Russian intrusions into the Balkans, from making the trip. Roosevelt was about to send Stalin a noncommittal message on the meeting. Before it was dispatched, however, Hopkins heard about the message, went to the Map Room to read it, asked that it be held up, and forthwith went to talk to Roosevelt, whom he found shaving. He pointed out to the president that Stalin might think that Churchill was speaking for Roosevelt. At that, Hopkins reported to Bohlen, Roosevelt became somewhat agitated and instructed Hopkins to stop the message.[134] In its place the following message was sent to Harriman to deliver personally to Stalin, bundled with the instructions to Harriman that follow it.

For Marshal Stalin from President Roosevelt
October 4, 1944
    While I had hoped that the next meeting could have been between you, Churchill and myself, I appreciate that the Prime Minister wishes to have an early conference with you.
    You, naturally, understand that in this global war there is literally no question, political or military, in which the United States is not interested. I am firmly convinced that the three of us, and only the three of us, can find the solution to the still unresolved questions. In this sense, while appreciating the Prime Minister's desire for the meeting, I prefer to regard your forthcoming talks with Churchill as preliminary to a meeting of the three of us which, so far as I am concerned, can take place any time after the elections here.
    In the circumstances, I am suggesting, if you and Mr. Churchill approve, that our Ambassador In Moscow be present at your coming conference as an observer for me. Naturally, Mr. Harriman would not be in a position to commit this Government relative to the important matters which you and the Prime Minister will, very naturally, discuss.
    You will, by this time, have received from General Deane, the state-

ment of our Combined Chiefs of Staff position relative to the war against Japan and I want to reiterate to you how completely I accept the assurances which you have given us on this point. Our three countries are waging a successful war against Germany and we can surely join together with no less success in crushing a nation that I am sure in my heart is as great an enemy of Russia as she is of ours.

Personal from the President to Ambassador Harriman.

The above message will indicate to you that I wish you to participate as an observer.

I can tell you quite frankly, but for you only and not to be communicated under any circumstances to the British or the Russians, that I would have very much preferred to have the next conference between the three of us for the very reasons that I have stated to the Marshal. I should hope that this bi-lateral conference be nothing more than a preliminary exploration by the British and the Russians leading up to a full dress meeting between the three of us. You, therefore, should bear in mind that there are no subjects of discussion that I can anticipate between the Prime Minister and Stalin in which I will not be greatly interested. It is of importance, therefore, that when this conference is over Mr. Hull and I have complete freedom of action.

I will expect you to come home immediately when the discussions are over and, naturally, you will keep Mr. Hull and me fully and currently advised during the talks.

Roosevelt

Stalin

· 247 ·

October 8, 1944

Personal from Premier Stalin to President Roosevelt

Your message of October 5 somewhat puzzled me. I supposed that Mr. Churchill was going to Moscow in accordance with the agreement reached with you at Quebec. It happened, however, that this supposition of mine does not seem to correspond to reality.

It is unknown to me with what questions Mr. Churchill and Mr. Eden are going to Moscow. So far I have not been informed about this by either one. Mr. Churchill, in his message to me, expressed a desire to come to Moscow, if there would not be any objections on my part. I, of course, gave my consent. Such is the matter in connection with Mr. Churchill's trip to Moscow.

In the future I will keep you informed about the matter, after the meeting with Mr. Churchill.

Stalin and Churchill

· 248 ·

At his first meeting with Stalin the evening of the day he arrived in Moscow, Churchill baldly proposed dividing up the Balkans as follows:

> Let us settle about our affairs in the Balkans. Your armies are in Romania and Bulgaria. We have interests, missions, and agents there. Don't let us get at cross-purposes in small ways. So far as Britain and Russia are concerned, how would it do for you to have ninety per cent predominance in Romania, for us to have ninety per cent of the say in Greece, and go fifty-fifty about Yugoslavia?

As this was being translated to Stalin, Churchill wrote out his proposal, adding to it a fifty-fifty split for Hungary and conceding 70 percent of Bulgaria. Then, according to Churchill, Stalin "took his blue pencil and made a large tick upon it. It was all settled in no more time than it takes to set down."[135]

In the first draft of the following cable Churchill wrote in the phrase "having regard to our varying duties among them," but the phrase was deleted after Stalin pointed out that it implied a sphere-of-influence arrangement. When Harriman heard this, he told Stalin that that would please Roosevelt because having all decisions made by the Big Three was of paramount importance. Harriman later told the president that "Stalin said he was glad to hear this, and, reaching behind the Prime Minister's back, shook my hand."[136]

October 10, 1944
To President Roosevelt from Marshal Stalin and Prime Minister Churchill.

1. In an informal discussion we have taken a preliminary view of the situation as it affects us and have planned out the course of our meetings,

social and others. We have invited Messrs. Mikolajczyk, Romer and Grabski to come at once for further conversations with the Polish National Committee.

We have agreed not to refer in our discussions to the Dumbarton Oaks issues, and that the (steps) shall be taken up when we three can meet together.

We have to consider the best way of reaching an agreed policy about the Balkan countries, including Hungary and Turkey, ~~having regard to our varying duties among them~~. We have arranged for Mr. Harriman to sit in as an observer at all the meetings, where business of importance is to be transacted, and for General Deane to be present whenever military topics are raised. We have arranged for technical contacts between our high officers and General Deane on military aspects, and for any meetings which may be necessary later in our presence and that of the two foreign secretaries together with Mr. Harriman.

We shall keep you fully informed ourselves about the progress we make.

2. We take this occasion to send you our heartiest good wishes and to offer our congratulations on the progress of the United States forces and upon the conduct of the war in the West by General Eisenhower.

Churchill. Stalin.

Stalin

· 249 ·

On October 12, after a delay of some days, Harriman learned that indeed Churchill had worked out a spheres-of-influence arrangement during the talks with Stalin. Harriman talked Churchill out of writing Stalin a letter nailing down this understanding, saying "that I was certain both Roosevelt and Hull would repudiate the letter, if it was sent."[137] The matter was never raised again.

October 19, 1944
Personal from Premier J. V. Stalin to President Franklin Roosevelt.

1. During the stay of Mr. Churchill and Mr. Eden in Moscow we have exchanged views on a number of questions of mutual interest. Ambassador Harriman has certainly, informed you about all important Moscow conversations. I also know that the Prime Minister had to send you his es-

timate of the Moscow conversations. On my part I can say that our conversations were extremely useful for the mutual ascertaining of views on such questions as the attitude towards the future of Germany, Polish question, policy in regard to the Balkan States, and important questions of further military policy. During the conversations it has been clarified that we can, without great difficulties, adjust our policy on all questions standing before us, and if we are not in a position so far to provide an immediate necessary decision of this or that task, as for example, on the Polish question, but nevertheless, more favorable perspectives are opened. I hope that these Moscow conversations will be of some benefit from the point of view that at the future meeting of three of us, we shall be able to adopt definite decisions on all urgent questions of our mutual interest.

2. Ambassador Gromyko has informed me about his recent conversation with Mr. Hopkins, in which Mr. Hopkins expressed an idea that you could arrive in the Black Sea at the end of November and meet with me on the Soviet Black Sea coast. I would extremely welcome the realization of this intention. From the conversation with the Prime Minister, I was convinced, that he also shares this idea. Thus the meeting of three of us could take place at the end of November in order to consider the questions which have been accumulated since Tehran. I would be glad to receive a message from you on this matter.

Roosevelt

· 250 ·

By this action Gen. Charles de Gaulle was recognized as the leader of the provisional government of France.

October 20, 1944
Personal for Marshal Stalin

We have been giving active consideration to the diplomatic recognition of the existing French authorities as the Provisional Government of France. The recent enlargement of the Consultative Assembly has made these authorities more representative of the French people. It is expected that in the very near future the French, with the agreement of General Eisenhower, will set up a real zone of the interior which will be under French administration and that when this is done it would be an appropriate time to recognize the French authorities as the Provisional Government of France. I am informing you in advance of our intentions in this regard in case you wish to take some similar action at the time the zone of the interior is set up under French administration.

Roosevelt

Stalin

· 251 ·

October 22, 1944
Personal from Premier Stalin to President Franklin Roosevelt

I received your message of October 21 about the intention to recognize the existing French authorities as a Provisional Government of France and to create an international zone under the French Administration's control. The British Government has also informed the Soviet Government about its desire to recognize the Provisional Government of France. As to the Soviet Government, it welcomes the decision to recognize the Provisional French Government and has already given an appropriate instruction to its representative in Paris.

Roosevelt

· 252 ·

October 23, 1944
Personal from The President for Marshal Stalin.

I am delighted to learn from your message dated October 19 and from reports by Ambassador Harriman of the success attained by you and Mr. Churchill in approaching an agreement on a number of questions that are of high interest to all of us in our common desire to secure and maintain a satisfactory and a durable peace. I am sure that the progress made during your conversations in Moscow will facilitate and expedite our work in the next meeting when the three of us should come to a full agreement on our future activities and policies and mutual interests.

We all must investigate the practicability of various places where our meeting in November can be held, such as accessibility, living accommodations, security, etc., and I would appreciates suggestions from you.

I have been thinking about the practicability of Malta, Athens, or Cyprus if my getting into the Black Sea on a ship should be impracticable or too difficult. I prefer traveling and living on a ship.

We know that the living conditions and security in Malta and Cyprus are satisfactory.

I am looking forward with much pleasure to seeing you again.

Please let me have your suggestions and advice.

Roosevelt

Stalin

· 253 ·

October 29, 1944

Personal from Premier J. V. Stalin to President F. D. Roosevelt.

I have received your message of October 25.

If the idea that was expressed earlier about the possibility of our meeting on the Soviet Black Sea coast appears to be acceptable for you I would consider it extremely desirable to realize this plan. The conditions for a meeting there are absolutely favorable. I hope that by that time it will be also possible to provide a safe entrance of your vessel into the Black Sea. Since the doctors do not recommend to undertake any big trips at the present time, I have to give consideration to that.

I shall be glad to see you as soon as you find it possible to undertake the trip.

Stalin

· 254 ·

November 9, 1944

President Roosevelt

Washington, D.C.

I am sending you my congratulations on the occasion of your re-election. I am sure that under your tried leadership the American people will complete, together with the peoples of the Soviet Union, Great Britain and other democratic countries, the cause of struggle against a common foe and will guarantee victory in the name of liberation of mankind from Nazi tyranny.

J. Stalin

Roosevelt

· 255 ·

———

Roosevelt held his first postelection cabinet meeting on November 10. As he entered, according to Stettinius, "the entire cabinet rose and clapped. The president was very cheerful and looked well. The president said he was like the old man Dante wrote about, who had gone to Hell four times."[138]

November 10, 1944
Personal from the President for Marshal Stalin.

I am very pleased to have your message of congratulations and happy that you and I can continue together with our Allies to destroy the Nazi tyrants and establish a long period of peace in which all of our peace-loving peoples, freed from the burdens of war, may reach a higher order of development and culture, each in accordance with its own desires.

Roosevelt

Roosevelt

· 256 ·

———

November 18, 1944
Personal from the President for Marshal Stalin.

All three of us are of one mind—that we should meet very soon, but problems chiefly geographical do not make this easy at this moment. I can, under difficulties, arrange to go somewhere now in order to get back here by Christmas, but, quite frankly, it will be far more convenient if I could postpone it until after the Inauguration which is on January twentieth.

My Navy people recommend strongly against the Black Sea. They do not want to risk a capital ship through the Aegean or the Dardanelles as it would involve a very large escort much needed elsewhere. Churchill has suggested Jerusalem or Alexandria, and there is a possibility of Athens, though this is not yet sure.

Furthermore, I have at this time a great hesitation in leaving here while my old Congress is in its final days, with the probability of its not adjourning finally until December fifteenth. Also I have to be here, under the

Constitution, to send the Annual Message to the new Congress which meets here in early January.

What I am suggesting is that we should all meet about the twenty-eighth or thirtieth of January, and I should hope that by that time you will have ~~road~~ *rail* travel to some port on the Adriatic and that we should meet you there or that you could come across in a few hours on one of our ships to Bari and then motor to Rome, or that you should take the same ship a little further and that we should all meet in a place like Taormina, in eastern Sicily, which should provide a fairly good climate at ~~this~~ *that* time.

Almost any place in the Mediterranean is accessible to me so that I can be within easy air distance of Washington in order to carry out action on Legislation—a subject with which you are familiar. I must be able to get Bills or Resolutions sent from here and returned within ten days.

I hope that your January military operations will not prevent you from coming at that time, and I do not think that we should delay the meeting longer than the end of January or early February.

Of course, if in the meantime the Nazi Army or people should disintegrate quickly, we should have to meet earlier, though I should much prefer the meeting at the end of January.

A further suggestion as to a place would be one on the Riviera but this would be dependent on the withdrawal of German troops from north-western Italy. I wish you would let me know your thoughts on this.

I hope to talk over many things with you. We understand each other's problems and, as you know, I like to keep these discussions informal, and I have no reason for formal agenda.

My Ambassador in China, General Hurley, is doing his best to iron out the problem between the Generalissimo and the forces in North China. He is making some progress but nothing has been signed yet.

My warmest regards to you.

Roosevelt

Stalin

· 257 ·

On November 21 Secretary of State Hull, who had been ailing for years and seriously ill for months and was in Bethesda Naval Hospital, resigned. Edward R. Stettinius, who had been acting secretary of state, was appointed in his place.

November 23, 1944
From Premier J. V. Stalin to President Roosevelt

It is greatly regretted that your naval organs doubt the expedience of your initial supposition that the Soviet coast of the Black Sea should be chosen as the meeting place for the three of us. The suggested by you date of the meeting at the end of January or beginning of February has no objections on my part, but at the same time I have in mind that we shall succeed in choosing as a meeting place one of the Soviet port cities. I still have to take into consideration the advice of the doctors about the danger of long trips.

I still hope, however, that we shall succeed, if not right now, then somewhat later to agree finally upon an acceptable for all of us meeting place.

I am sending you my very best wishes.

Stalin

· 258 ·

On December 2 Gen. Charles de Gaulle arrived in Moscow for four days of talks with Stalin. The Soviet Union had recognized de Gaulle as the leader of the Free French in 1941, and a squadron of French airmen was fighting bravely and suffering heavy casualties in the war. The Soviets had pressured the United States and Great Britain into early recognition of the de Gaulle government in Paris in August 1944.

De Gaulle, keenly aware that France did not measure up as an equal power in the eyes of Roosevelt and Churchill, tried in this visit to position himself, with Stalin, as representing one of the two military powers on the Continent that would keep Germany in check.

Stalin, according to the minutes of the meetings published by the Soviet Foreign Ministry in 1959, was profoundly unimpressed with de Gaulle, considering him an arrogant Frenchman representing a weak, defeated nation. Stalin first offered him a quid pro quo: "Let the French accept in Paris a representative of the Polish Committee of National Liberation, and we shall sign the Franco-Soviet Pact."[139] De Gaulle, however, after meeting the Lublin Poles, would not go that far. In the end the Russians decided to sign a Franco-

Soviet pact because, according to Alexander Werth, it might help the French Communists. The Communist leader Maurice Thorez, who had sat out the war in Moscow, had just returned to France; he would be appointed a minister of state by de Gaulle.[140]

Churchill, in favor of a tripartite pact between Great Britain, France, and Russia, was against a Franco-Soviet pact.

December 2, 1944
Strictly Personal from Premier J. V. Stalin to President Roosevelt.

According to all data General de Gaulle and his friends who arrived in the Soviet Union, will put two questions.

1. About the conclusion of Franco-Soviet pact of mutual assistance similar to Anglo-Soviet pact.

It is difficult for us to object. But I would like to know your opinion on this question. I ask you to give me your advice.

2. Probably General de Gaulle will raise a question about the change of the eastern frontier of France with expansion of the French frontier to the left bank of the Rhine. It is also known that there is a project about the establishment of the Rhine-Westphalian region under the international control.

It is possible that this control provides the participation of France. Thus the proposal of the French concerning the shift of the frontier to the Rhine will compete with the project of establishment of the Rhine region under the international control.

I ask your advice on this question as well.

I sent a similar message to Mr. Churchill.

Stalin

· 259 ·

December 3, 1944
Personal and Secret From Premier J. V. Stalin to the President, Mr. F. Roosevelt.

The meeting with General de Gaulle gave the possibility for a friendly exchange of opinions on the questions of Franco-Soviet relations. In the course of the conversation, as I had supposed, General de Gaulle, touched two main questions: about the frontier of France on the Rhine and about the conclusion of Franco-Soviet pact of mutual assistance similar to the Anglo-Soviet Treaty.

As to the frontier of France on the Rhine, I expressed the idea that this question cannot be solved without knowledge and consent of our main Allies, whose forces are carrying on the struggle for liberation against the Germans on the French territory. I stressed the complexity of the solution of this question.

In connection with the proposal of a Franco-Soviet pact I pointed to the necessity of close study of this question, the necessity of clarification of juridical nature of such pact, in particular such question of who will ratify this pact in France under the present conditions. Thus the Frenchmen should still give some explanations which we have not yet received from them.

In sending you this message I would appreciate your reply and your comments on these questions.

Similar message I sent to Mr. Churchill.

I send you my best wishes.

Roosevelt

· 260 ·

Roosevelt stipulated that this message be personally delivered to Stalin by Harriman so that Harriman could discuss and explain it to Stalin.

Stettinius's two pages of instructions to Harriman concluded:

We have great confidence in your ability to convince Marshal Stalin of the reasonableness of our views which we feel are fully as much in the interests of the Soviet Union as in those of all other states. We do not, of course, feel that we are in any sense asking simply for a yes or no answer, although we would naturally be highly gratified to ascertain that marshal Stalin agrees with our views. We agree entirely with the view which you emphasized in Washington that, even if you are not entirely successful at this time in persuading the marshal to adopt as his own the views expressed in the President's message, it is essential to keep the issue open and to avoid any crystallization of a negative attitude on the part of the Soviet Government on this vitally significant matter.

December 5, 1944

Personal and Secret for Marshal Stalin from President Roosevelt

In view of the fact that prospects for an early meeting between us are still unsettled and because of my conviction, with which I am sure you agree, that we must move forward as quickly as possible in the convening of a general conference of the United nations on the subject of international organization, I am asking Ambassador Harriman to deliver this message to you and to discuss with you on my behalf the important subject of voting procedure in the Security Council. This and other questions will, of course, have to be agreed between us before the general conference will be possible. I am also taking up this matter with Mr. Churchill.

After giving this whole subject further consideration, I now feel that the substance of the following draft provision should be eminently satisfactory to everybody concerned:

PROPOSAL FOR SECTION C OF THE
CHAPTER ON THE SECURITY COUNCIL

C. *VOTING*

1. Each member of the Security Council should have one vote.

2. Decisions of the Security Council on procedural matters should be made by an affirmative vote of seven members.

3. Decisions of the Security Council on all other matters should be made by an affirmative vote of seven members including the concurring votes of the permanent members; provided that, in decisions under Chapter VIII, Section A, and under paragraph 1 of Chapter VIII, Section C, a party to a dispute should abstain from voting.

You will note that this calls for the unanimity of the permanent members in all decisions of the Council which relate to a determination of a threat to the peace and to action for the removal such a threat or for the suppression of aggression or other breaches of the peace. I can see, as a practical matter, that this is necessary if action of this kind is to be feasible, and I am, therefore, prepared to accept in this respect the view expressed by your Government in its memorandum on an international security organization presented at the Dumbarton oaks meeting. This means of course, that in decisions of this character each permanent member would always have a vote.

At the same time, the Dumbarton Oaks proposals also provide in Chapter VIII, Section A, for judicial or other procedures of a recommendatory character which the Security Council may employ in promoting voluntary peaceful settlement of disputes. Here, too, I am satisfied that recommendations of the Security Council will carry far greater weight if they are concurred in by the permanent members. But I am also convinced that such procedures will be effective only if the Great Powers exercise moral leadership by demonstrating their fidelity to the principles of justice, and, therefore, by accepting a provision under which, with regard to such procedures, all parties to a dispute should abstain from voting. I firmly believe that willingness on the part of the permanent members not to claim for themselves a special position in this respect would greatly enhance their moral prestige and would strengthen their own position as the principal guardians of the future peace, without in any way jeopardizing their vital interests or impairing the essential principle that in all decisions of the Council which affect such interests of the Great Powers must act unanimously. It would certainly make the whole plan, which must necessarily assign a special position to the Great Powers in the enforcement of peace, far more acceptable to all nations.

Neither the Soviet nor the American memoranda presented at Dumbarton Oaks contained specific provisions for voting procedure on questions of this nature. Our representatives there were not, of course, in a position to reach a definite agreement on the subject. You and I must now find a way of completing the work which they have so well carried forward on our behalf.

If you should be inclined to give favorable consideration to some such approach to the problem of voting in the Council as I now suggest, would you be willing that there be held as soon as possible a meeting of representatives designated by you, by me, and by Mr. Churchill to work out a complete provision on this question and to discuss the arrangements necessary for a prompt convention of a general United Nations conference?

Roosevelt

· 261 ·

December 6, 1944
Personal from the President for Marshal Stalin.

Thank you for your two informative messages of December two and December three.

In regard to a proposed Franco-Soviet pact along the lines of the Anglo-Soviet pact of mutual assistance, this Government would have no objection in principle if you and General de Gaulle considered such a pact in the interests of both your countries and European security in general.

I am in complete agreement with your replies to General de Gaulle with regard to the post-war frontier of France. It appears to me at the present time that no advantage to our common war effort would result from an attempt to settle this question now and that its settlement subsequent to the collapse of Germany is preferable.

Roosevelt

Stalin

· 262 ·

————

A twenty-year alliance between France and Soviet Russia was quickly ratified by both countries.

December 10, 1944
Personal from Premier J. V. Stalin to President Franklin Roosevelt

Thank you for your reply on the French question. Together with General de Gaulle we came to a decision that the conclusion of the Franco-Soviet Pact of mutual assistance will be beneficial to the cause of the French-Soviet relations as well as for the European security in general. Today the Franco-Soviet Pact was signed.

As to the post-war border of France, the consideration of this question, as I have already written to you, has been postponed.

Roosevelt

· 263 ·

————

On November 24 Mikolajczyk resigned as prime minister of the Polish government-in-exile, stymied by two problems: the opposition of other cabinet ministers in his government to the ceding of any territory to Russia, and the insistence of the Soviet Union that the Soviet-backed Lublin faction have majority representation in the new government. Churchill had publicly pressured the Polish government-in-exile to accept the Curzon Line, and Mikolajczyk had begged Roosevelt "to throw the weight of your decisive influence and authority on the scale of events."[141] Roosevelt was later criticized for insufficient action on the issue, but Mikolajczyk, according to Hull, told Harriman the day before he resigned that he regretted asking the president to take up the question of Lwow, because even if Stalin had agreed, his colleagues still would not have accepted the boundary.[142]

The House of Commons had taken up the matter, and during the debate Churchill, supporting Mikolajczyk's position, worked out during his trip to Moscow, condemned the Polish Government in London for its unrealistic and inflexible position. Harriman, who did not receive Roosevelt's cable in Moscow until December 20, incorporated the State Department statement which follows it, issued on December 18, into Roosevelt's message.

December 16, 1944
Personal from the President for Marshal Stalin.

In view of the interest raised in this country by Prime Minister Churchill's statement in the House of Commons yesterday and the strong pressure we are under to make known our position in regard to Poland, I believe it may be necessary in the next few days for this government to issue some statement on the subject. This statement, if issued, will outline our attitude somewhat along the following lines.

The proposed statement, as you will note, will contain nothing, I am sure, that is not known to you as the general attitude of this Government and is I believe in so far as it goes in general accord with the results of your discussion with Prime Minister Churchill in Moscow in the autumn, and for this reason I am sure, you will welcome it.

I feel it is of the highest importance that until the three of us can get together and thoroughly discuss this troublesome question there be no action on any side which would render our discussions more difficult. I have seen indications that the Lublin Committee may be intending to give itself the status of a provisional government of Poland. I fully appreciate the desirability from your point of view of having a clarification of Polish authority before your armies move further into Poland. I very much hope, however, that because of the great political implications which such a step would entail you would find it possible to refrain from recognizing the Lublin Committee as a government of Poland before we meet, which I hope will be immediately after my inauguration on January 20. Could you not until that date continue to deal with the Committee in its present form. I know that Prime Minister Churchill shares my views on this point.

                                        Roosevelt

Department of State Press Release December 18, 1944

The United States Government's position as regards Poland has been steadfastly guided by full understanding and sympathy for the interests of the Polish people. This position has been communicated on previous occasions to the interested governments, including the Government of Poland. It may be summarized as follows:

1. The United States Government stands unequivocally for a strong, free, and independent Polish state with the untrammeled right of the Polish people to order their internal existence as they see fit.

2. It has been the consistently held policy of the United States Government that questions relating to boundaries should be left in abeyance until the termination of hostilities. As Secretary Hull stated in his address of April 9, 1944, "This does not mean that certain questions may not and should not in the meantime be settled by friendly conference and agreement." In the case of the future frontiers of Poland, if a mutual agreement is reached by the United Nations directly concerned, this Government would have no objection to such an agreement which could make an essential contribution to the prosecution of the war against the common enemy. If, as a result of such agreement, the Government and people of Poland decide that it would be in the interests of the Polish state to transfer national groups, the United States Government in cooperation with other governments will assist Poland, in so far as practicable, in such transfers. The United States Government continues to adhere to its traditional policy of declining to give guarantees for any specific frontiers. The United States Government is working for the establishment of a world security organization through which the United States together with other member states would assume responsibility for the preservation of general security.

3. It is the announced aim of the United States Government, subject to legislative authority, to assist the countries liberated from the enemy in repairing the devastation of war and thus to bring to their peoples the opportunity to join as full partners in the task of building a more prosperous and secure life for all men and women. This applies to Poland as well as the other United Nations.

The policy of the United States Government regarding Poland outlined above has as its objective the attainment of the announced basic principles of United States foreign policy.

Roosevelt

· 264 ·

The White House

To be sent: December 21, 1944

His Excellency
J. V. Stalin
   Prime Minister of the Union of
      Soviet Socialist Republics,
         Moscow.

It gives me great pleasure on this anniversary of Your Excellency's birth to extend to you my sincere congratulations and best wishes.

Franklin D. Roosevelt

Roosevelt

· 265 ·

Eisenhower thought the Ardennes Forest so heavily wooded as to be impassable, and so he stationed only four divisions to hold the line as the rest of the Allied forces charged ahead to the Saar. On December 16 German forces overwhelmed the four divisions in a surprise attack, capturing 10,000 soldiers and putting the small, vulnerable garrison of Allied soldiers guarding the town of Bastogne in harm's way. Eisenhower asked General Patton to alter direction and relieve Bastogne, which Patton accomplished within forty-eight hours. Low cloud cover had kept planes from attacking the German troops, but on December 23 the skies cleared, Allied planes could again command the air, and within days the tide of battle turned to the Allies. More than 100,000 German and 70,000 Allied soldiers died.

December 23, 1944
Personal from the President for Marshal Stalin.

I wish to direct General Eisenhower to send to Moscow a fully qualified officer of his staff to discuss with you Eisenhower's situation on the Western Front and its relation to the Eastern Front, in order that all of us may have information essential to our coordination of effort. We will maintain complete secrecy.

I hope you will see this officer of Eisenhower's staff and arrange to exchange with him information that will be of mutual benefit. *The situation in Belgium is not bad but it is time to talk of the next plan.*

In view of the emergency an early reply to this proposal is requested.

Roosevelt

Stalin

· 266 ·

December 25, 1944
Personal from Premier J. V. Stalin to President F. D. Roosevelt

I have received your message regarding sending to Moscow a competent officer from General Eisenhower.

Naturally, I agree with your proposal as well as I agree to meet the officer from General Eisenhower and to arrange an exchange of information with him.

Stalin

· 267 ·

December 26, 1944
Franklin D. Roosevelt
President of the United States of America
White House
Washington, D.C.

I beg you to accept my gratitude for congratulations and wishes addressed to me on the occasion of my birthday.

J. Stalin

Stalin

· 268 ·

December 26, 1944
Personal from Premier J. V. Stalin to President F. D. Roosevelt

On December 14 I have received from Mr. Harriman your message. I fully share your opinion that prior to convocation of a general conference of the United Nations on the question of an International Organization we should agree upon the principal questions not agreed upon in the course of the Dumbarton Oaks conversations and, in the first place, on the question of the procedure of voting in the Security Council. I have to remind you that in the original American draft was specially marked the necessity to work out special rules in regard to the procedure of voting in case of a dispute which involves directly one of several permanent numbers of the Council. In the British draft it was also stated that the general order of settlement of disputes between great powers, should such disputes arise, may prove unfit.

In this connection the first and second points of your proposal meet with no objections and can be accepted, bearing in mind that point two deals with procedure questions mentioned in chapter V, subdivision "D."

As regards point three of your proposal I have, to my regret, to inform you that with the proposed by you wording of this point I see no possibility of agreeing. As you yourself admit the principle of unanimity of permanent members is necessary in all decisions of the Council in regard to determination of a threat to peace as well as in respect to measures of elimination of such a threat or for suppression of aggression or other violations of peace. Undoubtedly, that when decisions on questions of such a nature are made there must be full agreement of powers which are permanent members of the Council bearing upon themselves the main responsibility for maintenance of peace and security.

It goes without saying that the attempt to prevent, on a certain stage, one or several permanent members of the Council from participating in voting on said questions, and theoretically it is possible to assume also a case when the majority of permanent members will find themselves prevented from participation in making decisions on a question, can have fatal consequences for the cause of preservation of international security. Such a situation is in contradiction with the principle of agreement and unanimity of decisions of the four leading powers and can lead to a situation when some great powers are put in opposition to other great powers and this may undermine the cause of universal security. In prevention of this small countries are interested not less than great powers since a split among great powers, united for tasks of maintenance of peace and security for all peace-loving countries, is pregnant with the most dangerous consequences for all these nations.

Therefore I have to insist on our former position on the question of voting in the Security Council. This position, as it seems to me, will provide the new International Organization with the unanimity of four powers, contributing to avoiding of attempts to put certain powers in opposition to other great powers which (unanimity) is necessary for their joint fight against aggression in the future. Naturally, such a situation would secure the interests of small nations in the cause of preservation of their security and would correspond to the interests of universal peace.

I hope that you will estimate the importance of the above-stated view in favor of the principle of unanimity of decisions of the four leading powers and that we shall find an agreed upon decision of this question as well as certain other questions which remain still unsolved. On the basis of such an agreed upon decision our representatives could work out a full draft on this question and discuss the measures necessary for an early convocation of a general conference of the United Nations.

Stalin

· 269 ·

Tomasz Arciszewski was an old Socialist, in Stalin's eyes even less acceptable than Mikolajczyk.

December 27, 1944
Personal from Premier J. V. Stalin to President F. D. Roosevelt

I have received your message on Polish matters on December 20.

As regards Mr. Stettinius' statement of December 18, I would prefer to express myself about this during our personal meeting. In any case the events in Poland have considerably moved ahead than it is reflected in the said statement.

A number of facts which took place during the time after the last visit of Mikolajczyk to Moscow and, in particular the radio-communications with Mikolajczyk's government intercepted by us from arrested in Poland terrorists—underground agents of the Polish émigré government—with all palpability proves that the negotiations of Mr. Mikolajczyk with the Polish National Committee served as a screen for those elements who conducted from behind Mikolajczyk's back criminal terrorist work against Soviet officers and soldiers on the territory of Poland. We cannot reconcile with such a situation when terrorists instigated by Polish emigrants kill in Poland soldiers and officers of the Red Army, lead a criminal fight against Soviet troops which are liberating Poland, and directly aid our enemies, whose allies they in fact are. The substitution of Mikolajczyk by Arzyshevsky [Arciszewski] and, in general, transpositions of ministers in the

Polish émigré government have made the situation even worse and have created a precipice between Poland and the émigré government.

Meanwhile, the Polish National Committee has made serious achievements in the strengthening of the Polish state and the apparatus of governmental power on the territory of Poland, in the expansion and strengthening of the Polish army, in carrying into practice of a number of important governmental measures and, in the first place, of agrarian reform in favor of the peasants. All this has lead to consolidation of democratic powers of Poland and to powerful strengthening of authority of the National Committee among the wide masses in Poland and among wide social Polish circles abroad.

It seems to me that now we should be interested in the support of the Polish National Committee and all those who want and are capable to work together with it and that is especially important for the Allies and for the solution of our common task—the speeding of the defeat of Hitlerite Germany. For the Soviet Union, which is bearing the whole burden for the liberation of Poland from German occupationists, the question of relations with Poland under present conditions is the talk of daily close and friendly relations with a power which has been established by the Polish people on its own soil and which has already grown strong and has its own army which together with the Red Army is fighting against the Germans.

I have to say frankly that if the Polish Committee of National Liberation will transform itself into a Provisional Polish Government then, in view of the above-said, the Soviet Government will not have any serious ground for postponement of the question of its recognition. It is necessary to bear in mind that in the strengthening of a pro-Allied and democratic Poland the Soviet Union is interested more than any other power not only because the Soviet Union is bearing the main brunt of the battle for liberation of Poland but also because Poland is a border state with the Soviet Union and the problem of Poland is inseparable from the problem of security of the Soviet Union. To this we have to add that the successes of the Red Army in Poland in the fight against the Germans are to a great degree dependent on the presence of peaceful and trustworthy rear in Poland, and the Polish National Committee fully takes into account this circumstance while the émigré government and its underground agents by their terroristic actions are creating a threat of civil war in the rear of the Red Army and counteract the successes of the latter. On the other hand, under the condition which exist in Poland at the present time there are no reasons for the continuation of the policy of support of the émigré government, which has lost all confidence of the Polish population in the country and besides creates a threat of civil war in the rear of the Red Army, violating thus our common interests of a successful fight against the Germans. I think that it would be natural, just and profitable for our common cause if the governments of the Allied countries as the first step have agreed on an immediate exchange of representatives with the Polish National Committee so that after a certain time it would recognized as the lawful government of Poland after the transformation of the National Committee into a provisional government of Poland. Otherwise I am afraid that the confidence of the Polish People in the Allied powers may weaken. I think that we cannot allow the Polish people to say that we are sacrificing the interests of Poland in favor of the interests of a handful of Polish emigrants in London.

Roosevelt

· 270 ·
_____

This message was the subject of intense discussion between the president, Stettinius, and Charles Bohlen.[143]

December 29, 1944
Personal from the President to Marshal Stalin.

I am disturbed and deeply disappointed over your message of December 27 in regard to Poland in which you tell me that you cannot see your way clear to hold in abeyance the question of recognizing the Lublin Committee as the provisional government of Poland until we have had an opportunity at our meeting to discuss the whole question thoroughly. I would have thought no serious inconvenience would have been caused your Government or your Armies if you could have delayed the purely juridical act of recognition for the short period of a month remaining before we meet.

There was no suggestion in my request that you curtail your practical relations with the Lublin Committee nor any thought that you should deal with or accept the London Government in its present composition. I had urged this delay upon you because I felt you would realize how extremely unfortunate and even serious it would be at this period in the war in its effect on world opinion and enemy morale if your Government should formally recognize one Government of Poland while the majority of the other United Nations including the United States and Great Britain continue to recognize and to maintain diplomatic relations with the Polish Government in London.

I must tell you with a frankness equal to your own that I see no prospect of this Government's following suit and transferring its recognition from the Government in London to the Lublin Committee in its present form. This is in no sense due to any special ties or feelings for the London Government. The fact is that neither the Government nor the people of the United States has as yet seen any evidence either arising from the manner of its creation or from subsequent developments to justify the conclusion that the Lublin Committee as at present constituted represents the people of Poland. I cannot ignore the fact that up to the present only a small fraction of Poland proper west of the Curzon line has been liberated from German tyranny, and it is therefore an unquestioned truth that the people of Poland have had no opportunity to express themselves in regard to the Lublin Committee.

If at some future date following the liberation of Poland a provisional government of Poland with popular support is established, the attitude of this Government would of course be governed by the decision of the Polish people.

I fully share your view that the departure of Mr. Mikolajczyk from the Government in London has worsened the situation. I have always felt that Mr. Mikolajczyk, who I am convinced is sincerely desirous of settling all points at issue between the Soviet Union and Poland, is the only Polish leader in sight who seems to offer the possibility of a genuine solution of the difficult and dangerous Polish question. I find it most difficult to believe from my personal knowledge of Mr. Mikolajczyk and my conversations with him when he was here in Washington and his subsequent efforts and policies during his visit at Moscow that he had knowledge of terrorist instructions.

I am sending you this message so that you will know the position of this Government in regard to the recognition at the present time of the Lublin Committee as the provisional government, I am more than ever convinced that when the three of us get together we can reach a solution of the Polish problem, and I therefore still hope that you can hold in abeyance until then the formal recognition of the Lublin Committee as a government of Poland. *I cannot, from a military angle, see any great objection to a delay of a month.*

Stalin

· 271 ·

———

Roosevelt sent a copy of this message from Stalin to Churchill, prefaced with the comment, "I am not replying to Stalin, but we may discuss the matter at the meeting," and closed with the warning, "I have not told Stalin that my message to him was shown to you."

January 1, 1945
From: Marshal Stalin
To: The President

I have received your message of December 31.

I am extremely sorry that I did not succeed in convincing you of the correctness of the position of the Soviet Government on the Polish question. Nevertheless, I hope that events will convince you that the Polish National Committee has all the time rendered and is continuing to render the Allies, in particular the Red Army, important assistance in the fight against Hitlerite Germany whereas the émigré Government in London is bringing disorganization into this struggle and this is aiding the Germans.

Of course, your suggestion to postpone for a month the recognition of the Provisional Government of Poland by the Soviet Union is perfectly understandable to me. But there is one circumstance which makes me powerless to fulfill your wish. The fact is that on December 27 the Presidium of the Supreme Soviet of the USSR to an appropriate request of the Poles has already informed them that it intends to recognize the Provisional Government of Poland as soon as it is formed. This circumstance makes me powerless to fulfill your wish.

Permit me to congratulate you on the New Year and to wish you health and success.

Stalin

Stalin

· 272 ·

———

The Russian offensive against Warsaw began on January 12. The Red Army quickly broke through German lines and entered the city on January 17 to find total destruction. "Nothing was left but ruins and ashes covered by snow. Badly starved and exhausted residents were making their way home," wrote a Russian soldier. Only 162,000 of the 1,310,000 prewar inhabitants were left.[144]

Meanwhile, American forces were desperately fighting the Wehrmacht in the Ardennes Forest in Belgium in what became known as the Battle of the Bulge, into which Hitler threw all his remaining soldiers.

To Air Marshal Arthur Tedder, Eisenhower's chief of staff, who arrived in Moscow on January 15, Stalin attempted to portray the Red Army offensive as timed to help the Allied armies caught in the Battle of the Bulge, but in fact Washington knew that the timing was helpful but coincidental. Wrote Admiral Leahy in his diary on January 1, "There is a feeling in this country that the effort of Russia in Poland has been and is being delayed to obtain political advantage, but from confidential information in my possession it appears practically certain that a Russian offensive in Poland will start in the very near future."[145]

January 15, 1945
From: Marshal Stalin
To: The President

Today, on January 15, I had a conversation with Marshal Tedder and the generals who accompanied him. As it seems to me, mutual information is sufficiently complete. The exhaustive answers have been given on the matters in question by both sides. I should say that Marshal Tedder makes the most favorable impression.

After four days of offensive operations on the Soviet German front, now I have a possibility to inform you that in spite of unfavourable weather the offensive of the Soviet troops is going on satisfactorily. The whole Central Front from the Carpathians to the Baltic Sea is moving westward. Although the Germans are resisting desperately, they, however, are forced to retreat. I have no doubt that the Germans will have to disperse their reserves between two fronts, as a result they will be obliged to abandon the offensive on the Western front. I am glad that these circumstances will relieve the situation of the Allied troops in the West and will accelerate the preparation of the offensive planned by General Eisenhower.

As to the Soviet troops, you may be sure, that they in spite of existing difficulties will do everything in their power so that the blow undertaken by them against the Germans would be most effective.

Roosevelt

· 273 ·

___

On January 9 Gen. Douglas MacArthur landed ten divisions at Lingayen on the main Philippine island of Luzon, the biggest assault force up until that time. The fighting was costly, difficult, and slow; thousands of Americans and hundreds of thousands of Filipinos would die before the island and its capital, Manila, were free.

January 17, 1945
From: The President
To: Marshal Stalin

Thank you for your encouraging message dated January 15 in regard to Air Marshal Tedder's conference with you, and in regard to the offensive of your Armies on the Soviet-German front.

The past performance of your heroic soldiers and their already demonstrated efficiency in this offensive, give high promise of an early success to our armies on both fronts.

By skillful coordination of our combined efforts, the time required to force a surrender upon our barbarian enemies will be radically reduced.

As you know, America is putting forth a great effort in the Pacific at a distance of 7,000 miles, and it is my hope that any early collapse of Germany will permit the movement of sufficient forces to the Pacific Area to quickly destroy the Japanese menace to all of our Allied Nations.

Roosevelt

Roosevelt

· 274 ·

___

Roosevelt's fourth inaugural, held on January 20 on the South Portico of the White House, was the last occasion when he donned his braces and delivered a speech standing up. Probably for this reason his speech was short, something over five minutes, but according to Hopkins he put more time and effort into its preparation than into any speech he had made in years. Roosevelt wore a light suit, no hat, and no coat although it was very cold. Wrote Robert Sherwood, "I thought he seemed immeasurably better in health and strength and spirits than when I had gone to see him after my return from London four months previously. I had watched him improve steadily throughout the campaign and now, at this Inaugural, I believed he was ready for anything that the next four years might bring."[146]

On the evening of January 22 Roosevelt and his party left Washington by special train on the first leg of the trip to Yalta.

January 22, 1945
Personal, from the President to Marshal Stalin.

I have decided not to have any press representatives at ARGONAUT [code name for Yalta] and to permit only a small group of uniformed service photographers from the American Navy to take the pictures that we will want.

Prime Minister Churchill agrees.

Roosevelt

Stalin

· 275 ·

Roosevelt had known for a month that Yalta would probably be chosen as the meeting place for the Big Three conference, presuming, as he told Stettinius, that Stalin was neither willing nor able to fly. As he explained it to Stettinius, "While he [Stalin] had offered Armenia and Sicily, it would probably end up in [Yalta] which is someplace where all the old Russian palaces used to be."[147] On January 23 the president boarded the USS *Quincy* at Newport News, Virginia, for the four thousand–mile trip to Malta. During the ten-day voyage, the blacked-out ship, escorted by destroyers and guarded by planes, zigzagged continually to elude any enemy submarines. Aboard the *Quincy* in the president's party were his daughter, Anna Boettiger; James Byrnes, then director of war mobilization; Ed Flynn, chairman of the Democratic Party; Adm. William Leahy; both his doctors, Vice Adm. Ross McIntire and Comm. H. G. Bruenn; and press secretary Steve Early.

January 23, 1945
From Premier J. V. Stalin to President Franklin D. Roosevelt

Received your cable regarding the presence of press and photo representatives in ARGONAUT. I do not have any objections against your proposals.

The same reply I sent to the Prime Minister's request.

Roosevelt

· 276 ·

Roosevelt was notified of Ambassador Oumansky's death and wrote this while on board the USS *Quincy*. The message was transmitted to one of the destroyers to send to the Map Room for transmission to the Kremlin; the destroyer detached itself from the other ships before sending it. All radio communications to and from the *Quincy* were handled in this manner so that there could be no hint of the president's whereabouts if a cable were intercepted.

January 26, 1945

Please accept my personal expression of deep regret at the death of your Ambassador to Mexico. We knew Mr. Oumansky well through his service as Ambassador in Washington where he made many friends.

Roosevelt

Stalin

· 277 ·

January 29, 1945
Personal from Premier J. V. Stalin to President F. D. Roosevelt

Thank you for the condolences expressed by you on the occasion of the fatal death of the Soviet Ambassador to Mexico, C. A. Oumansky, whose work was highly valued by the Soviet Government.

Stalin

· 278 ·

_____

January 30, 1945
From Premier Stalin to the President, Mr. F. Roosevelt

Please accept, Mr. President, my heartfelt congratulations and best wishes on the occasion of your birthday.

Roosevelt

· 279 ·

_____

The *Quincy* arrived at Malta on the morning of February 2. Waiting there were Secretary of State Stettinius, Harriman, Harriman's daughter Kathleen, Harry Hopkins, General Marshall, Admiral King, and the prime minister, who remained for lunch. "Conversations at this interesting luncheon," according to Admiral Leahy, were "as usual monopolized by the Prime Minister, who spoke about English problems in war time, the high purpose of the so called Atlantic Charter, and his complete devotion to the principles enunciated in America's Declaration of Independence."[148]

The C-54 dubbed the Sacred Cow transported the president and his personal party to Saki in the Crimea, where Foreign Minister Molotov, Ambassador Gromyko, and Russian military and naval officers waited to receive them. From there a motor caravan drove the president and his party the ninety miles to Yalta on a curving mountain road lined with Soviet soldiers, male and female, each standing within sight of the next, each snapping to salute as the president passed.

Roosevelt was quartered in the enormous Livadia Palace, built by the last tsar and used frequently as the summer palace of the royal family. As the Americans were told, the palace had been left in complete disrepair by the Germans and had been completely renovated in the three weeks before the conference. Stalin and his staff stayed at the Koreis Villa, Churchill at the Vorontsov Villa, twelve miles away. All the Americans assumed that everything they said was listened to; when they wanted to discuss something private, they went outside and spoke standing near one of the water fountains.[149]

February 2, 1945
Personal from the President for Marshal Stalin.

Please accept this expression of appreciation of your kind message of congratulations on my Birthday anniversary.

Roosevelt

· 280 ·

———

On the afternoon of February 4 Stalin and Molotov called on Roosevelt. According to Charles Bohlen, Roosevelt's translator, "Smiling broadly, the President grasped Stalin by the hand and shook it warmly. Stalin, his face cracked in one of his rare, if slight smiles, expressed pleasure at seeing the President again."[150]

This meeting was followed by a meeting of Roosevelt, Stalin, Churchill, and their military staffs. Stalin asked Roosevelt to preside, which he did at this first plenary meeting and all the following ones.

"As we left the conference table that day," wrote Charles Bohlen, "the Americans and the British faced a formidable task in trying to salvage anything on Poland. We were up against a simple fact: the Red Army held most of the country; Stalin had the power to enforce his will. But the President would not give up so easily."[151]

Before the third afternoon plenary session on February 6, Roosevelt wrote the following letter to Stalin on the subject of Poland. Later, at the meeting, he said that there were six or seven million Poles in the United States who wanted Lwow and the oilfields there to be part of Poland, although they accepted the Curzon Line as the eastern frontier. It would make life easier for him at home, Roosevelt continued, if Russia would "give something to Poland."[152] Further, he proposed that Polish leaders be summoned to build a Polish government based on five parties, including the Communists. At the next day's plenary session Molotov gave Stalin's answer: that the Curzon Line be accepted as the eastern Polish border and the Neisse as the western border, that a reorganized Polish government should be formed, that the foreign secretaries (Molotov, Harriman, and Clark Kerr, the British ambassador) "should study a method of enlarging the present government," and that the Polish leaders could not arrive in time for a discussion.[153]

Vincente Witos, the prewar leader of the Peasant Party, had remained in Poland during the German and Soviet occupation; Adam Sapieha was archbishop of Cracow, later cardinal; he also had also stayed in Poland. (See declaration on Poland, page 309.)

[Yalta]
February 6, 1945
My Dear Marshal Stalin;

I have been giving a great deal of thought to our meeting this afternoon, and I want to tell you in all frankness what is on my mind.

In so far as the Polish Government is concerned, I am greatly disturbed that the three great powers do not have a meeting of minds about the political setup in Poland. It seems to me that it puts all of us in a bad light throughout the world to have you recognizing one government while we and the British are recognizing another in London. I am sure this state of affairs should not continue and that if it does it can only lead our people to think there is a breach between us which is not the case. I am determined that there shall be no breach between ourselves and the Soviet Union. Surely there is a way to reconcile our differences.

I was very much impressed with some of the things you said today, particularly your determination that your rear must be safeguarded as your army moves into Berlin. You cannot, and we must not, tolerate any temporary government which will give your armed forces any trouble of this sort. I want you to know that I am fully mindful of this.

You must believe me when I tell you that our people at home look with a critical eye on what they consider a disagreement between us at this vital stage of the war. They, in effect, say that if we cannot get a meeting of minds now when our armies are converging on the common enemy, how can we get an understanding on even more vital things in the future.

I have had to make it clear to you that we cannot recognize the Lublin Government as now composed, and the world would regard as a lamentable outcome of our work here if we parted with an open and obvious divergence between us on this issue.

You said today that you would be prepared to support any suggestions for the solution of this problem which offered a fair chance of success, and you also mentioned the possibility of bringing some members of the Lublin government here.

Realizing that we all have the same anxiety in getting this matter settled, I would like to develop your proposal a little and suggest that we invite here to Yalta at once Mr. Bierut and Mr. Osobk-Morawski from the Lublin government and also two or three from the following list of Poles, which according to our information would be desirable as representatives of the other elements of the Polish people in the development of a new temporary government which all three of us could recognize and support: Bishop Sapieha of Cracow, Vincente Witos, Mr. [Zygmunt] Zurlowski, Professor [Franciszek] Buyak, and Professor [Stanislaw] Kutzeba. If, as a result of the presence of these Polish leaders here, we could jointly agree with them on a provisional government in Poland which should no doubt include some Polish leaders from abroad such as Mr. Mikolajczyk, Mr. Grabski and Mr. Romer, the United States Government, and I feel sure the British Government as well, would then be prepared to examine with you conditions under which they would dissociate themselves from the London government and transfer their recognition to the new provisional government.

I hope I do not have to assure you that the United States will never lend it support in any way to any provisional government in Poland that would be inimical to your interests.

It goes without saying that any interim government which could be formed as a result of our conference with the Poles here would be pledged to the holding of free elections in Poland at the earliest possible date. I know this is completely consistent with your desire to see a new free and democratic Poland emerge from the welter of this war.

Most sincerely yours,
Franklin D. Roosevelt

Roosevelt

· 281 ·

Roosevelt, saying there were two questions of a military nature regarding Europe that he wished to take up with the marshal, handed Stalin the following two memos, in English, with translations into Russian.

Stalin agreed to both requests and promised to give the necessary orders at once.[154]

February 7, 1945

The full potential of the United States air forces now based in South-eastern Italy is not being realized due to excessive distances from the only available bases to targets in enemy territory and bad weather that is frequently encountered over the Alps and the Northern Adriatic. The staging or basing of fighters in the Budapest area would be of particular importance in providing the heavy fighter escort which is now required on deep penetrations and which may be increasingly necessary with the recent revival of German fighter strength employing jet-propelled aircraft. Also, the staging of heavy bombers in the Budapest area would considerably increase the radius of action and bomb tonnage delivered against targets north of the Alps by United States air forces.

Therefore your agreement is requested to the provision of two air-dromes in the Budapest area for use by United States air units. If you agree, our military staffs can begin work on this project at once.

Roosevelt

· 282 ·

February 7, 1945

An urgent need exists for the earliest possible survey of targets bombed by the U.S. Strategic Air Forces, similar to the survey made of Ploesti. To be effective, investigation must be instituted before tangible evidence is destroyed and personnel present during the bombing are removed from the area.

Details of the survey requirements are being passed to Marshal Khud-yakov.

Franklin D. Roosevelt

Stalin

· 283 ·

Koreis, February 9, 1945

Dear Mr. Roosevelt,

Please accept my appreciation for the sentiments expressed by you in the name of the American people and the government of the USA in connection with the tragic death of the Soviet Ambassador in Mexico, C. A. Oumansky, his wife and assistants of the Soviet Embassy.

The Soviet Government accepts with thanks your proposal concerning the bringing to Moscow of their remains on an American military airplane.

Sincerely yours,
[signed] J. Stalin

President Franklin D. Roosevelt, "Livadia" Crimea

Roosevelt

· 284 ·

Roosevelt wrote a similar letter to Churchill, who wrote the following day that he would support him: "I have given consideration to your letter of February 10 about the political difficulties which might arise in the United States in connection with the ratification by the Senate of the Dumbarton Oaks Agreement because of the fact that the United States alone among the three Great Powers will have only one vote in the Assembly."[155] (All three leaders agreed that Great Britain controlled six votes.)

[Yalta]
February 10, 1945
President Roosevelt to Marshal Stalin
My Dear Marshal Stalin:

I have been thinking, as I must, of possible political difficulties which I might encounter in the United States in connection with the number of votes which the Big Powers will enjoy in the Assembly of the World Organization. We have agreed, and I shall certainly carry out that agreement, to support at the forthcoming United Nations Conference the admission of the Ukrainian and White Russian Republics as members of the Assembly of the World Organization. I am somewhat concerned lest it be pointed out that the United States will have only one vote in the Assembly. It may be necessary for me, therefore, if I am to insure whole hearted acceptance by the Congress and people of the United States of our participation in the World Organization, to ask for additional votes in the Assembly in order to give parity to the United States.

I would like to know, before I face this problem, that you would perceive no objection and would support a proposal along this line if it is necessary for me to make it at the forthcoming conference. I would greatly appreciate you letting me have your view in reply to this letter.

Most sincerely yours,

Franklin D. Roosevelt

Roosevelt and Stalin

· 285 ·

The president and the marshal agreed, after some discussion, that the Soviet Union would enter the war against Japan within two or three months after the surrender of Germany, as the Joint Chiefs of Staff had told Roosevelt was imperative to save American lives. In return, Roosevelt agreed to return to the Soviet Union the possessions and privileges that Japan had won from Russia in 1904. Stalin informed Roosevelt that he was going to begin moving twenty-five divisions across Siberia, which would presumably take three or four months. Roosevelt said that after the operation was complete, he would inform Chiang Kai-shek of the details of the agreement. The agreement, with details spelled out, was presented to Churchill the next day. He approved it, recalling later that it was "an American affair. . . . It was not for us to shape it."[156]

February 10, 1945

1. All of the islands of Sakhalin and the Kurile Islands will be returned to the Soviet Republics.

2. The Soviet Government will obtain the harbor of Port Arthur under a lease agreement.

3. Darien will be made a free port.

4. The Soviets will accomplish a lease of the Manchurian railroads such as they had prior to the Japanese invasion of Manchuria.

5. The existing autonomy of Outer Mongolia will be preserved.

6. The Soviet Government will join effort with the National Government of China in its war against Japan.

Stalin

· 286 ·

___

Koreis, February 11, 1945
President Franklin D. Roosevelt
Livadia Palace,
Yalta, Crimea
Dear Mr. Roosevelt:

I have received your letter of February 10. I entirely agree with you that, since the number of votes for the Soviet Union is increased to three in connection with the inclusion of the Soviet Ukraine and Soviet White Russia among the members of the assembly, the number of votes for the USA should also be increased.

I think that the number of votes for the USA might be increased to three as in the case of the Soviet Union and its two basic Republics. If it is necessary I am prepared officially to support this proposal.

With sincere respects
[signed] J. Stalin

Roosevelt

· 287 ·

___

The President sent off this message upon his safe arrival aboard ship.

February 12, 1945
Personal from the President for Marshal Stalin

Upon leaving the hospitable shores of the Soviet Union, I wish again to tell you how deeply grateful I am for the many kindnesses which you showed me while I was your guest to the Crimea. I leave greatly heartened as a result of the meeting between you, the Prime Minister and myself. I am sure that the peoples of the world will regard the achievements of this meeting, not only with approval, but as a genuine assurance that our three great nations can work as well in peace as they have in war.

Roosevelt

Roosevelt

· 288 ·

February 23, 1945
His Excellency Joseph V. Stalin
    Supreme Commander of the Armed Forces
        Of the Union of Soviet Socialist Republics
    In anticipation of our common victory against the Nazi oppressors, I wish to take this opportunity extend my heartiest congratulations to you as Supreme Commander on this the twenty-seventh anniversary of the founding of the Red Army.

The far reaching decisions we took at Yalta will hasten victory and the establishment of a firm foundation for a lasting peace. The continued outstanding achievements of the Red Army together with the all-out effort of the United Nations forces in the south and the west assure the speedy attainment of our common goal—a peaceful world based upon mutual understanding and cooperation.

Franklin D. Roosevelt

Stalin

· 289 ·

February 27, 1945
Franklin D. Roosevelt President of the United States of America
White House, Washington, D.C.
    I beg you, Mr. President, to accept my thanks for your friendly greeting on the occasion of the 27th Anniversary of the Red Army. I am confident that the further strengthening of the collaboration between our countries having found its expression in the decisions of the Crimean Conference will shortly bring about the complete collapse of our common enemy and the establishment of a stable peace based on the principle of the cooperation of all freedom-loving peoples.

J. Stalin

Roosevelt

· 290 ·

It had been agreed months earlier that all Soviet citizens liberated by the United States and all American citizens liberated by the Soviets would be held separately until they were repatriated, which to General Deane, in charge of providing clothing, food, and medicine for the many wounded American prisoners of war held in German prisons in Poland, meant immediate access to the Americans as they were released. This wasn't happening. Healthy Americans, having heard that they would encounter "hardships" in Soviet repatriation camps, were hitchhiking across Poland, were forced to bum rides and hide out until they reached Moscow, and were reporting that groups of Americans were stuck throughout Poland in need of help. General Deane requested of General [K. D.] Golubev, administrator of the Russian Repatriation Commission, permission to send small contact teams as close behind the Russian lines in Poland as possible and to fly in medical supplies to the American hospital at Poltava in the Ukraine. Golubev, constantly revising his figures as to how many American prisoners there were, finally, hesitantly, on February 19 told Deane that Odessa, in the Ukraine, had to be the assembling point for released Americans and allowed one small group of American officers to go to one location in Poland: Lublin. The American officers, once in Lublin, were not allowed to leave the city and were subjected to a variety of restrictions, although they were allowed to remain until all the former American prisoners of war were on their way to Odessa.[157]

March 3, 1945
From the President to Marshal Stalin

I have reliable information regarding the difficulties which are being encountered in collecting, supplying and evacuating American ex-prisoners of war and American aircraft crews who are stranded east of the Russian lines. It is urgently requested that instructions be issued authorizing ten American aircraft with American crews to operate between Poltava and places in Poland where American ex-prisoners of war and stranded airmen may be located. This authority is requested for the purpose of providing supplementary clothing, medical and food supplies for all American soldiers, to evacuate stranded aircraft crews and liberated prisoners of war, and especially to transfer the injured and sick to the American hospital at Poltava. I regard this request to be of the greatest importance not only for humanitarian reasons but also by reason of the intense interest of the American public in the welfare of our ex-prisoners of war and stranded aircraft crews. Secondly on the general matter of prisoners of war in Germany I feel that we ought to do something quickly. The number of these prisoners of war, Russian, British and U.S., is very large. In view of your disapproval of the plan we submitted what do you suggest in place of it?

Stalin

· 291 ·

March 5, 1945
Personal from Premier J. V. Stalin to President Franklin D. Roosevelt.

I received your message of March 4 concerning the question of prisoners of war. I, once again, consulted our local representatives who deal with these questions and have to inform you about the following.

The difficulties, which we had to meet on the first stages in the cause of speedy evacuation of American prisoners of war, when they were in the zone of active military operations have now considerably decreased. At the present time the organization on the affairs of foreign prisoners of war, specially formed by the Soviet Government, has an appropriate number of people, transport facilities and food stuffs, and each time when new groups of American prisoners of war are found, measures are urgently taken to render help to these prisoners of war and for their evacuation to the gathering points for the subsequent repatriation. According to information which is at present at the disposal of the Soviet Government, on the territory of Poland and in other places liberated by the Red Army, there are no groups of American prisoners of war, as all of them, except the single sick persons who are in the hospitals, have been sent to the gathering point in Odessa, where 1,200 American prisoners of war have already arrived and the arrival of the rest is expected in the nearest future.

In view of this under the present conditions there is no necessity to carry on flights of American planes from Poltava to the territory of Poland on the matters of American prisoners of war. You may feel assured that the appropriate measures will be urgently taken also in respect to crews of American planes having a forced landing. This, however, does not exclude the cases when the help of American planes may become necessary. In these cases Soviet military authorities will apply to the American military representatives in Moscow on the subject of sending American planes from Poltava.

Having at the present moment no proposals on the question of condition of Allied prisoners of war who are in the hands of the Germans, I want to assure you that on our part we shall do everything possible for the creation of favorable conditions for them, as soon as they will be on the territory which will be taken by the Soviet troops.

Roosevelt

·   292   ·

General Deane, sure that there were still stray Americans in Poland, requested of General Golubev permission to visit Poland. "I was eager to go to Poland and see the situation for myself." Golubev said that only the Foreign Office could grant the permit, so Harriman went to Vishinsky. Vishinsky said that the Polish government had to approve, which Harriman considered a ploy to make the United States recognize the Lublin government.

March 17, 1945
Personal from the President to Stalin.

With reference to the question of evacuation of American prisoners from Poland I have been informed that the arrangement for General Deane with a Soviet Army officer to make a survey of the U.S. prisoners of war situation has been cancelled. In your last message to me you stated that there was no need to accede to my request that American aircraft be allowed to carry supplies to Poland and to evacuate the sick. I have information that I consider positive and reliable that there are a very considerable number of sick and injured American in hospitals in Poland and also numbers of liberated U.S. prisoners in good health who are awaiting entrainment in Poland to transit camps in Odessa, or are at large in small groups that have not yet made contact with Soviet authorities.

Frankly I cannot understand your reluctance to permit American officers and means to assist their own people in this matter. This Government has done everything to meet each of your requests. I now request you to meet mine in this particular matter. Please call Harriman to explain my desires in detail.

Roosevelt

Stalin

· 293 ·

General Deane was not allowed into Poland. Eventually all the Americans liberated from German prison camps in Poland were found and sent to Odessa by the Russians. Soviet generals who lost battles sometimes did pay with their lives.

March 22, 1945
Personal from Premier J. V. Stalin to President Franklin D. Roosevelt

I have received your message concerning the evacuation from Poland of former American prisoners of war.

In regard to the information which you have about a seemingly great number of sick and wounded Americans who are in Poland, and also those who are waiting for departure for Odessa or who did not get in touch with Soviet authorities, I must say that that information is not exact. In reality, on the territory of Poland by March 16 there were only 17 sick Americans, except a number of Americans who are on the way to Odessa. Today I have received a report that very soon they (17 persons) will be taken to Odessa by planes.

In regard to a request contained in your message I must say that if that request concerned me personally I would readily agree even to the prejudice of my interests. But in this case the matter concerns the interests of the Soviet armies at the front and Soviet commanders, who do not want to have extra officers with them, having no relation to military operations but at the same time requiring care for their accommodation, for the organization of meetings and all kinds of connections for them, for their guard from possible diversions on the part of German agents who have not yet been caught, and other measures diverting commanders and officers under their command from their direct duties.

Our commanders pay with their lives for the state of matters at the front and in the immediate rear. And I do not consider it possible to limit their rights in any degree.

In addition to this I have to say that former American prisoners of war liberated by the Red Army are in Soviet prisoner-of-war camps in good conditions, at any rate in better conditions than former Soviet prisoners of war in American camps where they have been partially placed together with German prisoners of war and where some of them were subjected to unfair treatment and unlawful inconveniences up to beating as it was reported to the American Government more than once.

Roosevelt

· 294 ·

Conversations had been initiated between Gen. Karl Wolff, ranking SS officer in Italy, and Allen Dulles, OSS chief in Switzerland, regarding the possible surrender of German troops in northern Italy. Harriman, involved in the matter and privy to all the details, on March 12 informed Molotov of the surrender discussions and further that Field Marshal Sir Harold Alexander was sending his American deputy chief of staff, Gen. Lyman Lemnitzer, and the chief British intelligence officer, Gen. Sir Terence Airey, disguised as civilians, across the Swiss border to talk to Wolff in three days. Molotov replied that "the Soviet Government would like officers representing the Soviet Military Command to participate in these negotiations." Harriman consulted with Deane, Marshall, and the Joint Chiefs of Staff; all agreed that Soviet participation was undesirable, that the Russians "might jeopardize the surrender by their 'embarrassing demands.'" Harriman, too, thought that the Russians should be excluded from the talks. "The Soviets would never allow our officers, I am satisfied, to participate in a parallel situation on the eastern front. Indeed I doubt whether they would even let us know of any negotiations for a surrender." Molotov called the refusal "utterly unexpected and incomprehensible."[158]

Molotov's withdrawal from the San Francisco Conference was the result.

March 24, 1945
Personal from the President to Marshal Stalin
Ambassador Gromyko has just informed the State Department of the composition of the Soviet delegation to the San Francisco Conference. While we have the highest regard for Ambassador Gromyko's character and capabilities and know that he would ably represent his country, I cannot help being deeply disappointed that Mr. Molotov apparently does not plan to attend. Recalling the friendly and fruitful cooperation at Yalta be-

tween Mr. Molotov, Mr. Eden, and Mr. Stettinius, I know the Secretary of State has been looking forward to continuing the joint work in the same spirit at San Francisco for the eventual realization of our mutual goal, the establishment of an effective international organization to insure a secure and peaceful future for the world.

Without the presence of Mr. Molotov the Conference will be deprived of a very great asset. If his pressing and heavy responsibilities in the Soviet Union make it impossible for him to stay for the entire Conference, I very much hope that you will find it possible to let him come at least for the vital opening sessions. Since all sponsoring powers and the majority of other countries attending will be represented by their Ministers of Foreign Affairs, I am afraid that Mr. Molotov's absence will be construed all over the world as a lack of comparable interest on the part of the Soviet Government in the great objectives of this Conference.

Roosevelt

· 295 ·

———

Roosevelt had not been informed of the surrender negotiations. When he heard about them for the first time in late March, he summoned Leahy and Marshall into his office for an explanation. They told him that excluding the Soviets was Field Marshal Alexander's idea, endorsed by the Combined Chiefs of Staff, who suggested that including Russia would be a mistake—what might be accomplished in "four hours would take four months."[159] Roosevelt sought to allay Stalin's great fear that Great Britain and the United States were double-crossing the Soviets now that victory was imminent.

March 24, 1945
Personal from the President for Marshal Stalin.

I have received from Ambassador Harriman a letter addressed to him by Mr. Molotov regarding an investigation being made by Field Marshal Alexander into a reported possibility of obtaining the surrender of part or all of the German Army in Italy, in which letter Mr. Molotov demands that this investigation to be undertaken in Switzerland be stopped forthwith because of the non participation therein of Soviet officers.

I am sure that the facts of this matter, through misunderstanding, have not been correctly presented to you.

The facts are as follows: Some few days ago unconfirmed information was received in Switzerland that some German officers were considering the possibility of arranging for the surrender of German troops that are opposed to the British-American Armies in Italy commanded by Field Marshal Alexander.

When this information reached Washington, Field Marshal Alexander was authorized to send an officer, or officers, of his staff to Switzerland to ascertain the accuracy of the report, and if it appeared to be of sufficient promise, to arrange with any competent German officers for a conference with Field Marshal Alexander at his headquarters in Italy to discuss details of the surrender. *Soviet representatives would, of course, be present if such a meeting could be arranged.*

The Soviet Government was immediately informed of this investigation to be made in Switzerland and was later informed that it will be agreeable for Soviet officers to be present at Field Marshal Alexander's meeting with German officers when and if such a meeting is finally arranged *in Berne* to discuss details of a surrender *at Caserta.*

Attempts by our representatives to arrange a meeting with German officers have met with no success up to the present time, but there still appears to be a possibility of such a meeting.

You will, of course, understand that my government must give every assistance to all officers in the field in command of American Forces who believe there is a possibility of forcing the surrender of enemy troops in their area. It would be completely unreasonable for me to take any other attitude or to permit any delay which must cause additional and avoidable loss of life in the American Forces. You as a military man will understand the necessity for prompt action to avoid losing an opportunity. *It is in the same category as would be the sending of a flag of truce to your general at Koenigsberg or Danzig.*

In such a surrender of enemy forces in the field, there can be no political implications whatever and no violation of our agreed principle of unconditional surrender.

At any discussion of details of surrender by our commanders of American Forces in the field, I will be pleased to have the benefit of the experience and advice of any of your officers who can be present, but I cannot agree to suspend investigation of the possibility because of objection on the part of Mr. Molotov for some reason completely beyond my understanding.

I do not expect much from the reported possibility, but I hope you will, with the purpose of preventing misunderstanding between our officers, point out to the Soviet officials concerned the desirability and necessity of our taking prompt and effective action without any delay to accomplish the surrender of any enemy military forces in the field that are opposed to American Forces.

I am sure that when a similar opportunity comes on the Soviet front you will have the same attitude and will take the same action.

Roosevelt

Stalin

· 296 ·

Personal and Secret from Marshal J. V. Stalin to President F. D. Roosevelt March 27, 1945

We extremely value and attach great importance to the forthcoming Conference in San Francisco, called to found the international organization of peace and security for peoples but circumstances have developed in such a way that Mr. V. M. Molotov, really, is not able to participate in the Conference. I and Mr. Molotov regret it extremely but the convening, on request of the deputies of the Supreme Soviet, in April, of a sessions of the Supreme Soviet of the USSR where the presence of Mr. Molotov is absolutely necessary, is excluding the possibility of his participation even in the first meetings of the Conference.

You also know that Ambassador Gromyko has quite successfully accomplished his task in Dumbarton Oaks and we are confident that he will with great success head the Soviet delegation in San Francisco.

As regards various interpretations, you understand, this cannot determine the decisions which are to be made.

Stalin

· 297 ·

This telegram reached the president in Warm Springs.

March 29, 1945
Personal from Premier J. V. Stalin to President F. D. Roosevelt.

I gave consideration to the question you raised before me in the letter of March 25, 1945, and have found that the Soviet Government could not have given a different answer after the Soviet representatives were refused participation in the discussions in Bern with the Germans regarding the possibility of capitulation of German troops and opening the front to Anglo-American troops in Northern Italy.

I am not against and, more than this, I am fully for using the opportunity of disintegration in the German armies and to hasten their capitulation in any section of the front, to encourage them in the opening of the front for the Allies.

But I agree to negotiations with the enemy on such matter only in the case when these negotiations will not make the situation of the enemy easier, if there will be excluded a possibility for the Germans to maneuver and to use these negotiations for shifting of their troops to other sections of the front and, first of all, to the Soviet front.

Only with the purpose of creating such a guarantee was the participation of representatives of the Soviet Military Command in such negotiations with the enemy considered necessary by the Soviet Government, no matter where they would take place—in Bern or Caserta. I cannot understand why representatives of the Soviet Command were refused participation in these negotiations and in what way could they cause inconvenience to the representatives of the Allied Command.

For your information I have to tell you that the Germans have already made use of the negotiations with the Allied Command and during this period have succeeded in shifting three divisions from Northern Italy to the Soviet front.

The task of coordinated operations with a blow upon the Germans from the West, South and East, announced at the Crimea Conference is to bind the troops of the enemy to the place of their location and not to give the enemy any possibility to maneuver and shift troops in to the necessary for him direction. This task is being carried out by the Soviet Command. This is being violated by Fieldmarshal Alexander.

This circumstance is irritating the Soviet Command and creates ground for mistrust.

"As a military man," you write me, "you will understand, that it is necessary to act quickly in order not to miss an opportunity. It would be the same if your general at Koenigsberg or Danzig would be approached by the enemy with a white flag." It is regretted that an analogy does not suit this case. German troops at Koenigsberg and Danzig are surrounded. If they surrender they will do it in order to avoid annihilation but they cannot open a front to the Soviet troops as the front has moved away from them far to the West, to the Oder. An entirely different situation is that of the German troops in Northern Italy. They are not surrounded and they do not face annihilation. If the Germans in Northern Italy, in spite of this seek negotiations in order to surrender and to open the front to Allied troops, this means that they have different, more serious aims relating to the fate of Germany.

I have to tell you, that if on the Eastern front, somewhere on the Oder, similar conditions of a possibility of capitulation of the Germans and opening the front to Soviet troops would arise, I would not hesitate to inform immediately the Anglo-American Military Command to request it to send their representatives for participation in negotiations as in such cases the Allies should have no secrets from each other.

Roosevelt

· 298 ·

Roosevelt couldn't believe that Stalin had written the previous letter. He asked Harriman to find out whether Stalin was personally writing the messages. Harriman advised him that the words and reasonings were Stalin's.[160] It is possible that at this time Molotov was exacerbating Stalin's fears that the Allies might enter into surrender negotiations excluding the Soviet Union. The previous July, after the Allied forces had broken out of the Normandy beachhead, Molotov had said to Stalin, "Germany will try to make peace with Churchill and Roosevelt"; Stalin had replied, "Right, but Roosevelt and Churchill won't agree."[161] Molotov didn't want to go to the San Francisco Conference because he wanted to attend the meeting of the Supreme Soviet, scheduled for the same time, as Harriman noted at the time of his visit to Stalin following Roosevelt's death.[162]

March 31, 1945
Personal from the President for Marshal Stalin

It seems to me in the exchange of messages we have had on possible future negotiations with the Germans for surrender of their forces in Italy, that although both of us are in agreement on all the basic principles, the matter now stands in an atmosphere of regrettable apprehension and mistrust.

No negotiations for surrender have been entered into, and if there should be any negotiations they will be conducted at Caserta with your representatives present throughout. Although the attempt at Berne to arrange for the conduct of these negotiations has so far been fruitless, Marshal Alexander has been directed to keep you informed of his progress in this matter.

I must repeat that the meeting in Bern was for the single purpose of arranging contact with competent German military officers and not for negotiations of any kind.

There is no question of negotiating with the Germans in any way which would permit then to transfer elsewhere forces from the Italian front. Negotiations, if any are conducted, will be on the basis of unconditional surrender. With regard to the lack of Allied offensive operations in Italy, this condition has in no way resulted from any expectation of an agreement with the Germans. As a matter of fact, recent interruption of offensive operations in Italy has been due primarily to the recent transfer of Allied forces, British and Canadian divisions, from that front to France. Preparations are now made for an offensive on the Italian front about April 10th, but while we hope for successes, the operation will be of limited power due to the lack of forces now available to Alexander. He has seventeen dependable divisions and is opposed by twenty-four German divisions. We intend to do everything within the capacity of our available resources to prevent any withdrawal of the German forces now in Italy.

I feel that your information about the time of the movements of German troops from Italy is in error. Our best information is that three German divisions have left Italy since the first of the year, two of which have gone to the Eastern front. The last division of the three started moving about February 25, more than two weeks before anybody heard of any possibility of a surrender. It is therefore clearly evident that the approach made by German agents in Bern occurring after the last movement of troops began could not possibly have had any effect on the movement.

This entire episode has arisen through the initiative of a German officer reputed to be close to [SS and Gestapo chief Heinrich] Himmler and there, of course, is a strong possibility that his sole purpose is to create suspicion and distrust between the Allies. There is no reason why we should permit him to succeed in that aim. I trust that the above categorical statement of the present situation and of my intentions will allay the apprehensions which you express in your message of March 29.

Roosevelt

Roosevelt

· 299 ·

At the Yalta conference Roosevelt, Stalin, and Churchill had agreed to the following declaration on Poland:

A new situation has been created in Poland as a result of her complete liberation by the Red Army. This calls for the establishment of a Polish Provisional Government which can be more broadly based than was possible before the recent liberation of Western part of Poland. The Provisional Government which is now functioning in Poland should therefore be reorganized on a broader democratic basis with the inclusion of democratic leaders from Poland itself and from Poles abroad. this new Government should then be called the Polish Provisional Government of National Unity.

M. Molotov, Mr. Harriman and Sir A. Clark Kerr are authorized as a commission to consult in the first instance in Moscow with other members of the present Provisional Government and with other Polish democratic leaders from within Poland and from abroad, with a view to the reorganization of the present government along the above lines. This Polish Provisional Government of National Unity shall be pledged to the holding of free and unfettered elections as soon as possible on the basis of universal suffrage and secret ballot. In these elections all democratic and anti-Nazi parties shall have the right to take part and to put forward candidates.[163]

The following message was the result of a collaborative effort between the president and Winston Churchill, who suggested to Roosevelt that they jointly let Stalin know their views on the composition of the government of Poland. Roosevelt dictated a draft to Grace Tully and later worked over the draft at a meeting with Stettinius, Assistant Secretaries James C. Dunn, William L. Clayton, and Archibald MacLeish, along with Charles Bohlen and Leahy, on March 29, the day he left for Warm Springs, Georgia.[164] Roosevelt, as well as everyone around him, hoped that the restorative waters of the reknowned spa, where he expected to spend several weeks, would have a salutary effect on his health.

A copy of the draft message was sent to Churchill for his information and opinion. Churchill didn't think Roosevelt had gone far enough and suggested changes, which Roosevelt approved. The italicized sentences (not in the president's handwriting) are the ones added, Roosevelt wrote Churchill, "to cover the points you raise."[165]

March 31, 1945
Personal from the President to Marshal Stalin.

I cannot conceal from you the concern with which I view the development of events of mutual interest since our fruitful meeting at Yalta. The decisions we reached there were good ones and have for the most part been welcomed with enthusiasm by the peoples of the world who saw in our ability find a common basis of understanding the best pledge for a secure and peaceful world after this war. Precisely because of the hopes and expectations that these decisions raised, their fulfillment is being followed with the closest attention. We have no right to let them be disappointed. So far there has been a discouraging lack of progress made in the carrying out, which the world expects, of the political decisions which we reached at the Conference particularly those relating to the Polish question. I am frankly puzzled as to why this should be and must tell you that I do not fully understand in many respects the apparent indifferent attitude of your Government. Having understood each other so well at Yalta I am convinced that the three of us can and will clear away any obstacles which have developed since then. I intend, therefore, in this message to lay before you with complete frankness the problem as I see it.

Although I have in mind primarily the difficulties which the Polish negotiations have encountered, I must make a brief mention of our agreement embodied in the declaration on liberated Europe. I frankly cannot understand why the recent developments in Romania should be regarded as not falling within the terms of that agreement. I hope you will find time personally to examine the correspondence between our Governments on this subject.

However, the part of our agreements at Yalta which has aroused the greatest popular interest and is the most urgent relates to the Polish question. You are aware of course that the Commission which we set up has made no progress. I feel this is due to the interpretation which your Government is placing upon the Crimean decisions. In order that there shall be no misunderstanding I set forth below my interpretation of the points of the agreement which are pertinent to the difficulties encountered by the Commission in Moscow.

In the discussions that have taken place so far your Government appears to take the position that the new Polish Provisional Government of

National Unity which we agreed should be formed should be little more than a continuation of the present Warsaw Government. I cannot reconcile this with our agreement or our discussions. While it is true that the Lublin Government is to be reorganized and its members play a prominent role it is to be done in such a fashion as to bring into being a new Government. This point is clearly brought out in several places in the text of the agreement. I must make it quite plain to you that any such solution which would result in a continuance of the present Warsaw regime would be unacceptable and would cause the people of the United States to regard the Yalta agreement as a fraud *having failed*. It is equally apparent that for the same reason the Warsaw Government cannot under the agreement claim the right to select or reject what Poles are to be brought to Moscow by the Commission for consultation. Can we not agree that it is up to the Commission to select the Polish leaders to come to Moscow to consult in the first instance and invitations be sent out accordingly? If this could be done I see no great objection to having the Lublin group come first in order that they may be fully acquainted with the agreed interpretation of the Yalta decisions on this point. *It is of course understood that if the Lublin group comes first no arrangements would be made independently with them before the arrival of the other Polish leaders called for consultation.* In order to facilitate the agreement the Commission might first of all select a small but representative group of Polish leaders who could suggest other names for the consideration of the Commission. We have not and would not bar or veto any candidate for consultation which Mr. Molotov might propose being confident that he would not suggest any Poles who would be inimical to the intent of the Crimean decision. I feel that it is not too much to ask that my Ambassador be accorded the same confidence *and that any candidate for consultation presented by anyone of the commission be accepted by the others in good faith.* It is obvious to me that if the right of the Commission to select these Poles is limited or shared with the Warsaw Government the very foundation on which our agreement rests would be destroyed. While the foregoing are the immediate obstacles which in my opinion have prevented the Commission from making any progress in this vital matter there are two other suggestions which were not in the agreement but nevertheless have a very important bearing on the result we all seek. Neither of these suggestions has been as yet accepted by your Government. I refer to (1) that there should be the maximum of political tranquility in Poland and that dissident groups should cease any measure and countermeasures against each other. That we should respectively use our influence to that end seems to me so eminently reasonable. (2) It would also seem entirely natural in view of the responsibilities placed upon them by the agreement that representatives of the American and British members of the Commission should be permitted to visit Poland. *As you will recall Mr. Molotov himself suggested this at an early meeting of the Commission and only subsequently withdrew it.*

I wish I could convey to you how important it is for the successful development of our program of international collaboration that this Polish question be settled fairly and speedily. If this is not done all the difficulties and dangers to Allied unity which we had so much in mind in reaching our decision at the Crimea will face us in an even more acute form. You are, I am sure, aware that genuine popular support in the United States is required to carry out any Government policy foreign or domestic. The American people make up their own mind and no Governmental action can change it. I mention this fact because the last sentence of your message about Mr. Molotov's attendance at San Francisco made me wonder whether you give full weight to this factor.

Roosevelt

Stalin

· 300 ·

April 3, 1945

Personal from Marshal J. V. Stalin to President F. D. Roosevelt

I have received your message on the question of negotiations in Bern. You are absolutely right that in connection with the affair regarding negotiation of the Anglo-American Command with the German Command somewhere in Bern or some other place "has developed an atmosphere of fear and distrust deserving regrets."

You insist that there have been no negotiations yet.

It may be assumed that you have not been fully informed. As regards my military colleagues, they, on the basis of data which they have on hand, do not have any doubts, that the negotiations have taken place and that they have ended in agreement with the Germans, on the basis of which the German Commander on the Western front—Marshal Kesselring, has agreed to open the front and permit the Anglo-American troops to advance to the East, and the Anglo-Americans have promised in return to ease for the Germans the peace terms.

I think that my colleagues are close to truth. Otherwise one could not have understood the fact that the Anglo-Americans have refused to admit to Bern representatives of the Soviet Command for participation in the negotiations with the Germans.

I also cannot understand the silence of the British who have allowed you to correspond with me on this unpleasant matter, and they themselves remain silent, although it is known that the initiative in this whole affair with the negotiations in Bern belongs to the British.

I understand that there are certain advantages for the Anglo-American troops as a result of these separate negotiations in Bern or in some other place since the Anglo-American troops get the possibility to advance into the heart of Germany almost without any resistance on the part of the Germans, but why was it necessary to conceal this from the Russians and why your Allies—the Russians, were not notified?

As a result of this at the present moment the Germans on the Western front in fact have ceased the war against England and the United States. At the same time the Germans continue the war with Russia, the Ally of England and the United States. It is understandable that such a situation can in no way serve the cause of preservation of the strengthening of trust between our countries.

I have already written to you in my previous message and consider it necessary to repeat it here that I personally and my colleagues would never have made such a risky step, being aware that a momentary advantage, no matter what it would be, is fading before the principle advantage on the preservation and strengthening of trust among the Allies.

Roosevelt

· 301 ·

———

Stalin received this message on April 5. That afternoon Molotov received the Japanese ambassador, Naotaka Sato, and informed him that the Soviet government wished to denounce the neutrality pact with Japan that had been signed in April 1941. "Japan, an ally of Germany, is helping the latter in her war against the USSR," Molotov said to Mr. Sato, adding, "Japan is fighting against the United States and Britain, which are allies of the Soviet Union." The news was announced on all Soviet radio stations that evening.[166]

April 4, 1945
Personal from the President for Marshal Stalin

I have received with astonishment your message of April 3 containing an allegation that arrangements which were made between Field Marshals

Alexander and Kesselring at Bern, "permitted the Anglo-American troops to advance to the East and the Anglo-Americans promised in return to ease for the Germans the peace terms."

In my previous messages to you in regard to the attempts made in Bern to arrange a conference to discuss a surrender of the German Army in Italy, I have told you that,

(1) No negotiations were held in Bern;

(2) That the meeting had no political implications whatever;

(3) That in any surrender of the enemy army in Italy there could be no violation of our agreed principle of unconditional surrender;

(4) That Soviet officers would be welcomed at any meeting that might be arranged to discuss surrender.

For the advantage of our common war effort against Germany, which today gives excellent promise of an early success in a disintegration of the German armies, I must continue to assume that you have the same high confidence in my truthfulness and reliability that I have always had in yours.

I have also a full appreciation of the effect your gallant army has had in making possible a crossing of the Rhine by the forces under General Eisenhower and the effect that your forces will have hereafter on the eventual collapse of the German resistance to our combined attacks.

I have complete confidence in General Eisenhower and know that he certainly would inform me before entering into any agreement with the Germans. He is instructed to demand and will demand unconditional surrender of enemy troops that may be defeated on his front. Our advances on the Western Front are due to military action. Their speed has been attributable mainly to the terrific impact of our air power resulting in destruction of German communications, and to the fact that Eisenhower was able to cripple the bulk of the German Forces on the Western front while they were still West of the Rhine.

I am certain that there were no negotiations in Bern at any time, and I feel that your information to that effect must have come from German sources which have made persistent efforts to create dissention between us in order to escape in some measure for responsibility for their war crimes. If that was Wolff's purpose in Bern your message proves that he has had some success.

With a confidence in your belief in my personal reliability and in my determination to bring about together with you an unconditional surrender of the Nazis, it is astonishing that a belief seems to have reached the Soviet Government that I have entered into an agreement with the enemy without first obtaining your full agreement.

Finally I would say this, it would be one of the great tragedies of history if at the very moment of victory now within our grasp, such distrust, such lack of faith should prejudice the entire undertaking after the colossal losses of life, matériel and treasure involved.

Frankly I cannot avoid a feeling of bitter resentment toward your informers, whoever they are, for such vile misrepresentations of my actions or those of my trusted subordinates.

Roosevelt

Stalin

· 302 ·

April 7, 1945
Personal and Secret from Marshal J. V. Stalin to President F. D. Roosevelt

I have received your message of April 5th.

1. In my message of April 3 I spoke not about honesty and dependability. I never doubted your honesty and dependability, as well as the honesty and dependability of Mr. Churchill. I speak about the fact that in the course of this correspondence between us has been revealed a difference of opinions as to what can an Ally allow himself to do in respect to the other Ally and what he should not allow himself to do. We, Russians, believe that in the present situation at the fronts when the enemy is confronted by the inevitability of capitulation, at any meeting with the Germans on questions of capitulation by representatives of one of the Allies arrangements have to be made for the participation in this meeting of representatives of the other Ally. At any rate this is absolutely necessary if this Ally is seeking participation in such a meeting. Americans, however, and the Englishmen think differently, considering the Russian point of view wrong. Proceeding from this fact they rejected the Russians the right of participation in the meeting with the Germans in Switzerland. I have already written to you and consider it not unnecessary to repeat that the Russians in a similar situation under no circumstances would have refused the Americans and Englishmen the right for participation in such a meeting. I continue to consider the Russian point of view as the only right one as it excludes any possibility of mutual distrust and does not permit the enemy to sow distrust among us.

2. It is difficult to agree that lack of resistance on the part of the Germans on the Western front can be explained only that they are defeated. The Germans have on the Eastern front 147 divisions. They could without

harm to their cause take from the Eastern front 15–20 divisions and shift them to the aid of their troops on the Western front. However, the Germans did not do it and are not doing it, They continue to fight savagely with the Russians for some unknown junction Zemlianitsa in Czechoslovakia which they need as much as a dead man needs poultices, but surrender without any resistance such important towns in Central Germany as Osnabrük, Mannheim, Kassel. Don't you agree that such a behavior of the Germans is more than strange and incomprehensible.

3. As regards my informers, I may assure that they are very honest and modest people who carry out their duties accurately and have no intentions of insulting anyone. These people have been manyfold tested by us by their deeds. Judge for yourself. In February 1945, General Marshall has given a number of important information to the General Staff of the Soviet troops where he, on the basis of date he had on hand, warned the Russians that in March there will be two serious counter-attacks of the Germans on the Eastern front one of which will be directed from Pomerania on Torun and the other from the region of Moravska Ostrava on Lodz. In fact, however, it proved that the principal blow of the Germans was being prepared and was realized not in the above-mentioned regions but in an entirely different region, namely in the region of Lake Balaton, to the South-west of Budapest. As it is known the Germans have concentrated in this region up to 35 divisions, including 11 tank divisions. This was one of the most serious blows in the course of the war with such great concentration of tank forces. Marshal [F. I.] Tolbukhin succeeded in avoiding a catastrophe and in complete defeat of the Germans later, because my informers have uncovered, true a little late, this plan of the main blow of the Germans and immediately informed Marshal Tolbukhin. Thus I had another occasion to convince myself in the accuracy and knowledge of Soviet informers.

For your orientation in this matter I am enclosing a letter of the Chief of the General Staff of the Red Army, Army General [A. E.] Antonov, addressed to Major-General Dean[e].

Major General John R. Dean
Head of the United States Military Mission in the USSR
March 30, 1945
Dear General Dean:

Please bring to the attention of General Marshall the following.

On February 20, 1945, I received from General Marshall's communication, transmitted to me by General Dean, that the Germans are forming two groupings on the Eastern front for a counter-offensive: one in Pomerania for a blow in the direction of Torun and another in the region of Vienna, Moravska Ostrava for an offensive in the direction of Lodz. Besides, the southern grouping was supposed to include the 6th tank army "SS." I received similar information on February 12 from Colonel Brinkman, head of the army section of the British Military Mission. I am extremely grateful to General Marshall for the information called to assist our common aims, which he so kindly put at our disposal. At the same time I consider it my duty to inform General Marshall that the military actions on the Eastern front in the course of March have not confirmed the information submitted by him as these battles showed that the main grouping of German troops including the 6th tank army "SS," was concentrated not in Pomerania and not in the region of Moravska Ostrava, but in the region of Lake Balaton, from where the Germans attacked with the purpose to reach the Danube and to force it south of Budapest.

This fact shows that the information used by General Marshall did not correspond to the actual course of events on the Eastern front in March.

A possibility is not excluded that some of the sources of this information aimed to disorientate the Anglo-American Command as well as the Soviet Command and to divert the attention of the Soviet Command from the region where the principal offensive operation of the Germans was being prepared on the Eastern front.

In spite of the above-said I ask General Marshall, if possible, to continue to inform us regarding available data about the enemy. I consider it my duty to inform General Marshall regarding the above with the only purpose that he could make certain conclusions regarding the source of this information.

I beg you to transmit to General Marshall my respect and gratitude.

Sincerely yours,
Antonov, Army General
Chief of Staff of the Red Army

Stalin

· 303 ·

Harriman denied that he ever made the statement that Stalin attributes to him, "It is possible that no member of the Provisional Government will be included in the composition of the Polish government of national unity."

Roosevelt received this message on April 10.

EMBASSY OF THE

UNION OF SOVIET SOCIALIST REPUBLICS

WASHINGTON 6, D.C.

April 9, 1945

My dear Mr. President:

I am forwarding herewith a message from Marshal J. V. Stalin on the Polish question. I have also instructions to forward to you a copy of Marshal Stalin's message to Prime-Minister Churchill on the Polish question.

Respectfully yours,

A. Gromyko

Ambassador

April 7, 1945

From: Marshal Stalin

To: The President

In connection with your message of April 1 I consider it necessary to make the following remarks on the question of Poland.

Matters on the Polish question have really reached a dead end.

What are the reasons for it? The reasons for it are that the Ambassadors of the United States and England in Moscow—members of the Moscow Commission have departed from the principles of the Crimea Conference and have introduced into the matter new elements not provided by the Crimea Conference.

Namely: a) At the Crimea Conference all three of us considered the Provisional Government of Poland as the government functioning in Poland at the present time which is subject to reconstruction and which should serve as kernel of the new government of national unity. But the Ambassadors of the United States and England in Moscow depart from this principle, ignore the existence of the Provisional Polish Government, do not notice it, at the best—put a sign of equality between singletons from Poland and from London and the Provisional Government of Poland. Besides, they consider that the reconstruction of the Provisional Government should be understood as its liquidation and formation of an entirely new government. Besides, the matter reach such a state when Mr. Harriman stated in the Moscow Commission: "It is possible that no member of the Provisional Government will be included in the composition of the Polish government of national unity."

Naturally, such a position of the American and British Ambassadors cannot but cause indignation on the part of the Polish Provisional Government. As regards the Soviet Union, it certainly cannot agree with such a position, as it would mean direct violation of the decisions of the Crimea Conference.

b) At the Crimea Conference all three of us agreed that not more than five persons from Poland and three persons from London should be called for consultation. But the Ambassadors of the United States and England in Moscow have departed from this position and demand that each member of the Moscow Commission be given the right to invite an unlimited number of people from Poland and from London.

Naturally the Soviet Government could not agree with this as the summons of people should be carried out according to decisions of the Crimea Conference, not by individual members of the Commission, but by the Commission as a whole, namely by the Commission as such. But the request of an unlimited number of persons summoned for consultation contradicts the plans of the Crimea Conference.

c) The Soviet Government proceeds from the fact that in accordance with the meaning of the decisions of the Crimea Conference such Polish leaders should be involved for consultations who, firstly, recognize the decisions of the Crimea Conference, including the decision on the Curzon Line, and, secondly, are really striving to establish friendly relations between Poland and the Soviet Union. The Soviet Government insists on this as blood of the Soviet troops abundantly shed for the liberation of Poland and the fact that in the course of the last 30 years the territory of Poland has been used by the enemy twice for attack upon Russia, - all this obliges the Soviet Government to strive that the relations between the Soviet Union and Poland be friendly.

But the Ambassadors of the United States and England in Moscow do not take this into consideration and strive that Polish leaders should be invited for consultation regardless of their attitude towards the decisions of the Crimea Conference and the Soviet Union.

Such, in my opinion, are the reasons hindering the solution of the Polish question on the basis of mutual agreement.

In order to leave the dead end and reach a harmonious decision it is necessary, in my opinion, to undertake the following steps:

1) To agree that the reconstruction of the Provisional Polish Government means not its liquidation but just its reconstruction by way of broadening it, bearing in mind that the kernel of the future Polish Government of National Unity should be the Provisional Polish Government.

2) To return to the projections of the Crimea Conference and to summon only eight Polish leaders, five of whom should be called from Poland and three from London.

3) To agree that, under any conditions, a consultation with representatives of the Provisional Polish Government should be carried out, bearing in mind that this consultation with them should be carried out first of all as the Provisional Polish Government is the greatest force in Poland as compared to those singletons who will be called from London and from Poland and whose influence on the population of Poland cannot be compared with the tremendous influence which the Provisional Polish Government enjoys in Poland.

I draw you attention to this point as, in my opinion, any other decision on this point can be perceived in Poland as an insult to the Polish people and as an attempt to force upon Poland a government formed without taking into consideration the public opinion of Poland.

4) To summon for consultation from Poland and from London only such leaders who recognize decisions of the Crimea Conference on Poland are really striving to establish friendly relations between Poland and the Soviet Union.

5) To carry out the reconstruction of the Provisional Polish Government by substituting some of the present ministers of the Provisional Government by new ministers from among Polish leaders not participating in the Provisional Government.

As regards the numerical correlation of old and new ministers in the composition of the Polish Government of national unity, there could be established approximately a similar correlation which was realized in respect to the Government of Yugoslavia.

I think that, taking into consideration the above-stated remarks, a harmonious decision on the Polish question can be reached in a short time.

Roosevelt

· 304 ·

———

Roosevelt had two major speeches to give. The first, on Jefferson's birthday, April 13, would be carried by all the major radio networks; the second, on April 25, was his speech opening the United Nations Conference in San Francisco. On April 11 Roosevelt dictated the final draft of the Jefferson Day speech to his secretary Dorothy Brady, later penciling in the final sentence. It was a strong plea for an end to war.

The work, my friends, is peace. More than an end of this war—an end to the beginnings of all wars. Yes, an end, forever

to this impractical, unrealistic settlement of the differences between governments by the mass killing of peoples. Today, as we
move against the terrible scourge of war . . . I ask you to keep up
your faith. I measure the sound, solid achievement that can be
made at this time by the straight-edge of your own confidence
and resolve. And to you, and to all Americans who dedicate
themselves with us to the making of an abiding peace, I say: The
only limit to our realization of tomorrow will be our doubts of
today. *Let us move forward with strong and active faith.*[167]

Papers dealing with the San Francisco Conference covered the
president's desk: the agenda, the seating of member nations, even
airport security procedures. The Jefferson speech done, he advised
his other secretary, Grace Tully, to be ready to begin work the next
morning on the speech to the conference.[168]

Roosevelt also sent two messages on April 11. The first one to
Churchill was again a plea to get along with Stalin:

I would minimize the general Soviet problem as much as possible because these problems, in one form or another, seem to
arise every day and most of them straighten out as is the case of
the Bern meeting.
    We must be firm, however, and our course thus far is cor-
rect.[169]

The second, to Stalin, went to Harriman in Moscow for presentation.

April 11, 1945
Personal from the President for Marshal Stalin
    Thank you for your frank explanation of the Soviet point of view of
the Bern incident which now appears to have faded into the past without
having accomplished any useful purpose.
    There must not, in any event, be mutual mistrust and minor misunder-
standings of this character should not arise in the future. I feel sure that
when our armies make contact in Germany and join in a fully coordinated
offensive the Nazi Armies will disintegrate.
                                                        Roosevelt

Instead of presenting the cable to the Kremlin as he ordinarily
would have done, Harriman cabled Roosevelt "respectfully" sug-

gesting that delivery of the cable to Stalin be delayed so that the president and the prime minister could take the same line to the marshal, and that the word "minor" be deleted because, Harriman wrote, "I must confess that the misunderstanding appeared to me to be of a major character."[170]

The cable reached the Map Room and was dispatched to Warm Springs in the early hours of April 12. Leahy knew that the president didn't agree. He suggested, for Roosevelt's approval, the following message for Roosevelt to send Harriman: "Churchill is therefore fully informed and there is no necessity of your delaying delivery of my message to Stalin. Your second question. I do not wish to delete the word 'minor' as it is my desire to consider the Bern misunderstanding a minor incident." Leahy's message, given the referral number MR-OUT-411 by the Map Room staff, was sent to Warm Springs by the Map Room at 10:50 A.M.

Roosevelt had awakened that morning a bit later than usual with a "slight" headache plus a "sort of stiffness" in his neck, he told Dr. Bruenn. Bruenn massaged his neck and took his blood pressure, which was 180 over 110 to 120. Bruenn also noted "the usual evidence of arteriosclerosis."[171]

The president spoke with Dewey Long, in charge of travel arrangements at the White House, instructing him to set up the most direct itinerary, not the scenic route, out to San Francisco. Madame Elizabeth Shoumatoff was in the fourth day of painting the president's portrait. As Roosevelt worked with Hassett over his papers—later than usual because the mail plane had been held up by bad weather—Shoumatoff "interrupted the paper work constantly; measured the President's nose; made other facial measurements; asked the Boss to turn this way and that," much to Hassett's annoyance. Tully realized that it would be lunchtime before Hassett and the president were finished; she decided to wait until after Roosevelt's postluncheon nap before going to take dictation.

At 1:06 P.M. the Map Room received Roosevelt's reply to Leahy's telegram. "Reference MR-OUT-411 Approved." Nine minutes after that, at 1:15, the president said, "I have a terrific pain in the back of my head."[172] He lost consciousness, never to regain it. At 3:30 he died.

Averell Harriman, in Moscow when Franklin Roosevelt died, heard the news in the early morning hours and called Molotov to tell him. By that time it was 3:00 A.M. Moscow time, but Molotov insisted, in spite of the hour, on immediately paying a call on Harriman to express his sympathy. "He seemed deeply moved and disturbed. He stayed for some time talking about the part President Roosevelt had played in the war and in the plans for peace, of the respect Marshal Stalin and all the Russian people had had for him and how much Marshal Stalin had valued his visit to Yalta," Harriman recalled.[173]

Harriman paid a call on Marshal Stalin the next day. He briefed Stalin on President Truman and the uncertainties and changes that his sudden accession to the presidency would naturally create. Stalin interrupted him. "President Roosevelt has died but his cause must live on. We shall support President Truman with all our forces and all our will."

Their talk turned to the San Francisco Conference, and to Roosevelt's disappointment that Molotov was not going to be present and his worry that Molotov's absence might be misconstrued as suggesting a rift between Russia and the other powers, or that Russia did not consider the United Nations of paramount importance. Harriman suggested to Stalin that to have Molotov present in San Francisco would be "the most effective way to assure the American public and the world at large of the desire of the Soviet Government to continue collaboration with us and the other United Nations." While they talked, Molotov kept muttering, according to Harriman, "Time, time, time." Overruling Molotov, "Marshal Stalin then stated categorically that Mr. Molotov's trip to the United States, although difficult at this time, would be arranged."[174]

Ten days later Molotov was in Washington at a meeting with Harry Truman on his way to the San Francisco Conference. The meeting went badly. Truman talked, his voicing rising sharply, about the importance of carrying out all agreements signed at Yalta, but insisted that it was "not a one-way street."

Molotov, according to Charles Bohlen, who was translating the Russian's words, tried to steer the conversation away from Yalta and talk about the war with Japan, but Truman dismissed him, saying, "That will be all, Mr. Molotov. I would appreciate it if you would transmit my views to Mr. Stalin."

"I have never been talked to like that in my life," Molotov replied.

"Carry out your agreements, and you won't get talked to like that," shot back Truman.[175]

Harriman, listening to the interchange, later wrote, "I was a little taken aback, frankly, when the President attacked Molotov so vigorously. . . . I did regret that Truman went at it so hard because his behavior gave Molotov an excuse to tell Stalin that the Roosevelt policy was being abandoned. I regretted that Truman gave him the opportunity. I think it was a mistake."[176] Leahy, also present, thought that the "not at all diplomatic" president left Molotov only two courses of action: "either to approach closely to our expressed policy in regard to Poland, or to drop out of the Association of Nations [United Nations]."[177]

Among the things the Soviets knew about Truman was that two days after Germany invaded Russia he had decided, according to the *New York Times,* that "if we see that Germany is winning we ought to help Russia and if Russia is winning we ought to help Germany and that way let them kill as many as possible although I don't want to see Hitler victorious under any circumstance. Neither of them think anything of their pledged word."[178]

On May 8 Germany surrendered. The Kremlin, perhaps not trusting their allies, waited a day before announcing the surrender to make sure that the Germans did not go on fighting in the east. On May 28 Stalin told Harry Hopkins, in Moscow attempting to smooth relations between Stalin and Truman, that per the agreement at Yalta, the Soviet Union would declare war on Japan on August 8. The Russian entry into the Pacific war was still deemed crucial to the Joint Chiefs of Staff, who assumed that it would force Japan to surrender, thereby avoiding the bloody prospect everyone dreaded: invading Japan.

On August 6 "Little Boy," the first atomic bomb, was dropped on Hiroshima. On August 8 the Soviet Union declared war on Japan.

On August 9 at 1 A.M. one million Soviet troops invaded eastern

Manchuria. Later that day the second atomic bomb, "Fat Man," annihilated Nagasaki. On August 10 Japan surrendered.

Dropping the bombs had unintended consequences both in the United States and in the Soviet Union. Americans never realized the significance of Russia's entry into the war, never appreciated the fact that the Soviet Union had moved a million men across Siberia, were never aware that Russia had been expected to bear the brunt of the casualties if and when there was an invasion of Japan, never realized that the Russian invasion had just as much to do with the Japanese surrender as the atomic bombs.

Russians, for their part, were afraid that the United States had dropped "Fat Man" to put them in their place.

As August progressed there were many people in the Soviet Union and in the United States who thought that the two countries might be able to work in partnership, that America could lend money to Russia that would enable the stricken country to reconstitute its industrial base.

On September 2, V-J day, Stalin went on the air in the Soviet Union to announce the end of the war. "Utterly defeated on the seas, on land and surrounded on all sides by the armed forces of the United Nations, Japan acknowledged her defeat and laid down arms." In closing, perhaps as a last salute to Roosevelt's Four Policemen, he said, "Glory to the armed forces of the Soviet Union, the United States of America, China and Great Britain which have won over Japan."[179]

That same day Truman went on the air in the United States to announce the end of the war with Japan. Buried halfway through his speech was mention of "gallant Allies in this war." He never named them. His closing words were: "God's help has brought us to this day of victory. With His help we will attain that peace and prosperity for ourselves and all the world in the years ahead."[180]

On March 6, 1946, Winston Churchill gave his speech in Fulton, Missouri, warning that an "iron curtain" was descending across Europe. On March 13 Stalin's response was published in *Pravda*. He called Churchill's speech "a dangerous act, calculated to sow seeds of dissent and hinder collaboration among the allied nations. It has harmed the cause of peace and security. Mr. Churchill has now adopted the position of a war monger."[181]

On January 8, 1945, Molotov had presented to Harriman a request for $6 billion in postwar credits over thirty years at an interest rate of 2½ percent. Morgenthau was in favor of the loan, but Roosevelt stated on January 19 that he did not want to act on the matter of postwar financing until he saw Stalin and discussed the issue with him; for some reason the loan was not discussed at Yalta. The Russians brought the loan request up again in August 1945, and on September 17 Stalin told a delegation of congressmen that the Soviet Union wanted to borrow $6 billion from the United States. He said, the *New York Times* reported, that Russia faced many years of building to repair her war damage and raise living standards, and that the Soviets needed economic aid, especially from the United States.[182] Nothing happened. According to Arthur Schlesinger, Jr., "Washington inexplicably mislaid the request. . . . It did not turn up again until March 1946. Of course this was impossible for the Russians to believe."[183]

On April 12, 1946, *Pravda* observed the anniversary of Roosevelt's death with a laudatory article about the president. "The Soviet people saw in Mr. Roosevelt a friend of the Soviet Union," the article said, and it went on to describe him as "an enemy of isolationism as well as an opponent of 'those non-isolationists who considered and still consider today that the United States policy must consist of power politics with the aim of establishing the domination of American interests throughout the world.'"[184]

President Truman's speech at the opening of the San Francisco Conference had been a heartfelt plea for peace. He repeated words of his speech to Congress nine days earlier, the day after Roosevelt's funeral:

> Nothing is more essential to the future peace of the world than continued cooperation of the nations which had to muster the force necessary to defeat the conspiracy of the Axis powers to dominate the world.
>
> While these great states have a special responsibility to enforce the peace, their responsibility is based upon the obligations resting upon all states, large and small, not to use force in international relations except in defense of law.[185]

Appendix

Roosevelt-Stalin Discussion of Basing American Forces on Soviet Territory

Admiral Leahy, U.S. chief of staff, and Gen. Alexei Antonov, Soviet chief of staff, met at 3 P.M. on Thursday, February 8, to plan for the final phase of the war on Japan. When told by the Americans that they wanted to base some operations on Russian territory, General Antonov and his staff replied that only Stalin could give permission for such a thing.

As a result, immediately after the meeting, and prior to the plenary session scheduled for 4 P.M., Roosevelt and Stalin met to discuss this matter.

Following is the conversation, as recorded by Admiral Leahy:

The President said that with the fall of Manila the war in the Pacific was entering into a new phase and that we hoped to establish bases on the Bonins and on the islands near Formosa. He said the time had come to make plans for additional bombing of Japan. He hoped that it would not be necessary actually to invade the Japanese islands and would do so only if absolutely necessary. The Japanese had 4,000,000 men in their army and he hoped by intensive bombing to be able to destroy Japan and its army and thus save American lives.

Marshal Stalin said he did not object to the United States having bases at Komsomolsk or at Nikolaesk. He said the first was on the lower reaches of the Amur River and the second at its mouth. He said that in regard to the bases on Kamchatka he thought we would have to leave that until a later stage since the presence of the Japanese Consul there made it difficult at this time to make the necessary arrangements. At any rate, he added, the other two bases in the Maritime Provinces were nearer.

Marshal Stalin added that there had been one phrase in regard to "commercial routes" in the President's letter on the subject which had not been clear to him.

The President said he had had in mind the importance of the supply routes across the Pacific and Eastern Siberia to the Soviet Union and he felt that once war broke out between Japan and the Soviet Union it would become very important but also very difficult to get by the Japanese Islands.

Marshal Stalin indicated that he recognized the importance of these supply routes and again repeated that he had no objection to the establishment of American bases in the Maritime Provinces.[1]

Agreement Regarding Soviet Entry into War Against Japan

The leaders of the three Great Powers—the Soviet Union, the United States of America and Great Britain—have agreed that in two or three months after Germany has surrendered and the war in Europe has terminated the Soviet Union shall enter into the war against Japan on the side of the Allies on condition that:

1. The *status quo* in Outer-Mongolia (The Mongolian People's Republic) shall be preserved;

2. The former rights of Russia violated by the treacherous attack of Japan in 1904 shall be restored, viz:

(a) the southern part of Sakhalin as well as all the islands adjacent to it shall be returned to the Soviet Union,

(b) the commercial port of Dairen shall be internationalized, the preeminent interests of the Soviet Union in this port being safeguarded and the lease of Port Arthur as a naval base of the USSR restored,

(c) the Chinese-Eastern Railroad and the South-Manchurian Railroad which provides an outlet to Dairen shall be jointly operated by the establishment of a joint Soviet-Chinese Company it being understood that the preeminent interests of the Soviet Union shall be safeguarded and that China shall retain full sovereignty in Manchuria;

3. The Kuril islands shall be handed over to the Soviet Union

It is understood, that the agreement concerning Outer-Mongolia and the ports and railroads referred to above will require concurrence of Generalissimo Chiang Kai-Shek. The President will take measures in order to obtain this concurrence on advice from Marshal Stalin.

The Heads of the three Great Powers have agreed that these claims of the Soviet Union shall be unquestionably fulfilled after Japan has been defeated.

For its part the Soviet Union expresses its readiness to conclude with the national Government of China a pact of friendship and alliance between the USSR and China in order to render assistance to China with its armed forces for the purpose of liberating China from the Japanese yoke.[2]

Abbreviations

FDRL   Franklin D. Roosevelt Library, Hyde Park, N.Y.
FRUS   U.S. State Department, *Foreign Relations of the United States*
HH   Harry Hopkins papers, FDRL
MR   Map Room papers, FDRL
NYT   *New York Times*
PPF   President's personal file, FDRL
PSF   President's secretary's files, FDRL
SC   *Stalin's Correspondence with Roosevelt and Truman, 1941–1945: Correspondence Between the Chairman of the Council of Ministers of the U.S.S.R. and the Presidents of the U.S.A. and the Prime Ministers of Great Britain During the Great Patriotic War of 1941–1945* (Capricorn Books, 1965)

Notes

Introduction

1. Lash, *Roosevelt and Churchill*, 369.
2. Quoted in Volkogonov, *Stalin*, 391.
3. Sherwood, *Roosevelt and Hopkins*, 303–4.
4. Kennedy, *Freedom from Fear*, 486–87.
5. Lash, *Roosevelt and Churchill*, 364.
6. Quoted in Sherwood, *Roosevelt and Hopkins*, 10.
7. Schlesinger, *Coming of the New Deal*, 587.
8. George M. Elsey Papers, Small Collections, FDRL.
9. Quoted in Dallek, *Roosevelt and Foreign Policy*, vii.
10. Deane, *Strange Alliance*, 9.
11. Quoted in Dallek, *Roosevelt and Foreign Policy*, 343.
12. Ibid., 420.
13. Deane, *Strange Alliance*, 23.
14. Rosenman, *Working with Roosevelt*, 404.
15. Ross T. McIntire with George Creel, *White House Physician* (New York: Putnam, 1946), 170.
16. Quoted in Sherwood, *Roosevelt and Hopkins*, 138.
17. McIntire with Creel, *White House Physician*, 171.
18. Warren F. Kimball, ed., *Churchill and Roosevelt: The Complete Correspondence*, vol. 1, *Alliance Emerging* (Princeton: Princeton University Press, 1984), 5.
19. Records of the President's Soviet Protocol Committee, FDRL.
20. Quoted in Dallek, *Roosevelt and Foreign Policy*, 293.
21. Quoted in Kennedy, *Freedom from Fear*, 485.
22. Deane, *Strange Alliance*, 89.
23. Ibid., 49.
24. Quoted in Dunn, *Caught Between Roosevelt and Stalin*, 240.
25. De Santis, *Diplomacy of Silence*, 25.

26. Tyler Kent papers, FDRL.

27. Davies to Roosevelt, January 18, 1939, HH.

28. Papers as President, FDRL.

29. Tyler Kent papers, FDRL.

30. Deane, *Strange Alliance*, 88.

31. Montefiore, *Stalin*, 390, note.

32. Records of the President's Soviet Protocol Committee, May 29, 1942, FDRL.

33. Ibid.

34. J. H. Burns, Russia memo for the president, August 3, 1942, PSF.

35. Quoted in Pierrepont Moffat to Sumner Welles, November 2, 1938, Tyler Kent papers, FDRL.

36. Davies, *Mission to Moscow*, 317, 318.

37. Stephen T. Early file; Davies to Early, March 9, 1937, FDRL.

38. Bohlen, *Witness to History*, 45.

39. Davies to Roosevelt, February 4, 1937, PSF.

40. Bohlen, *Witness to History*, 53.

41. Quoted in Dunn, *Caught Between Roosevelt and Stalin*, 123.

42. Roosevelt to Stalin, April 11, 1942; see message 22 in this book.

43. Quoted in Sherwood, *Roosevelt and Hopkins*, 635.

44. Standley, *Admiral Ambassador to Russia*, 295.

45. Harriman and Abel, *Special Envoy*, 179.

46. Standley, *Admiral Ambassador to Russia*, 295.

47. Maj. Gen. J. H. Burns, Letter of recommendation for the Distinguished Service Medal for Faymonville, to the Adjutant General, United States Army, June 20, 1946, HH.

48. Quotations from Standley, *Admiral Ambassador to Russia*, 320, 315.

49. Quoted ibid., 341.

50. Hull to Roosevelt, June 9, 1943, PSF.

51. Quoted in Isaacson and Thomas, *Wise Men*, 156.

52. Interview, "H. G. Wells versus Stalin, July 23rd, 1934," *Modern Monthly*, December, 1934, 591.

53. Dunn, *Caught Between Roosevelt and Stalin*, 136.

54. Quoted in Montefiore, *Stalin*, 486.

55. *FRUS* 1939, vol. 1.

56. Berezhkov, *At Stalin's Side*, 240.

57. Prime Minister's personal minutes, letter to the Foreign Secretary, January 4, 1944, Foreign Office, London.

58. Churchill to Stalin, November 23, 1943, *Stalin's Correspondence with Churchill and Attlee, 1941–1945* (New York: Capricorn, 1965), 177.

59. Bohlen, *Witness to History*, 146.

60. Deane, *Strange Alliance*, 44, 43.

61. Quoted in Ian Grey, *Stalin: Man of History* (Garden City, N.Y.: Doubleday, 1979), 386.

62. Quoted in Bohlen, *Witness to History*, 150.

63. Quoted in Rosenman, *Working with Roosevelt*, 407.

64. Sherwood, *Roosevelt and Hopkins*, 390.

65. Quoted in Harriman and Abel, *Special Envoy*, 444.

66. Quoted in Kimball, *Churchill and Roosevelt*, 3: 618.

67. Bohlen, *Witness to History*, 181.

68. Stalin to Roosevelt, April 7, 1945, MR.

69. Quoted in Kennedy, *Freedom from Fear*, 802.

70. Bohlen, *Witness to History*, 192.

71. McIntire with Creel, *White House Physician*, 211.

72. Papers of William D. Leahy, Library of Congress Microform Publication, reel 4, February 11, 1945.

73. George F. Kennan, *Russia and the West Under Lenin and Stalin* (Boston: Little, Brown, 1961), 378.

74. Statement of W. Averell Harriman, Special Assistant to the President, regarding our wartime relations with the Soviet Union, particularly as they concern the agreements reached at Yalta. To the Committees on Armed Services and Foreign Relations of the Senate, FDRL.

75. Harriman and Abel, *Special Envoy*, 442.

76. *NYT*, May 10, 1945; Kennan, *Memoirs*, 242.

77. William D. Leahy, *I Was There* (New York: Arno, 1979), 101.

78. Berezhkov, *At Stalin's Side*, 205.

79. Deane, *Strange Alliance*, 20.

80. Sherwood, *Roosevelt and Hopkins*, 91.

Correspondence

1. Quoted in Montefiore, *Stalin*, 352.

2. Quoted in Volkogonov, *Stalin*, 391.

3. Quoted in Montefiore, *Stalin*, 365.

4. Cited ibid., 374.

5. Dallek, *Roosevelt and Foreign Policy*, 279.

6. Sherwood, *Roosevelt and Hopkins*, 323.

7. Cited in Lash, *Roosevelt and Churchill*, 444.

8. Quoted in Sherwood, *Roosevelt and Hopkins*, 344.

9. MR.

10. Hull, *Memoirs*, 2: 980.

11. Cordell Hull, notes, PSF.

12. Dallek, *Roosevelt and Foreign Policy*, 295.

13. Sherwood, *Roosevelt and Hopkins*, 386.

14. Harriman and Abel, *Special Envoy*, 84.

15. Quoted in Montefiore, *Stalin*, 390.

16. Quoted in Sherwood, *Roosevelt and Hopkins*, 396.

17. Ibid., 395.

18. Montefiore, *Stalin*, 403.

19. SC, note, 286.

20. Memo, Hopkins, October 30, 1941, HH. 21. *FRUS 1941*, 1: 852.

21. *FRUS 1941*, 1: 852.

22. Dunn, *Caught Between Roosevelt and Stalin*, 142.

23. Harriman and Abel, *Special Envoy*, 93.

24. Montefiore, *Stalin: The Court of the Red Tsar*, 405.

25. Kennedy, *Freedom from Fear*, 529.

26. PSF.

27. Hull, *Memoirs*, 2: 1117.

28. Loewenheim, Langley, and Jonas, *Roosevelt and Churchill*, 19.

29. Sherwood, *Roosevelt and Hopkins*, 561.

30. Quoted in Deane, *Strange Alliance*, 89.

31. Quoted in Dallek, *Roosevelt and Foreign Policy*, 337.

32. Quoted in Sherwood, *Roosevelt and Hopkins*, 390.

33. Quoted in Dallek, *Roosevelt and Foreign Policy*, March 11, 1942, 338.

34. Kimball, *Churchill and Roosevelt*, 1: 421.

35. Feis, *Churchill-Roosevelt-Stalin*, 341.

36. Loewenheim, Langley, and Jonas, *Roosevelt and Churchill*, 202.

37. Quoted in Sherwood, *Roosevelt and Hopkins,* 538.

38. Standley, *Admiral Ambassador,* 153.

39. Quoted in Sherwood, *Roosevelt and Hopkins,* 528.

40. Kimball, *Churchill and Roosevelt,* 1: 473.

41. Molotov and Hopkins quoted in Sherwood, *Roosevelt and Hopkins,* 563, 577.

42. Loewenheim, Langley, and Jonas, *Roosevelt and Churchill,* 219.

43. *FRUS* 1942, 3: 598.

44. Quoted in Sherwood, *Roosevelt and Hopkins,* 591.

45. Quoted in Harriman and Abel, *Special Envoy,* 143.

46. Quoted in Sherwood, *Roosevelt and Hopkins,* 604.

47. Ibid.

48. Quoted in Harriman and Abel, *Special Envoy,* 147.

49. Telegram to Willkie, August 3, 1942, Manuscripts Department, Lilly Library, Bloomington, Ind.

50. Cable of Harriman to Roosevelt, quoted in Sherwood, *Roosevelt and Hopkins,* 617.

51. Harriman and Abel, *Special Envoy,* 154.

52. Harriman and Abel, *Special Envoy,* 160.

53. Quoted in Volkogonov, *Stalin,* 459.

54. William D. Leahy, *I Was There* (New York: Arno, 1979), 122.

55. Quoted in Sherwood, *Roosevelt and Hopkins,* 634.

56. Werth, *Russia at War,* 517.

57. Quoted in *FRUS* 1942, 3: 654.

58. Quoted in Kennedy, *Freedom from Fear,* 578.

59. For a discussion of Eisenhower's deal with Darlan, see Dallek, *Roosevelt and Foreign Policy,* 364.

60. Quoted in Montefiore, *Stalin,* 431.

61. Quoted in Werth, *Russia at War,* 465.

62. Ibid., 466–67.

63. Quoted ibid., 464.

64. Quoted in Kennedy, *Freedom from Fear,* 583.

65. Quoted in Harriman and Abel, *Special Envoy,* 198.

66. Hull, *Memoirs,* 2: 1570.

67. Quoted in Rosenman, *Working with Roosevelt,* 367.

68. *NYT,* February 3, 1943.

69. Cited in Kimball, *Churchill and Roosevelt,* 2: 134–35.

70. Quoted in Rosenman, *Working with Roosevelt,* 403.

71. See Harriman and Abel, *Special Envoy,* 302.

72. Sudaplatov and Sudoplatov, *Special Tasks,* 276. Russian President Boris Yeltsin released the documents to Lech Walesa, president of Poland, in 1992.

73. MacLean, *Joseph E. Davies,* 100.

74. Kimball, *Churchill and Roosevelt,* 2: 283.

75. Volkogonov, *Stalin,* 486; Alexander Dallin and F. I. Firsov, eds., *Dimitrov and Stalin, 1934–1943: Letters from the Soviet Archives* (New Haven: Yale University Press, 2000), 252–53.

76. Hull, *Memoirs,* 2: 1252.

77. Quoted in MacLean, *Joseph E. Davies,* 100.

78. Standley to the Secretary of State, May 25, 1943, PSF.

79. Davies to Roosevelt, May 29, 1943, PSF.

80. Kennedy, *Freedom from Fear,* 589.

81. Standley to the President, June 5, 1943, MR.

82. Memo from FDR to Gen. H. H. Arnold, June 10, 1943, MR; memo from Arnold to FDR, June 14, 1943, MR.

83. Werth, *Russia at War,* 630.

84. Quoted in Kennedy, *Freedom from Fear,* 595.

85. See Sherwood, *Roosevelt and Hopkins,* 745.

86. Kimball, *Churchill and Roosevelt,* 2: 591.

87. See Harriman and Abel, *Special Envoy,* 226.

88. Cited in Hull, *Memoirs,* 2: 1231.

89. Stalin to Churchill, August 31, 1943, *Stalin's Correspondence with Churchill and Attlee,* 152.

90. Quoted in Julius W. Pratt, *The American Secretaries of State* (New York: Cooper Square, 1964), 13: 616.

91. Hull, *Memoirs,* 2: 1255.

92. Quoted in Volkogonov, *Stalin,* 233.

93. Harriman and Abel, *Special Envoy,* 241.

94. Moran, *Churchill at War,* 159.

95. Harriman and Abel, *Special Envoy,* 236.

96. Ibid., 238.

97. Werth, *Russia at War,* 681.

98. Hull, *Memoirs,* 2: 1309–10.

99. Sherwood, *Roosevelt and Hopkins,* 757.

100. President's diary of the trip, FDRL.

101. Kimball, *Churchill and Roosevelt,* 2: 596.

102. Quoted in Harriman and Abel, *Special Envoy,* 258.

103. Roosevelt, *As He Saw It,* 173.

104. Dimitrov, *Diary,* 145.

105. Sherwood, *Roosevelt and Hopkins,* 777.

106. Quoted in Ian Grey, *Stalin: Man of History* (Garden City, N.Y.: Doubleday, 1979), 386.

107. Harrison Salisbury, *Russia on the Way* (New York: Macmillan, 1946), 428.

108. Harriman and Abel, *Special Envoy,* 278.

109. Quoted in Sherwood, *Roosevelt and Hopkins,* 787.

110. Deane, *Strange Alliance,* 107.

111. Rosenman, *Working with Roosevelt,* 411.

112. The Avalon Project at Yale Law School, The Tehran Conference.

113. Roosevelt, *Personal Letters,* to cousin Laura Delano, 2: 1483.

114. See Kimball, *Churchill and Roosevelt,* 2: 672.

115. Harriman and Abel, *Special Envoy,* note, 295.

116. Kimball, *Churchill and Roosevelt,* 2: 694.

117. *SC,* 291.

118. Harriman and Abel, *Special Envoy,* 297.

119. Harriman to FDR, February 2, 1944, MR.

120. Unidentified clipping, FDRL.

121. *Complete Presidential Press Conferences of Franklin D. Roosevelt* (New York: Da Capo, 1972), March 3, 1944, no. 939.

122. Harriman and Abel, *Special Envoy,* 294, 295.

123. Cable from Harriman to the President, June 28, 1944, MR.

124. "Polish President Names New Heir," *NYT,* June 21, 1944.

125. Dimitrov, *Diary,* 323–24.

126. Quoted in Bishop, *FDR's Last Year,* 96.

127. Werth, *Russia at War,* 807.

128. Montefiore, *Stalin,* 475; Harriman and Abel, *Special Envoy,* 336–37.

129. Edward J. Rozek, *Allied Wartime Diplomacy: A Pattern in Poland* (New York: Wiley, 1958), 237–42, quoted in Harriman and Abel, *Special Envoy,* 334.

130. Ibid., 339.

131. Stettinius, *Diaries,* 144.

132. Schlesinger, *Act of Creation,* 50; Stettinius, *Diaries,* 113.

133. Quoted in Stettinius, *Diaries,* 128, 130.

134. Bohlen, citing Hopkins in *Witness to History,* 162–63. Hopkins and Bohlen each claim to have helped draft the message.

135. Quoted in Harriman and Abel, *Special Envoy,* 356–57.

136. Ibid., 357.

137. Ibid., 357–58.

138. Stettinius, *Diaries,* 167.

139. Quoted in Werth, *Russia at War,* 842–83.

140. Ibid., 834.

141. Quoted in Stettinius, *Diaries,* 162.

142. Hull, *Memoirs,* 2: 1448.

143. Stettinius, *Diaries,* 209.

144. Beevor, *Berlin,* 22.

145. Papers of William D. Leahy, Library of Congress Microform Publication, reel 4, January 1, 1945.

146. Sherwood, *Roosevelt and Hopkins,* 846.

147. Stettinius, *Diaries,* 202.

148. Papers of William D. Leahy, Library of Congress Microform Publication, reel 4, February 2, 1945.

149. Author's interview with Kathleen Harriman Mortimer.

150. Bohlen, *Witness to History,* 180.

151. Ibid., 188.

152. Harriman and Abel, *Special Envoy,* 406.

153. Leahy, *Diary,* February 7, 1944, 22.

154. *FRUS: Conferences at Malta and Yalta,* 308; Leahy, *Diary,* February 8, 1944, 25.

155. Kimball, *Churchill and Roosevelt,* 3: 532.

156. Quoted in Dallek, *Roosevelt and Foreign Policy,* 518–19. See Appendix for text of the formal agreement.

157. Harriman and Abel, *Special Envoy,* 422–23; Deane, *Strange Alliance,* 196–97.

158. Quoted in Harriman and Abel, *Special Envoy,* 432–33.

159. Quoted in Bishop, *FDR's Last Year,* 509.

160. Ibid., 309.

161. Quoted in Montefiore, *Stalin,* 475.

162. Harriman and Abel, *Special Envoy,* 442–43.

163. Protocol of the Proceedings of the Crimea Conference March 24, 1947, FDRL.

164. Bishop, *FDR's Last Year,* 521; Leahy, *Diary,* March 31, 1945, 49.

165. Kimball, *Churchill and Roosevelt,* 3: 601–2.

166. "Pact with Japan Voided by Soviet," *NYT,* April 6, 1945.

167. Draft, undelivered Jefferson Day address, Master Speech File, FDRL.

168. Tully, *F.D.R.,* 360.

169. Kimball, *Churchill and Roosevelt,* 3:630.

170. Quoted in Harriman and Abel, *Special Envoy,* 439.

171. Bishop, *FDR's Last Year,* 573.

172. Quoted in Hassett, *Off the Record with FDR,* 336.

173. Harriman and Abel, *Special Envoy,* 440.

174. Ibid., 442–43.

175. Quoted in Isaacson and Thomas, *The Wise Men,* 266–67.

176. Harriman and Abel, *Special Envoy,* 454.

177. Leahy, *Diary,* April 23, 1945, 63.

178. "Our Policy Stated," *NYT*, June 24, 1941.

179. "Text of the Address by Truman Proclaiming V-J Day," *NYT*, September 2, 1945.

180. Ibid.

181. Quoted in Grey, *Stalin*, 438.

182. "Stalin Recalls Plea for Huge Tax Credit," *NYT*, September 18, 1945.

183. Schlesinger, *Cycles of American History*, 185; *NYT*, March 3, 1946.

184. Quoted in "Pravda Asks Unity in Roosevelt Name," *NYT*, April 13, 1946.

185. "Text of Address at Opening of United Nations Conference in San Francisco," *NYT*, April 25, 1945.

Appendix

1. Leahy, *Diary*, February 8, 1944, 24.

2. *FRUS, The Conferences at Malta and Yalta, 1945*, 984.

Selected Bibliography

Aid, Matthew M., and Cees Wiebes, eds. *Secrets of Signals Intelligence During the Cold War and Beyond.* London: Frank Cass, 2001.

Beevor, Antony. *Berlin: The Downfall, 1945.* London: Penguin, 2003.

Berezhkov, Valentin. *At Stalin's Side: His Interpreter's Memoirs from the October Revolution to the Fall of the Dictator's Empire.* Trans. Sergei V. Mikhehev. New York: Carol, 1984.

Bishop, Jim. *FDR's Last Year: April 1944–April 1945.* New York: William Morrow, 1974.

Bohlen, Charles E. *Witness to History, 1929–1969.* New York: Norton, 1973.

Bullitt, Orville H., ed. *For the President, Personal and Secret: Correspondence Between Franklin D. Roosevelt and William C. Bullitt.* Boston: Houghton Mifflin, 1972.

Conquest, Robert. *Stalin: Breaker of Nations.* New York: Viking, 1991.

Dallek, Robert. *Franklin D. Roosevelt and American Foreign Policy, 1932–1945.* New York: Oxford University Press, 1979.

Davies, Joseph E. *Mission to Moscow.* New York: Simon and Schuster, 1941.

Deane, John R. *The Strange Alliance: The Story of Our Efforts at Wartime Co-operation with Russia.* New York: Viking, 1950.

De Santis, Hugh. *The Diplomacy of Silence: The American Foreign Service, the Soviet Union, and the Cold War, 1933–1947.* Chicago: University of Chicago Press, 1983.

Deutscher, Isaac. *Stalin: A Political Biography.* Harmondsworth, U.K.: Penguin, 1966.

Dimitrov, Georgi. *The Diary of Georgi Dimitrov, 1933–1949.* New Haven: Yale University Press, 2003.

Djilas, Milovan. *Conversations with Stalin.* New York: Harcourt Brace Jovanovich, 1962.

Dunn, Dennis J. *Caught Between Roosevelt and Stalin: America's Ambassadors to Moscow.* Lexington: University Press of Kentucky, 1998.

Feis, Herbert. *Churchill-Roosevelt-Stalin: The War They Waged and the Peace They Sought.* Princeton: Princeton University Press, 1967.

Harriman, W. Averell, and Elie Abel. *Special Envoy to Churchill and Stalin, 1941–1946.* New York: Random House, 1975.

Hassett, William D. *Off the Record with FDR, 1942–1945.* New Brunswick, N.J.: Rutgers University Press, 1958.

Herring, George C. *Aid to Russia, 1941–1946*. New York: Columbia University Press, 1973.

Hull, Cordell. *The Memoirs of Cordell Hull*. New York: Macmillan, 1948.

Isaacson, Walter, and Evan Thomas. *The Wise Men: Six Friends and the World They Made*. New York: Simon and Schuster, 1986.

Jones, Robert Hugh. *The Roads to Russia: United States Lend-lease to the Soviet Union*. Norman: University of Oklahoma Press, 1969.

Kennan, George F. *Memoirs, 1925–1950*. Vol. 1. Boston: Little, Brown, 1967.

Kennedy, David M. *Freedom from Fear: The American People in Depression and War, 1929–1945*. New York: Oxford University Press, 1999.

Kimball, Warren F., ed. *Churchill and Roosevelt: The Complete Correspondence*. 3 vols. Princeton: Princeton University Press, 1984.

Lash, Joseph P. *Roosevelt and Churchill, 1939–1941: The Partnership That Saved the West*. New York: Norton, c. 1976.

Loewenheim, Francis L., Harold D. Langley, and Manfred Jonas, eds. *Roosevelt and Churchill: Their Secret War Time Correspondence*. New York: Da Capo, 1990.

Lukacs, John. *Churchill: Visionary. Statesman. Historian*. New Haven: Yale University Press, 2002.

MacLean, Elizabeth Kimball. *Joseph E. Davies: Envoy to the Soviets*. Westport, Conn.: Praeger, 1992.

Maisky, Ivan M. *Memoirs of a Soviet Ambassador*. New York: Norton, 1976.

Montefiore, Simon Sebag. *Stalin: The Court of the Red Tsar*. New York: Knopf, 2004.

Moran, Lord. *Churchill at War, 1940–45*. New York: Carol and Graf, 2002.

Nisbet, Robert. *Roosevelt and Stalin: The Failed Courtship*. Washington, D.C.: Regnery Gateway, 1988.

Perkins, Francis. *The Roosevelt I Knew*. New York: Viking, 1946.

Roosevelt, Elliott. *As He Saw It*. New York: Duell, Sloan and Pearce, 1946.

Roosevelt, Franklin Delano. *F.D.R.: His Personal Letters, 1928–1945*. Vol. 2, ed. Elliott Roosevelt. New York: Duell, Sloan and Pearce, 1950.

Rosenman, Samuel Irving. *Working with Roosevelt*. New York: Harper and Brothers, 1952.

Schlesinger, Arthur M., Jr. *The Age of Roosevelt*. Vol. 2, *The Coming of the New Deal*. Boston: Riverside, 1959.

———. *The Cycles of American History*. Boston: Houghton Mifflin, 1986.

Schlesinger, Stephen C. *Act of Creation: The Founding of the United Nations*. Boulder, Colo.: Westview, 2003.

Sherwood, Robert E. *Roosevelt and Hopkins*. Rev. ed. New York: Universal Library, 1950.

Stafford, David. *Roosevelt and Churchill: Men of Secrets*. Woodstock, N.Y.: Overlook, 2000.

Stalin, Joseph. *Stalin's Correspondence with Churchill and Attlee, 1941–1945: Correspondence Between the Chairman of the Council of Ministers of the U.S.S.R. and the Presidents of the U.S.A. and the Prime Ministers of Great Britain During the Great Patriotic War of 1941–1945*. New York: Capricorn, 1965.

———. *Stalin's Correspondence with Roosevelt and Truman, 1941–1945: Correspondence Between the Chairman of the Council of Ministers of the U.S.S.R. and the Presidents of the U.S.A. and the Prime Ministers of Great Britain During the Great Patriotic War of 1941–1945*. New York: Capricorn, 1965.

Standley, W. H. *Admiral Ambassador to Russia*. Chicago: Regnery, 1955.

Stettinius, Edward R. *The Diaries of Edward R. Stettinius, Jr., 1943–1946*. Ed. Thomas M. Campbell and George C. Herring. New York: New Viewpoints, 1975.

———. *Roosevelt and the Russians: The Yalta Conference*. New York: Doubleday, 1949.

Stimson, Henry L., and McGeorge Bundy. *On Active Service in Peace and War*. New York: Harper and Brothers, 1948.

Sudoplatov, Pavel, and Anatoli Sudaplatov, with Jerrold L. Schecter and Leona P. Schecter. *Special Tasks: The Memoirs of an Unwanted Witness—A Soviet Spymaster.* Boston: Little, Brown, 1995.

Tittmann, Harold H., Jr. *Inside the Vatican of Pius XII.* Ed. Harold H. Tittman III. New York: Image, Doubleday, 2004.

Tully, Grace. *F.D.R.: My Boss.* Chicago: People's Book Club, 1949.

Volkogonov, Dmitri. *Stalin: Triumph and Tragedy.* Weidenfeld, N.Y.: Grove, 1988.

Werth, Alexander. *Russia at War, 1941–1945.* New York: Avon, 1965.

Document Source Notes

1. Sherwood, *Roosevelt and Hopkins,* 321–22.
2. Sherwood, *Roosevelt and Hopkins,* 342–43.
3. PSF.
4. PSF.
5. PSF.
6. PSF.
7. PSF.
8. PSF.
9. PSF.
10. PSF.
11. PSF.
12. *FRUS 1941,* 1: 856–57.
13. PSF.
14. PSF.
15. PSF.
16. PSF.
17. PSF.
18. *FRUS 1942,* 3: 690–91.
19. HH.
20. HH.
21. PSF.
22. PSF.
23. PSF.
24. Standley, *Admiral Ambassador to Russia,* 152–53.
25. MR.
26. Sherwood, *Roosevelt and Hopkins,* 546.
27. MR.
28. PSF.
29. MR.
30. MR.
31. PSF.
32. MR.
33. SC.
34. MR.
35. MR.
36. MR.
37. PSF.
38. MR.
39. MR.
40. MR.
41. MR.
42. MR.
43. MR.
44. MR.
45. SC.
46. MR.
47. MR.
48. PSF.
49. MR.
50. MR.
51. MR.
52. MR.

53. MR.
54. MR.
55. MR.
56. MR.
57. *FRUS 1942*, 3: 659.
58. MR.
59. MR.
60. MR.
61. MR.
62. MR.
63. MR.
64. MR.
65. MR.
66. MR.
67. MR.
68. MR.
69. MR.
70. MR.
71. House Joint Resolution 371, December 16, 1942. *Congressional Record*, 77th Congress, 2nd session, House vol. 88, part 7, p. 2624; SC.
72. MR.
73. MR.
74. PSF.
75. United States Department of Defense, *The Entry of the Soviet Union into the War Against Japan: Military Plans, 1941–1945* (Washington, D.C.: U.S. Department of Defense, 1955), 14.
76. MR.
77. MR.
78. MR.
79. MR; *FRUS, The Casablanca Conference*, vol. 3, 803–6.
80. MR.
81. PSF.
82. MR.
83. MR.
84. MR.
85. MR.
86. MR.
87. MR.
88. SC.
89. MR.
90. MR.
91. MR.
92. MR.
93. PSF.
94. MR.
95. MR.
96. MR.
97. MR.
98. MR.
99. MR.
100. MR.
101. MR.
102. MR.
103. MR.
104. MR.
105. MR.
106. MR.
107. MR.
108. MR.
109. MR.
110. MR.
111. MR.
112. MR.
113. HH.
114. MR.
115. MR.
116. MR.
117. MR.
118. MR.
119. MR.
120. MR.
121. MR.
122. MR.
123. MR.
124. MR.
125. MR.
126. MR.
127. MR.
128. MR.
129. MR.
130. MR.
131. MR.
132. MR.
133. MR.
134. MR.
135. MR.
136. MR.
137. MR.
138. MR.
139. MR.
140. MR.
141. MR.
142. MR.
143. Berezhkov, *At Stalin's Side*, 263–64.
144. MR.
145. MR.
146. MR.
147. MR.
148. MR.

149. MR.
150. MR.
151. MR.
152. MR.
153. MR.
154. *FRUS, Conferences at Cairo and Teheran*, 617–19.
155. *FRUS, Conferences at Cairo and Teheran*, 618–19.
156. *FRUS, Conferences at Cairo and Teheran*, 619.
157. PPF.
158. MR.
159. MR.
160. MR.
161. MR.
162. MR.
163. MR.
164. MR.
165. MR.
166. MR.
167. MR.
168. MR.
169. MR.
170. MR.
171. MR.
172. MR.
173. PPF.
174. MR.
175. MR.
176. MR.
177. MR.
178. MR.
179. MR.
180. MR.
181. MR.
182. MR.
183. MR.
184. MR.
185. MR.
186. MR.
187. MR.
188. MR.
189. MR.
190. MR.
191. MR.
192. MR; Kimball, *Churchill & Roosevelt*, 3: 48–49.
193. MR.
194. MR.
195. MR; Kimball, *Churchill & Roosevelt*, 3: 61.

196. MR.
197. MR.
198. MR.
199. MR.
200. MR.
201. MR.
202. MR.
203. MR.
204. MR.
205. MR.
206. MR.
207. PPF.
208. MR.
209. MR.
210. MR.
211. MR.
212. MR.
213. PSF.
214. MR.
215. MR.
216. MR.
217. MR.
218. MR.
219. MR.
220. MR.
221. MR.
222. PPF.
223. MR.
224. MR.
225. MR.
226. PSF.
227. MR.
228. MR.
229. MR.
230. MR.
231. MR.
232. MR.
233. MR.
234. MR.
235. MR.
236. MR.
237. MR.
238. MR.
239. MR.
240. MR.
241. MR.
242. MR.
243. MR.
244. MR.
245. MR.
246. MR.
247. MR.

248. MR.
249. MR.
250. MR.
251. MR.
252. MR.
253. MR.
254. MR.
255. MR.
256. MR.
257. MR.
258. MR.
259. MR.
260. MR.
261. MR.
262. MR.
263. MR.
264. PPF.
265. MR.
266. MR.
267. MR.
268. MR.
269. MR.
270. MR.
271. MR.
272. MR.
273. MR.
274. MR.
275. MR.
276. MR.
277. MR.
278. MR.

279. MR.
280. Hopkins, FDRL.
281. SC.
282. SC.
283. PSF.
284. *FRUS, Conferences at Malta and Yalta,* 966–67.
285. Leahy, *Diary,* February 10, 1945; Papers of William D. Leahy, Library of Congress Microform Publication, reel 4, February 10, 1945.
286. Hopkins, FDRL.
287. MR.
288. MR.
289. PSF.
290. MR.
291. MR.
292. MR.
293. MR.
294. MR.
295. MR.
296. MR.
297. MR.
298. MR.
299. MR.
300. MR.
301. MR.
302. MR.
303. MR.
304. MR.

Index